IMAGES
of America

SECURITY-WIDEFIELD

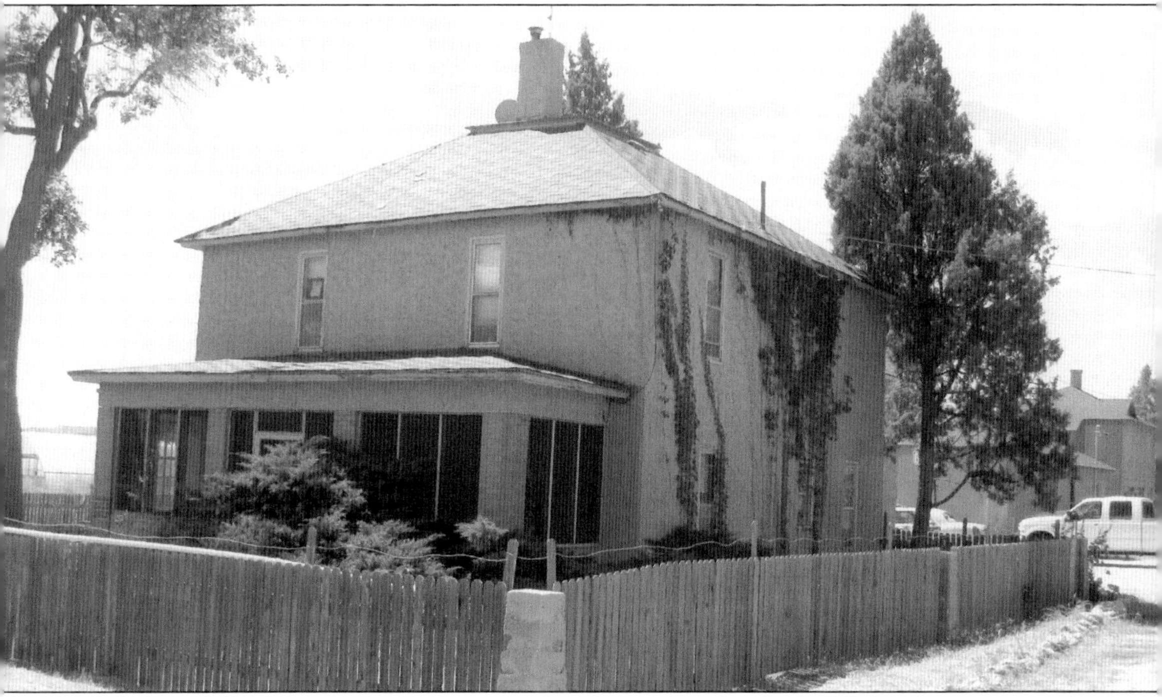

The Venetucci farmhouse is one of the two oldest structures in the Security-Widefield area. It was built before 1936, which was when Nick Venetucci moved in with his family. His home in the Fountain Valley was surrounded by pastoral farmland. Now, the almost constant noise of the highway reminds the visitor that during Venetucci's nearly 70 years in this house, he saw many changes. Eventually, his was the only farm remaining in the north end of the valley. (Mary Alice [Janitell] Scuderi.)

On the Cover: Widefield School District bus driver Ray Reams stands outside his bus in the 1940s. He picked up children in the southwestern corner of the district and dropped them off at the Widefield School, one of three small schoolhouses in the district. The school district stretched 37 miles east to the Lincoln County line, with additional school buildings located in the rural communities of Truckton and Drennan. (Dave and Sarah Wilson.)

IMAGES
of America

SECURITY-WIDEFIELD

Angela Thaden Hahn

ARCADIA
PUBLISHING

ISBN 978-1-4671-3092-9

Published by Arcadia Publishing
Charleston, South Carolina

Printed in the United States of America

Library of Congress Control Number:

For all general information, please contact Arcadia Publishing:
Telephone 843-853-2070
Fax 843-853-0044
E-mail sales@arcadiapublishing.com
For customer service and orders:
Toll-Free 1-888-313-2665

Visit us on the Internet at www.arcadiapublishing.com

To my mom and dad, Les and Nancy Thaden, for raising my brothers and me in Security-Widefield, one of the most desirable communities in America.

Contents

Acknowledgments

For sharing their stories and knowledge with me, I thank Walt Belveal, Sandie Comstock, Phil Cozzi, Dan Furzi, Mel McFarland, Ben Pinello, Chuck Poncelow, Miguel Santiago, Robert Sennert, and Mollie Wingate.

I thank the librarians and secretaries at Widefield School District 3; the staffs at the local news office, museum, senior center, and libraries; Jeanie Olive at Fountain Valley School; Patrick Hamilton at Venetucci Farm and Pinello Ranch; the Widefield High School 1966–1979 Facebook group; my editors, Mom and Tom; and my supporters Dixie and Mike.

To gather facts, I consulted old *Gazette Telegraph* articles and pages from the federal census. The writings of H. Kay Larson (*Valley of the Fountain,* 1969) and Kitty (aka "Kittie") Paster Fryhofer (*When I Was a Little Girl in the Pikes Peak Region*, 1951) were also quite helpful.

The images in this publication come from the following individuals and organizations, many of whom also shared their stories: Angela Thaden Hahn (ATH); Beverly (Sproul) Kelly (BK); Beverly Weinert (BW); Carole Jackson and Harold Colbert (CJ); Dede Blanchard (DB); Dave and Julie Groff (DG); Fort Carson Museum (FCM); Fountain Creek Nature Center (FCNC); Fountain Valley Historical Society and Museum (FVM); *Fountain Valley News* (FVN); Fountain Valley School (FVS); Fountain Valley Senior Center (FVSC); Bureau of Land Management General Land Office Records (GLO); Janet (Wallis) Altmann (JA); Jeff and Donna (Lamerson) Noth (JN); Joe Pyle (JP); John and Ruth Sinnes (JS); Kathy Duran (KD); Lonis and Jeanne Brown (LB); Mary Alice (Janitell) Scuderi (MAS); Mildred Chenowith (MC); MemorialLibrary.com (ML); Martin and Esther Simon (MS); Mark Watson (MW); Nancy Bright Thaden (NBT); Pikes Peak Community Foundation (PPCF); Special Collections, Pikes Peak Library District (PPLD); Rudy Legleiter (RL); Ray Sigala and family (RS); Sinton Dairy (SD); St. Dominic Parish (SDP); Security Fire Department (SFD); Security Lions Club (SLC); Scott O'Malley Agency (SOA); Security Public Library (SPL); St. Raphael's Episcopal Church (SRE); Dave and Sarah Wilson (SW); Tom and Binnie Kennedy (TK); Ursula Zimkas (UZ); Widefield Community Center (WCC); and Widefield School District 3 (WSD).

INTRODUCTION

Security-Widefield appears as an oasis in the sandy hills along the ancient Fountain Valley. Locals like to refer to the Fountain Valley as simply "the Valley." It stretches between the historic towns of Colorado Springs and Fountain. Long before white men entered the valley, Ute Indians camped along its river in the spring and autumn among the tall cottonwoods and thick willow trees. French fur trappers named the river la Fontaine qui Bouille, which is usually translated as "the fountain which boils." Its continual flow provided necessary water for travelers and their stock as they journeyed on the dusty road between Colorado City and Pueblo. The river is known as Fountain Creek today. It meanders quietly most of the year through the valley, providing essential life-giving water as it has for hundreds of years.

In the 1860s, eager homesteaders arrived in the attractive valley, while nomadic Indians still roamed the wide fields. Early pioneer Kitty Paster Fryhofer wrote that her family fled, with other frightened families, to a big, strong ranch house a few miles south, toward Fountain, whenever they received warnings of an Indian uprising. This was probably one of four such forts in the valley described in early writings. Even though the last Indian attacks in the Pikes Peak region occurred in 1868 along Monument Creek to the north, wary settlers remained ever watchful for years afterward. Incidentally, there was never any recorded trouble in the valley, and homesteaders eventually learned they had nothing to fear from the Utes.

A half century later, eastern educators discovered the beautiful, rolling hill country east of the Widefield School and determined to create a boarding school experience for boys in the wide-open spaces of the romanticized West. The Fountain Valley Boys School opened to 53 students, who came from as far away as Connecticut and California. It is easy for locals to forget that tucked in the community's backyard is a private school that has seen little structural change since its beginning.

At this same time, the agriculturally rich valley thrived with its large acreages of cattle ranches, dairies, and truck farms, some of which surrounded the dot on the map known as Widefield. Some of the valley's successful farmers included Italian immigrants who came to America during the great exodus from Southern Europe at the turn of the last century. As soon as they cleared customs, many of these foreigners boarded trains and headed west to the Pikes Peak region's coal mines in Papeton, Franceville, and Pikeview. Colorado Springs was just a young college town on the railroad at the time, but the city eventually grew to absorb these former mining communities. Most Italians had worked the land in their home country and, believing that land was the best investment, desired to buy farms in the Fountain Valley with their carefully saved pick-and-shovel earnings.

In 1912, Italian immigrant Alfonso Pinello moved from Franceville and acquired a 299-acre ranch with his cousin Angelo Pinello. Their new place was located on the old Denver-to-Pueblo road, across from Skinner, in the vicinity of present-day Highway 85 and the Academy Boulevard interchange. According to Pinello descendants, the cousins came from Rome, and the family spoke Italian at home. The children did not learn English until they entered school. The large family always had plenty to eat, though they may not have had much money, and no one ever left the farm hungry. Transient hobos knew they could satisfy their empty stomachs at the Pinello Ranch, and they customarily chopped wood or performed some other chore to pay for the much-appreciated meal. Farm boys stationed at Camp Carson spent their three-day passes working at the Pinello Ranch so they could earn some extra cash and eat some delicious Italian food. The Pinello Ranch was later purchased in the 1970s by Colorado Springs Utilities for its access to water. It is now leased to the Pikes Peak Community Foundation to serve as a ranch and wildlife refuge that teaches the community about sustainable agriculture.

The agrarian Fountain Valley remained unaltered until 1941 when, in answer to the bombing at Pearl Harbor, the War Department began construction on several Army posts throughout the country, including Camp Carson at the foot of Cheyenne Mountain. At the war's end, many troops and their families moved into the area, creating a shortage in available housing. Meanwhile, a yellow schoolhouse and a combination grocery store/filling station/post office sat on the high bank above Fountain Creek. These places made up the spot on Old Pueblo Road known as Widefield.

Suburbs began springing up all over the United States in the 1950s with affordable new homes to entice returning war veterans to take advantage of the GI Bill. In 1953, Ed Hayes bought a dairy farm and partnered with engineer William Horak and the Robert Willis Agency to form the Security Development Corporation. The name they chose symbolized security for families living in affordable homes, conveniently located near a city, and with the promise of a comfortable retirement. The sandy land on which the developers chose to build was home to field mice and cottontails, prickly pear and yucca, and spiderwort and sandspurs. Security Village began with a few homes along Security Boulevard and Willis, Hayes, and Easy Streets. People smiled at the thought of living on Easy Street in Security, Colorado. Those who came to live in Security were hardworking people from all occupations. Security Boulevard promised to look like a grand thoroughfare when the cottonwood trees, transplanted as young saplings from the river, grew tall and shady.

Fred Sproul, owner of American Builders, took over the development of Security Village and continued the housing development from Grand Boulevard north to Bradley Road. Working-class people were attracted to the reasonably priced housing with the big backyards, and eager families moved into the region weekly. American Builders stepped up its home production by sending heavy equipment the entire length of one side of the street to dig a continuous trench for the basements. Behind it, cement crews poured foundations, followed by the framers, plumbers, electricians, and roofers. On the weekends, new homeowners arrived with their U-Haul trailers to unload their furniture and belongings into the finished houses. The building crews then headed down the other side of the street, throwing up new homes in their wake. People who lived in Security in those early days say American Builders finished seven homes each week. In 1957, the development corporation changed its name to Sproul Homes. Many of the streets in Security were named for members of the Sproul family.

For a time, Security was known as Garden City as a result of the extensive landscaping undertaken by the many residents and the beautiful parks built by American Builders. The neighborhood flourished with shrubs, trees, flowers, and grass. South Security even had its own bird park at the Sinnes home on Security Boulevard, where the sounds of exotic birds were often heard.

A few years later, Arizona land developer Jules Watson recognized an opportunity in the Pikes Peak region with the expansion and growth of the little Army post that had officially become Fort Carson. In 1957, he formed the Widefield Homes development company on a 120-acre tract of land on the former Dent Ranch and truck farm. These new ranch-style and bi-level homes were larger than the houses in Security, and the first models, showcasing homes built of brick, were located at 107, 111, and 112 Amherst Street. One of the features making Widefield Homes so affordable was the option to purchase a house with an unfinished basement or lower level. The home buyer could purchase a big home and live upstairs, and the lower level could be finished later when more funds were available. Realizing the neighborhoods would be more attractive with the inclusion of schools, parks, churches, and businesses, the developers of both Security and Widefield made provisions for these amenities.

By 1951, the western part of the school district began to anticipate some growth, while the eastern section continued to remain sparsely populated. In the interest of both sections of the district, it was divided, and Widefield District's new board of education consisted of three members—John Janitell, president; Mrs. Roy Barnes, secretary; and Louie Pinello, treasurer. With the sudden influx of families in the late 1950s, it became necessary to address the educational needs of the children. Most had just moved in and were of elementary age. The little yellow, two-room schoolhouse was no longer sufficient.

Modern schools appeared in rapid succession, and construction continued on the existing buildings with added gymnasiums, lockers, lunchrooms, and office spaces, even as new schools were being built. In an effort to keep up with the steady growth over the next two decades, classes were held in rented homes, portable modular buildings, and in split sessions at existing schools. Eventually, the school district totaled 10 elementary schools, 3 junior high schools, 2 high schools, and 1 charter school.

For 40 years, most of Security-Widefield's teenagers attended classes at the only high school, home of the Gladiators. This mascot was chosen by the school's first students because true gladiators of Roman days entertained spectators with their fierce fighting.

In 1956, the Widefield School District principal earned $4,500; a teacher's salary amounted to $3,600. At $6,000, the superintendent earned a little under twice the amount of a teacher's pay. Secretaries and bus drivers worked for $150 per month, and custodians earned $300 during the same pay period. In 1960, a teacher's average class size amounted to 36 students. Individuals who served on the school board during these early days of rapid growth included Louie Pinello, Rodger Fay, Robert Brown, James O'Donnell, Clarence Foster, Robert Poole, and Reba Pyle. The number of graduating seniors almost tripled from 25 in 1959 to 70 in 1961.

The year 1956 seems to be the magical point when Security boomed into existence outside of its housing area. Security developer Fred Sproul and, later, Widefield developer Jules Watson often made loans to prospective business owners and donated land for much-needed churches and schools in anticipation of a vigorous community. Both men have forever been respected for their generosity and honesty by the businessmen of the community. A handshake sealed many deals, which manifested trust, pride, and professionalism. A few of those businesses assisted by Fred Sproul remarkably remain in operation today, three generations later.

During those first few decades, Security-Widefield was very much a small town. Most business owners lived in the community with customers as neighbors, and the stores were often referred to by the owners' names. For instance, on her errand day, a mother might drop the family car off at Groff's for an engine repair and then walk her son over to Manny's for a haircut. She might stop by Noth's to pick up her husband's boots and step inside Ralph's to buy herself a pair of new shoes. In Duckwall's, she would find fabric to sew a dress for her daughter, and at Anthony's, she could find some underclothing. After picking up her car, she might finish out her errands with a visit to Simm's for the week's groceries.

In addition to the business area, many of Security's earliest churches and organizations established themselves in the mid-1950s. The Knights of Columbus Security Council 4636, one of the oldest organizations in Security, stays busy with activities such as the Tootsie Roll drive, which collects funds to benefit children with special needs. The Knights also prepare Thanksgiving dinner for the area's elderly neighbors and host Christmas parties for the children. Likewise, the Security Lions Club, organized in 1957, has been involved in many philanthropic projects, such as Bowling for the Blind. The club has collected old eyeglasses and cases and Campbell's Soup labels to raise funds for playground equipment for the Colorado School for the Deaf and Blind.

Typically, church members assembled in homes or school buildings for a year or two until their sanctuaries were completed. Some of these original buildings now host other religious sects, but a few of the original congregations have remained constant through the years. The Latter-day Saints and Jehovah's Witnesses now meet as two of the newest congregations in Security.

As the two communities of Security and Widefield joined together on many fronts, they were often spoken of in the same breath. Naturally, the combined communities became known by their combined moniker, Security-Widefield. However, there are still many occasions when one refers to only half of the community.

In the 1980s, Colorado lottery funds were made available to towns, cities, and counties for park improvements, but this did not include the parks uniquely maintained by Widefield School District. In 1987, community center director Dan Furzi went to the area's state representative, who sponsored a bill tweaking the disbursement of lottery funds to include school districts. Much-needed improvements were immediately made to the community center fields and pool.

Quite a few of the current citizens of Security-Widefield moved here in the early days as very small children with their families. When these children grew up, many of them married and raised their own families in their beloved hometown. Three generations later, children now experience the joy of growing up in this delightful community.

Notably, Security-Widefield survives without a mayor or a town council of any kind. The community functions well through its fire board, water boards, and school board, and citizens consistently vote down the notion of incorporation, choosing instead to remain subject to the county. New people moving into this community discover the secrets of Security-Widefield that longtime residents have known for years.

One

A Wide Field

Highway 85, as it is called today, rambles through the Fountain Valley on the east side of Fountain Creek from Colorado Springs to Fountain. A main thoroughfare is often the oldest element in a region, and so it is with this road, which started as the Indian trail that came out of Ute Pass. The path evolved into a wagon road used for freighters, stagecoaches, and covered wagons. Railroad gangs laid tracks next to the road in the 1870s and 1880s, providing a more modern form of transportation. A paving crew came through in 1930 to iron out some of the curves in the old road, creating a smooth highway suitable for motorcars. Finally, in the late 1950s, a freeway was built on the west side of the river to connect the Front Range with the rest of the country's interstate system.

When early homesteaders discovered this fertile valley, they dug wells to water crops and livestock. A network of hand-dug irrigation ditches diverted precious life-giving water from the river to green fields and pastures. The first ditch in the Widefield area was dug by early ranchers P.D. Miller and R. Stubbs prior to 1866. Later, the Fountain Ditch brought water to farms and ranches east of Widefield. Remnants of this ditch system are scattered throughout the area and can be seen along roadways and in parks.

The homesteaders' children received their educations in the Widefield School District, created in 1874. Sometime in the 1870s, Adam Paster and his sons, living along the creek not far from Stubbs, worked on the construction of the Widefield School. At this time, Ute Indians still frequented the area, sometimes peering into the windows of the school and startling the children.

Big changes came to the valley when the federal government exercised its power of eminent domain and bought up a large swath of ranches. Among those affected were the Oaks and Venetucci families. They lost the western portions of their ranches, which reached far into the western hills that had been claimed for a new military post.

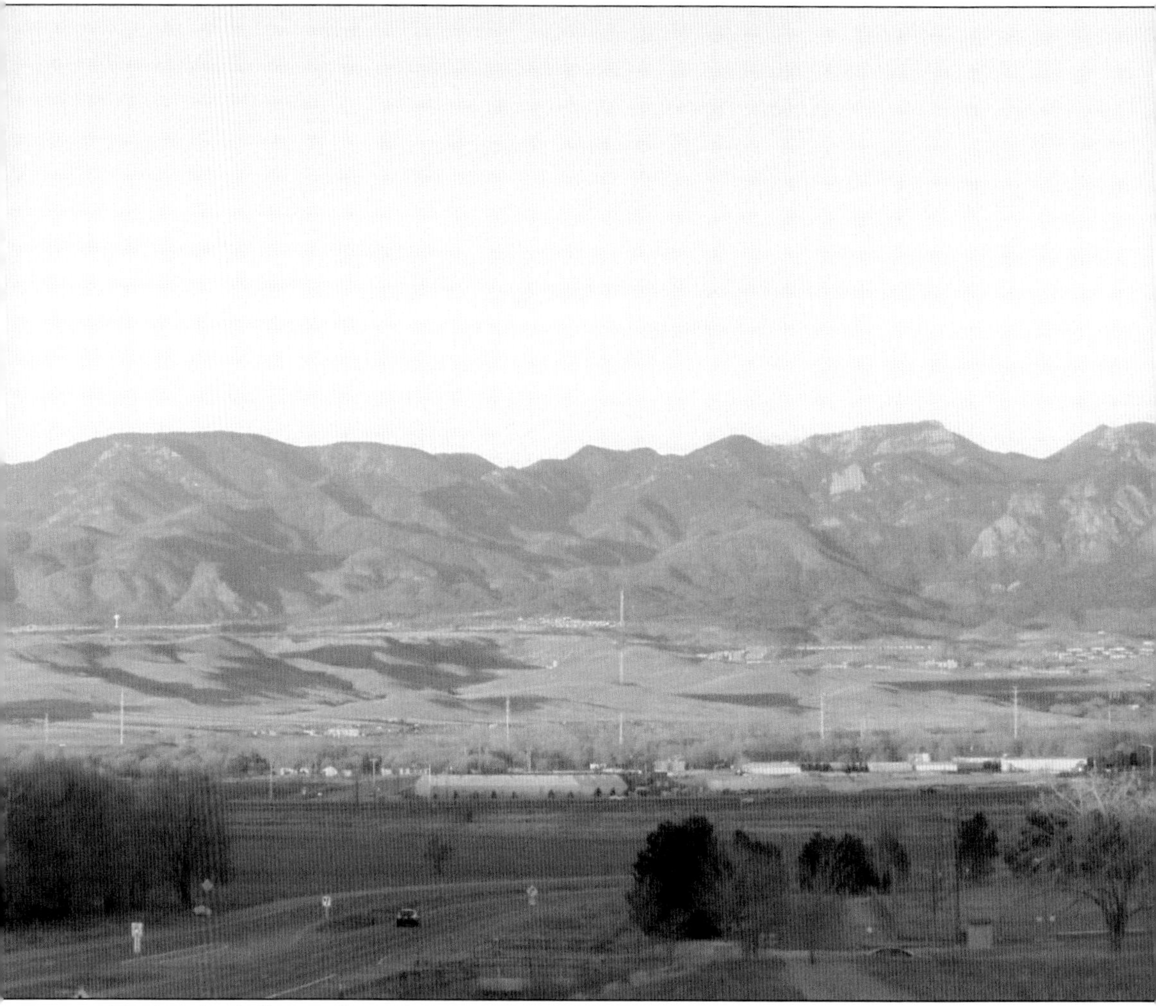

Treeless foothills rise above the river's west banks. A creek trickles from the mountains through a break in the hills (center) and joins the waters of Fountain Creek. Early writings describe this grassy little valley as Lanahan Hollow, where Henry Hutchin operated a stagecoach station on the east side of the river in the 1860s along the route then known as the Colorado and Pueblo Road. Hutchin's niece Anna Terrell visited his family as a teenager in 1868. On one such visit, she and her cousins sat atop a roof and watched a small detachment of cavalry ride northward on the

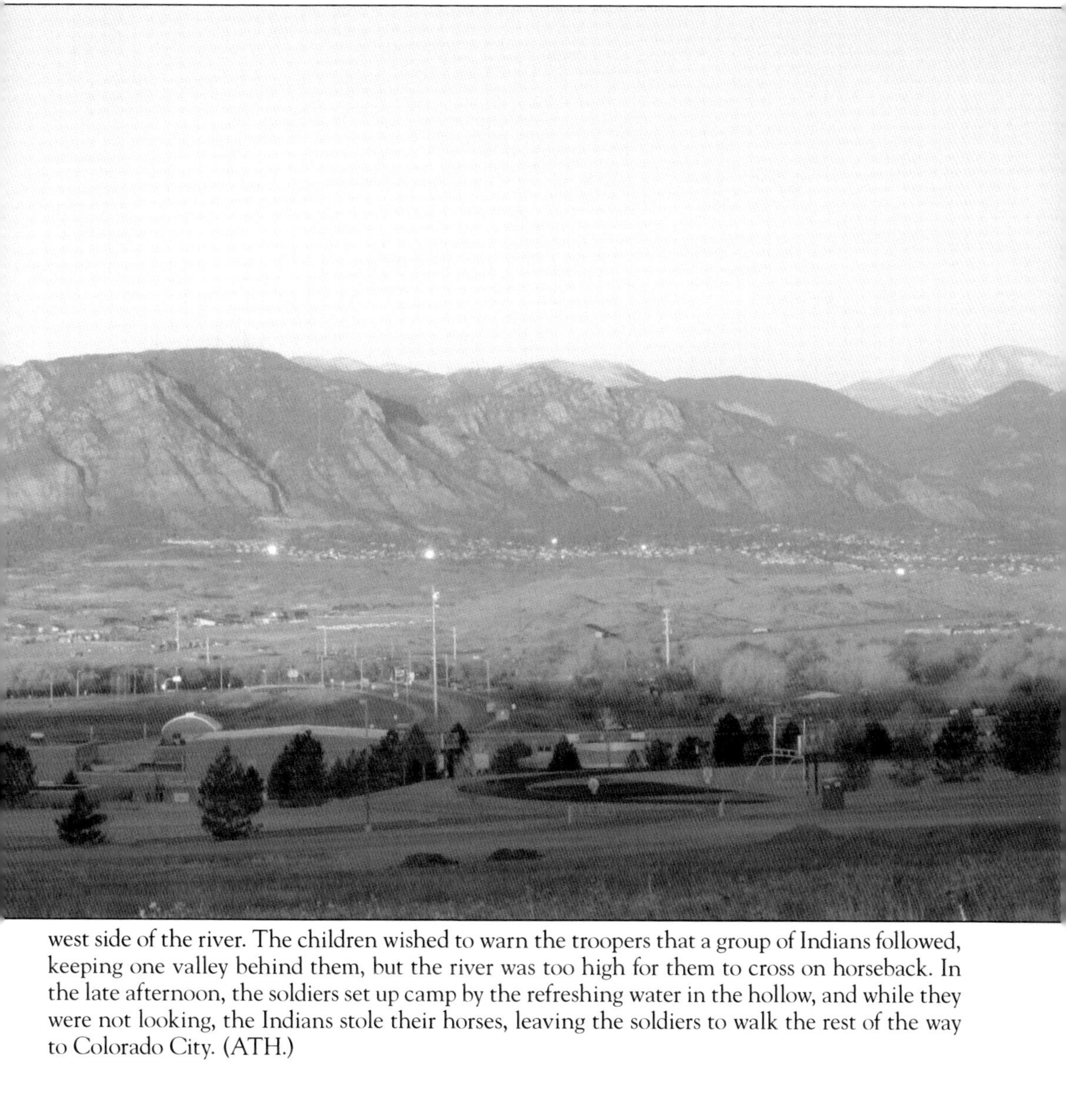

west side of the river. The children wished to warn the troopers that a group of Indians followed, keeping one valley behind them, but the river was too high for them to cross on horseback. In the late afternoon, the soldiers set up camp by the refreshing water in the hollow, and while they were not looking, the Indians stole their horses, leaving the soldiers to walk the rest of the way to Colorado City. (ATH.)

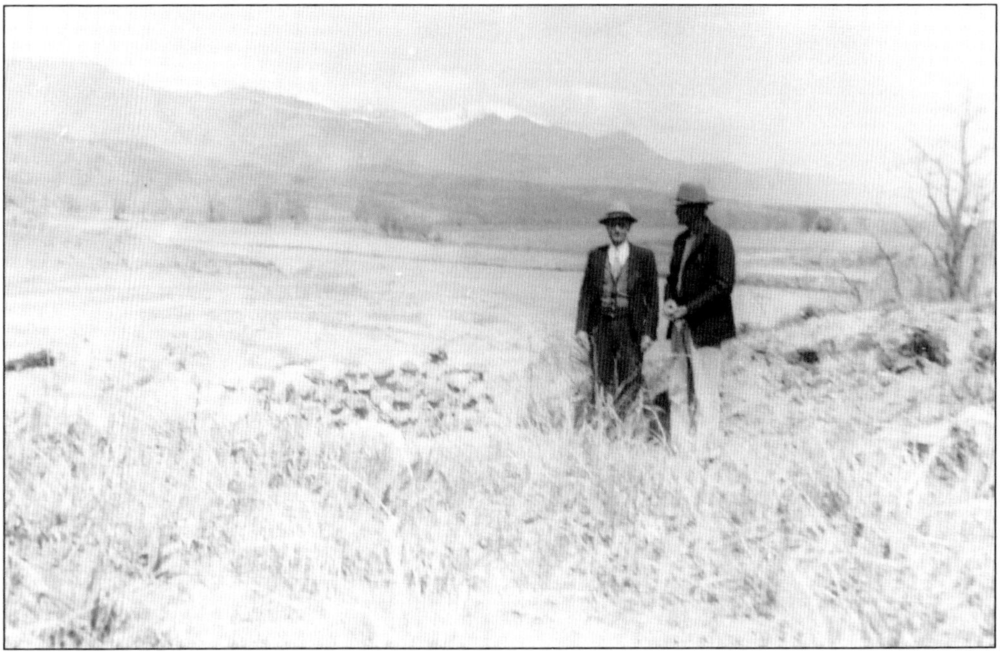

Two men stand next to what has been identified as the ruins of an old stage station. Careful observation puts the location of this rock ruin in the vicinity of Fountain Mesa Road between Mesa Road and Mesa Ridge Parkway. Indeed, an 1866 plat survey map shows that a road branched off the Colorado and Pueblo Road in a northeastern direction through this spot on its way to Jimmy's Camp Creek. (PPLD.)

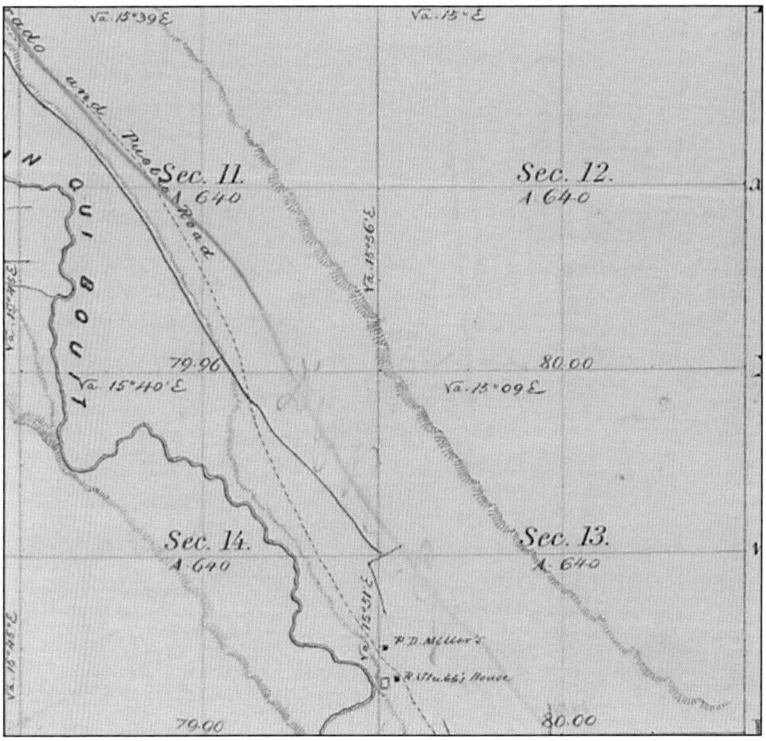

This 1863 plat survey map shows little settlement in the area where Security and Widefield began. The homesteads of P.D. Miller and R. Stubbs were located on the high riverbank behind the present-day Walmart across from Security. Today, this four-section area is bounded roughly on the north by Leta Drive, on the south by Fontaine Boulevard, and on the east by Grinnell Boulevard. (GLO.)

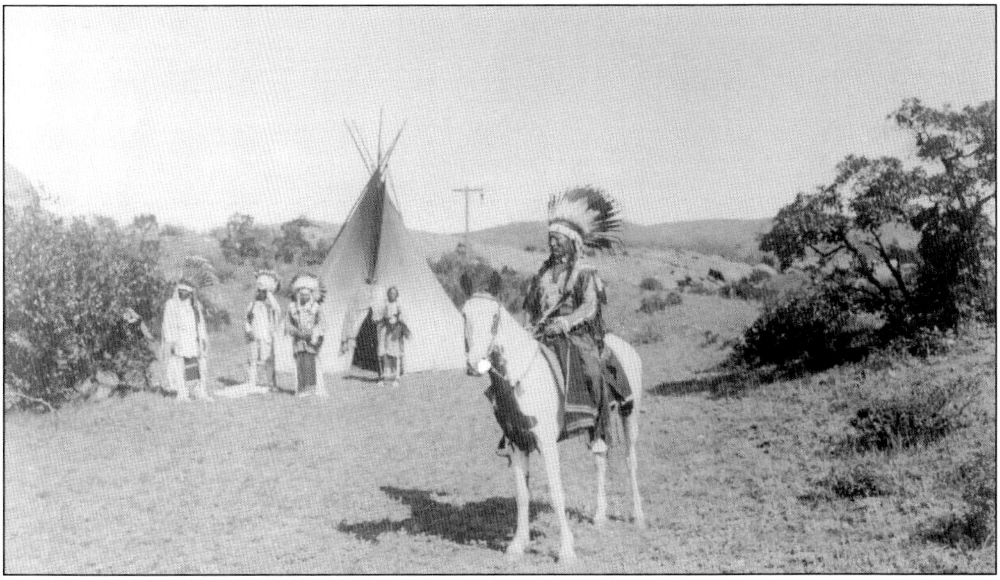

Ute Indians frequently traveled the Fountain Valley. During the 1870s, Kitty Paster and her family looked forward to the biannual Ute migration when Indians camped in the creek bottoms on her family's ranch near present-day Widefield. Neighboring families came to watch the peaceful Indians in their daily activities. Light trading took place, and friendships formed between Indians and homesteaders. (Photograph by Stewarts Commercial Photographers, 013-288, courtesy of PPLD.)

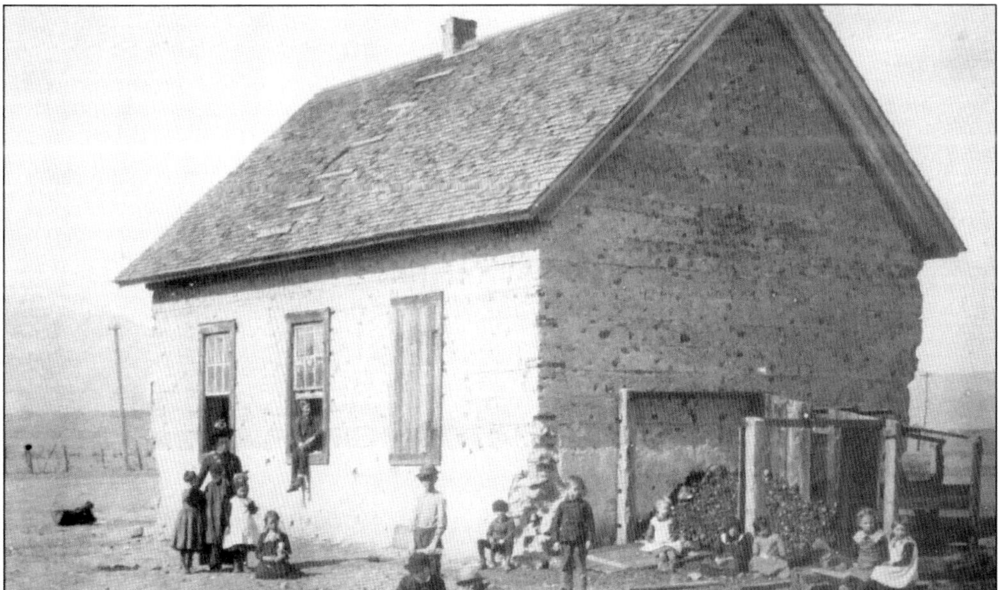

R. Stubbs represented the Widefield community on the three-member school board, and Widefield students attended this one-room schoolhouse made of grout on the site of the present old Widefield School building. A term used by early locals, grout referred to a mixture of sand, cementitious material, different-sized stones, and water. The teacher in this photograph is reported to be Kitty Paster Fryhofer, who taught in 1887 and attended the school as a student. (WSD.)

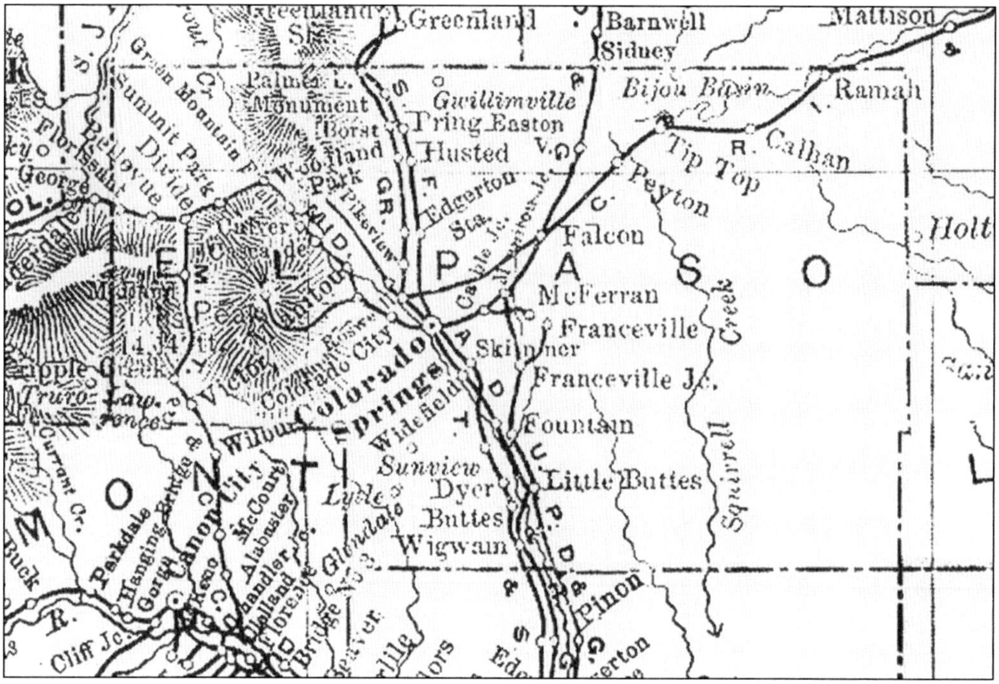

By 1896, Widefield was a whistle stop along the Denver & Rio Grande Railroad in the approximate location of the Main Street intersection in Security. At the intersection of Bradley Road and Highway 85 was a stop on the Santa Fe Railway known as Skinner. Local cattlemen brought their beeves to the stockyards at Skinner to be shipped elsewhere. Later, the railroad added a small station at Crews, south of Widefield. Other rail stops mentioned in this book are Pikeview and Franceville. (ML.)

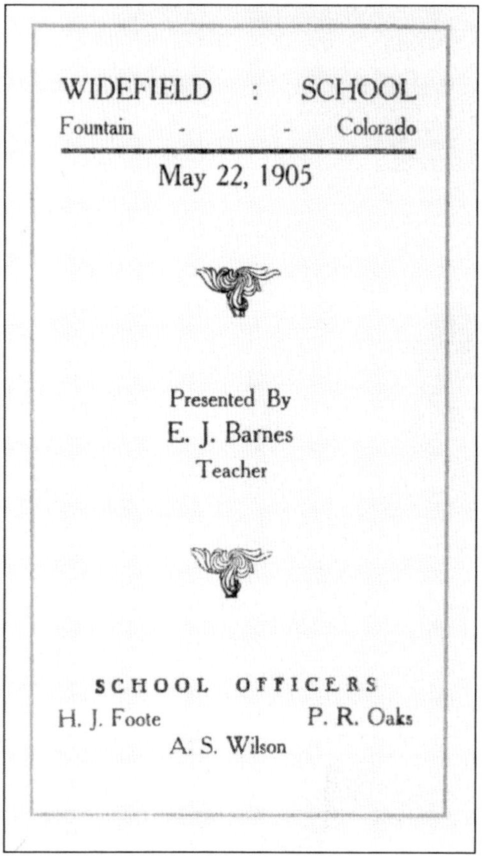

WIDEFIELD : SCHOOL

Fountain - - - Colorado

May 22, 1905

Presented By

E. J. Barnes

Teacher

SCHOOL OFFICERS

H. J. Foote P. R. Oaks

A. S. Wilson

In the spring of 1905, Widefield students held their graduation exercises. At this time, Widefield was included in one of Fountain's precincts. School officer Peter Oaks owned land west of the present nature center, and school officer Seward Wilson operated a dairy farm at the south end of present-day Widefield. There were 15 students attending Widefield School in 1905, including children from the Wilson and Oaks families. (FCNC.)

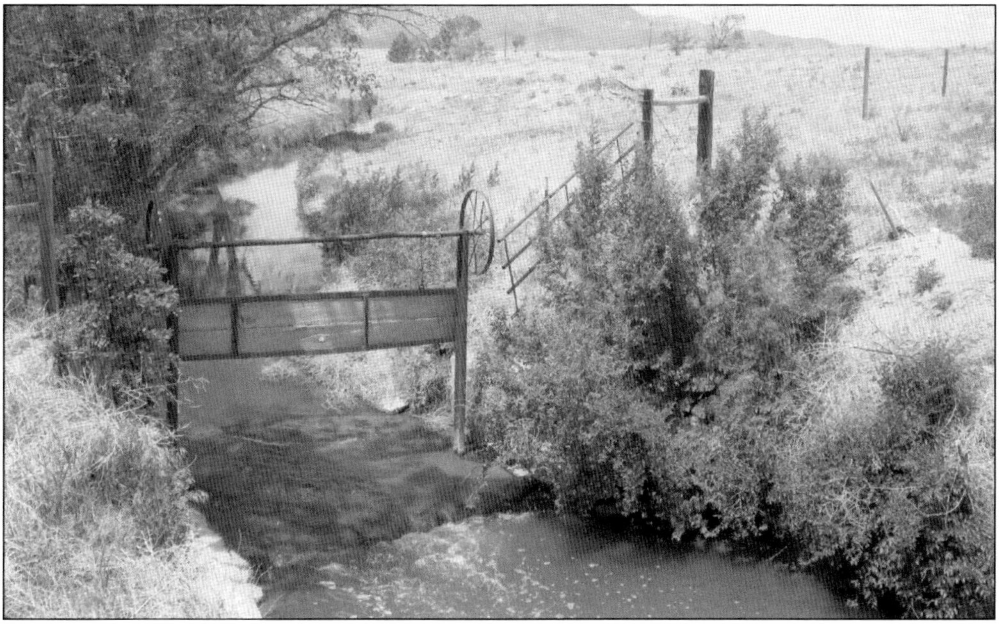

Water diverted from Fountain Creek flows in the Fountain Ditch just before running under the one-lane bridge on Bradley Road. The stream continues eastward to fill the Big Johnson Reservoir. Water in the arid west is a precious resource, and every effort was made to capture and conserve it. Farmers and ranchers purchased shares in the ditch, which allowed them to water their fields and livestock. (ATH.)

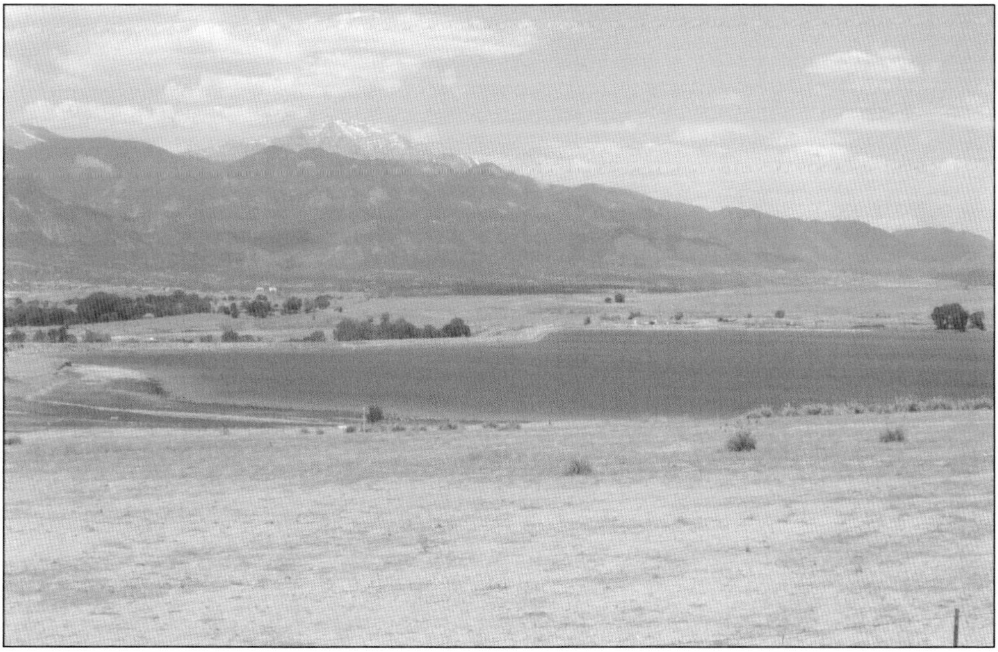

Construction on the Big Johnson Reservoir began in 1905 as part of the Fountain Valley Land & Irrigation Company for the purpose of storing irrigation water. The reservoir feeds the Fountain Ditch as it continues southward. Bringing water to thousands of acres east of the river resulted in larger crop yields, especially in sugar beets. (ATH.)

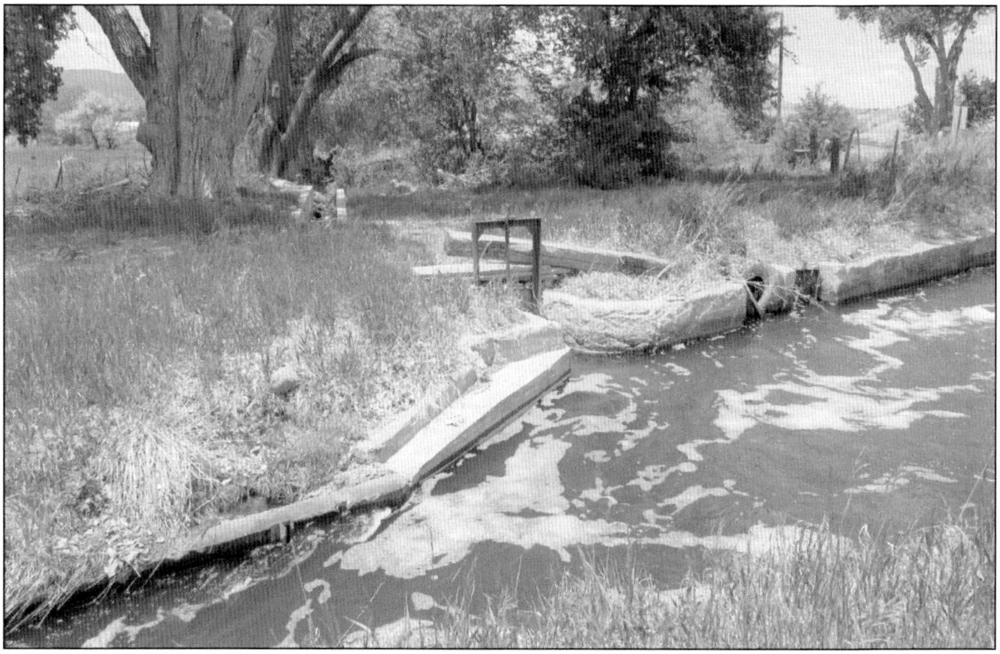

Ditch water flows away from the Big Johnson dam. Some is allowed to trickle down into McCray Reservoir, locally known as Carp Lake. From there, the water flows through Crews Gulch and back into Fountain Creek from which it originated. But most of the water from Big Johnson continues down the Fountain Ditch, which slithers its way south to Fountain and beyond. (ATH.)

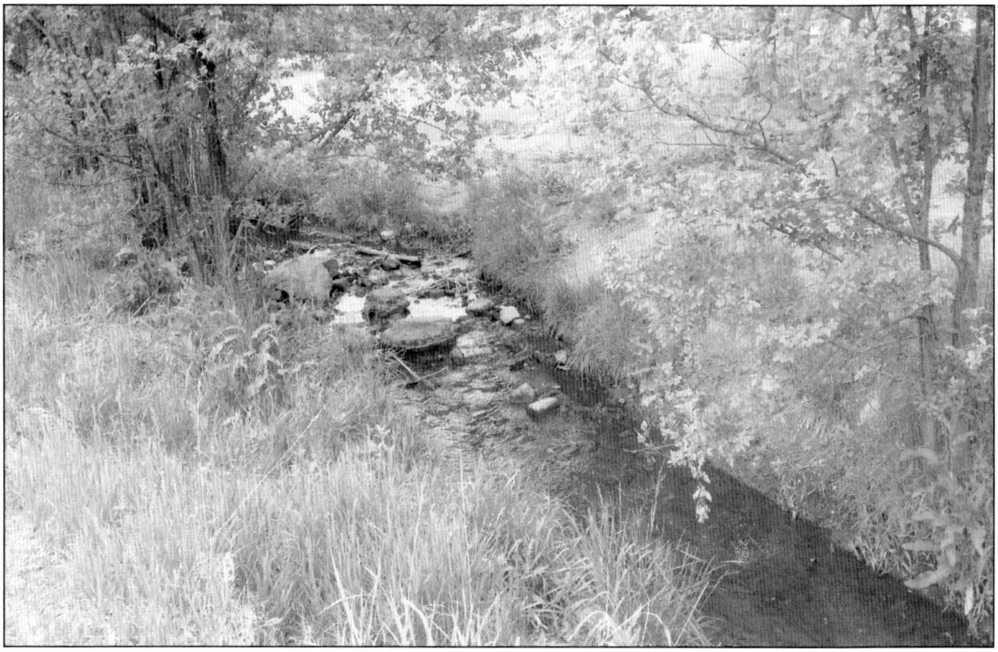

Water dribbles through Crews Gulch as it makes its unhurried way through Widefield Park from Carp Lake to Fountain Creek. In the arid prairie, any source of water is valued by wildlife, livestock, and farmers. The boys from the Wilson Ranch often found their dairy cattle in the luscious grasses along this creek. (ATH.)

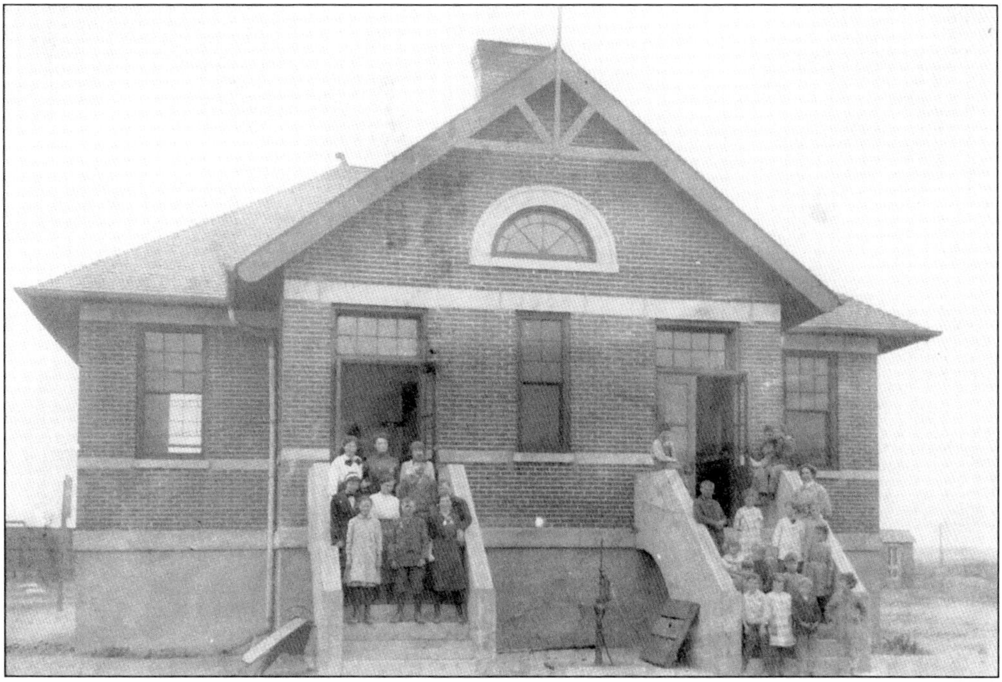

Two classes stand on the steps of the brick, two-room schoolhouse constructed in 1912 on the site of the old grout building. Once known as Widefield School, it stands on the Old Widefield Road and is now used for another purpose. Until the late 1950s, students in grades one through six attended this brick schoolhouse and then spent their high school years at Fountain schools. (FVM)

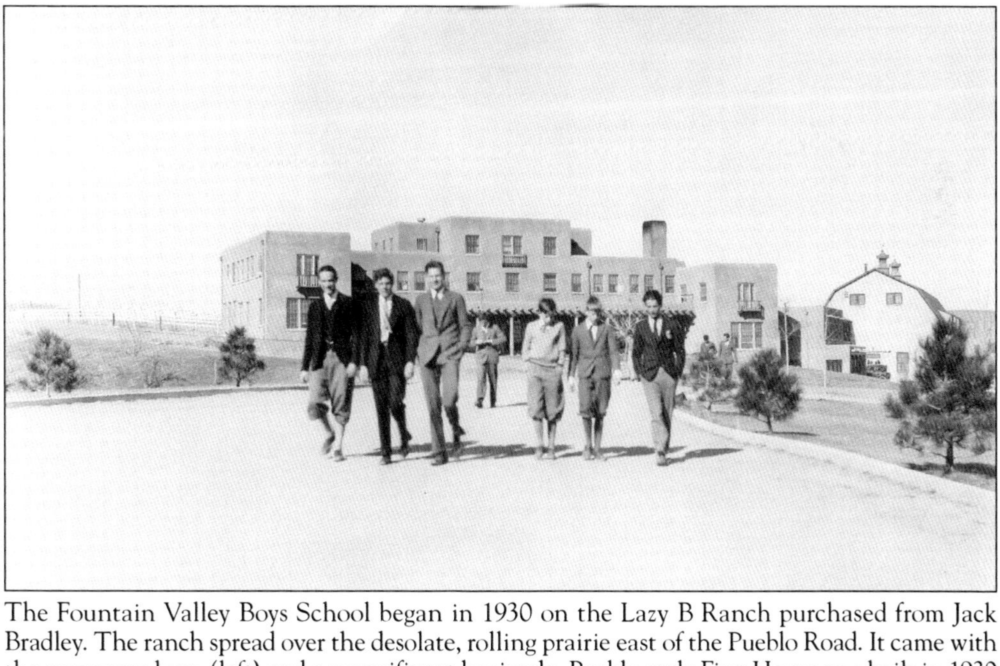

The Fountain Valley Boys School began in 1930 on the Lazy B Ranch purchased from Jack Bradley. The ranch spread over the desolate, rolling prairie east of the Pueblo Road. It came with the enormous barn (left) and a magnificent hacienda. Pueblo-style First House was built in 1930 and later named Sage Hall. Subsequent structures have been added over the years, all built in Southwestern architecture. (Photograph by Laura Gilpin, courtesy of FVS.)

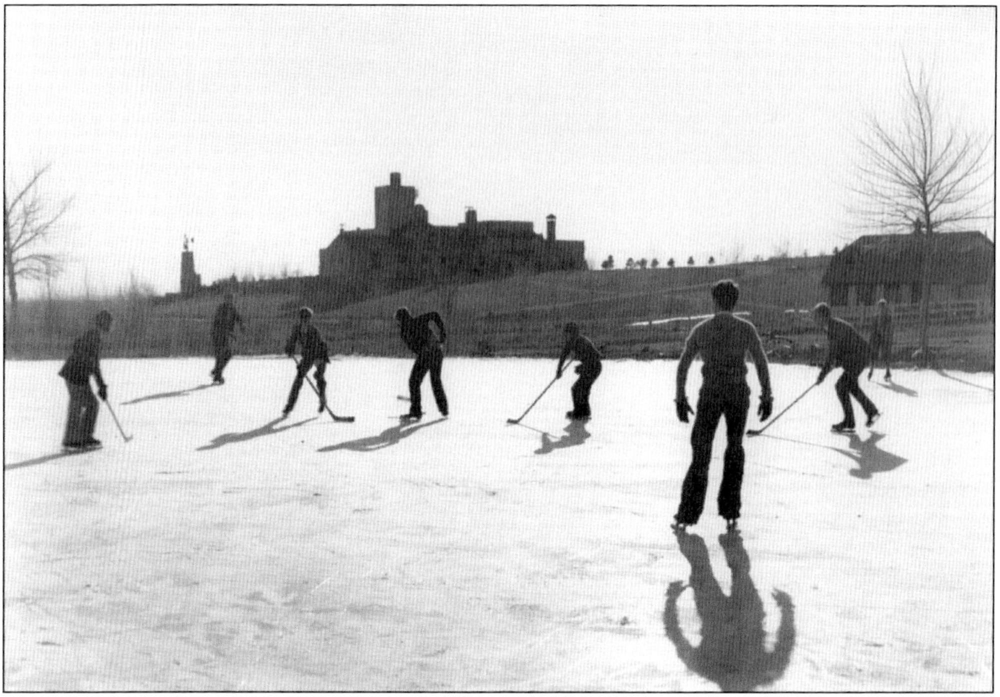

Students at the Fountain Valley Boys School play hockey on the outdoor rink in 1938. This pond was located next to the ranch's original hacienda and was filled with the help of water rights from nearby Big Johnson Reservoir. Hockey was a popular sport, and the school's team participated in interscholastic competitions at the Broadmoor Ice Palace. (Photograph by Laura Gilpin, courtesy of FVS.)

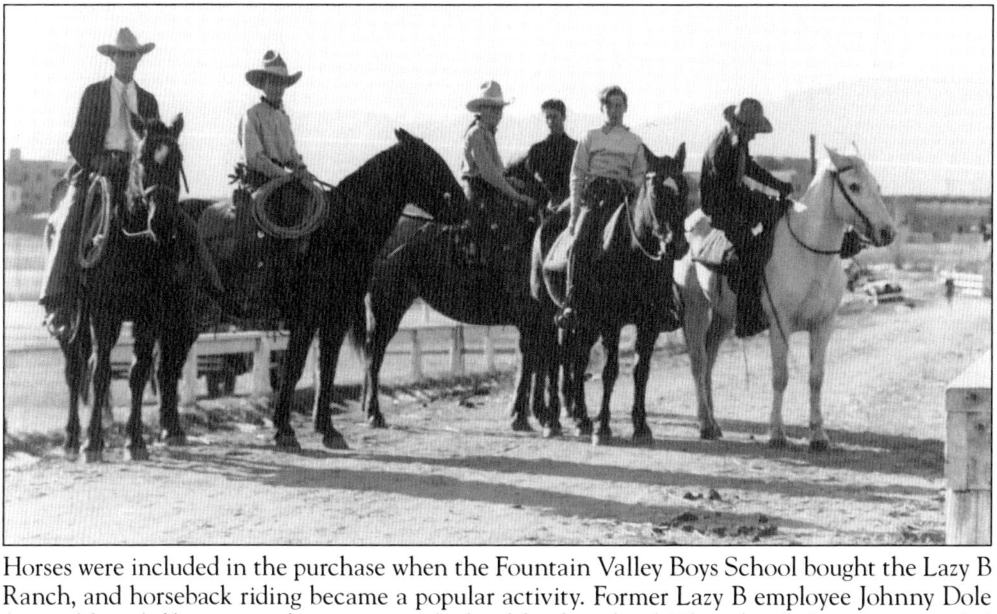

Horses were included in the purchase when the Fountain Valley Boys School bought the Lazy B Ranch, and horseback riding became a popular activity. Former Lazy B employee Johnny Dole (second from left) continued to maintain the herd for the school. The school's founders intended to provide an Eastern boarding school experience in a Western atmosphere. (Photograph by Laura Gilpin, courtesy of FVS.)

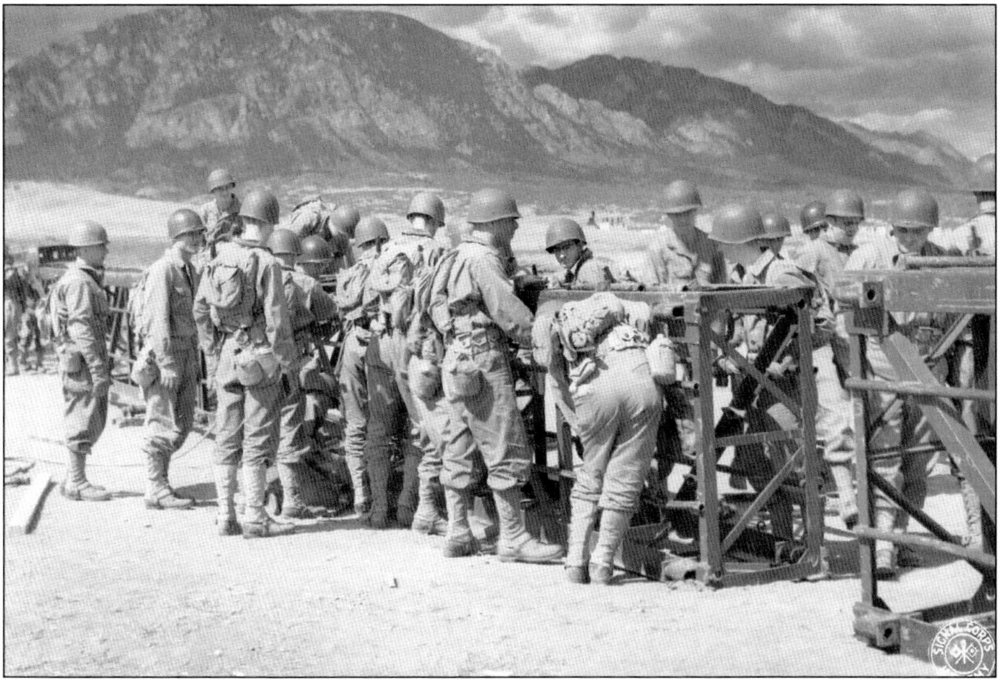

On former ranchlands, soldiers of the 89th Infantry Division Engineers at Camp Carson gather for training in 1943. Heavy-equipment parts were transported by air in metal crates and dropped at locations where the engineers assembled them for use in building roads and bridges. (FCM.)

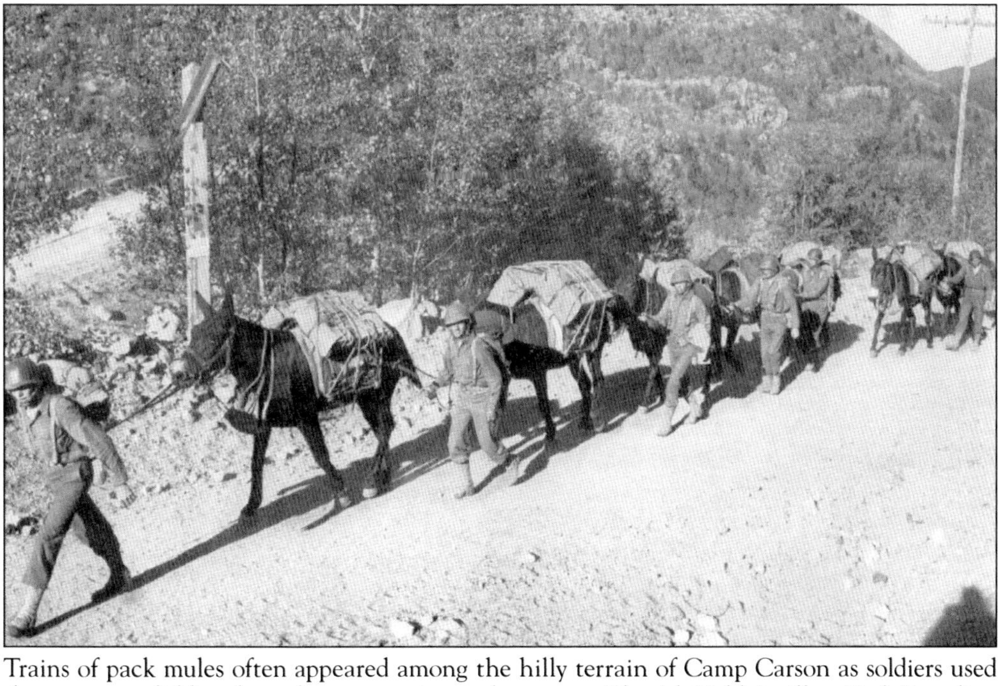

Trains of pack mules often appeared among the hilly terrain of Camp Carson as soldiers used them to carry field packs and maneuver in rough country. The 4th Field Artillery Pack Battalion arrived at the Mountain Post in 1947. The mule battalion saw service in the Philippines and the Panama Canal Zone and supported winter maneuvers at Camp Hale. (FCM.)

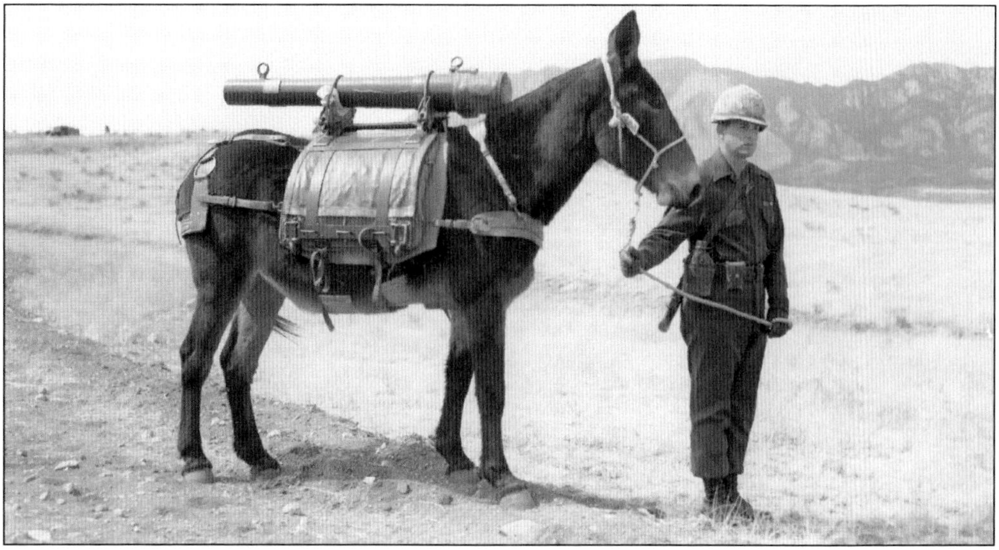

The Army used mules to transport supplies, artillery, and their own feed. Mule handlers at Camp Carson learned how to break wild mules and care for them. They also learned how to load the animals with packs, which required specialized rope knotting. Soldiers with a farming background were valued for this particular assignment. (FCM.)

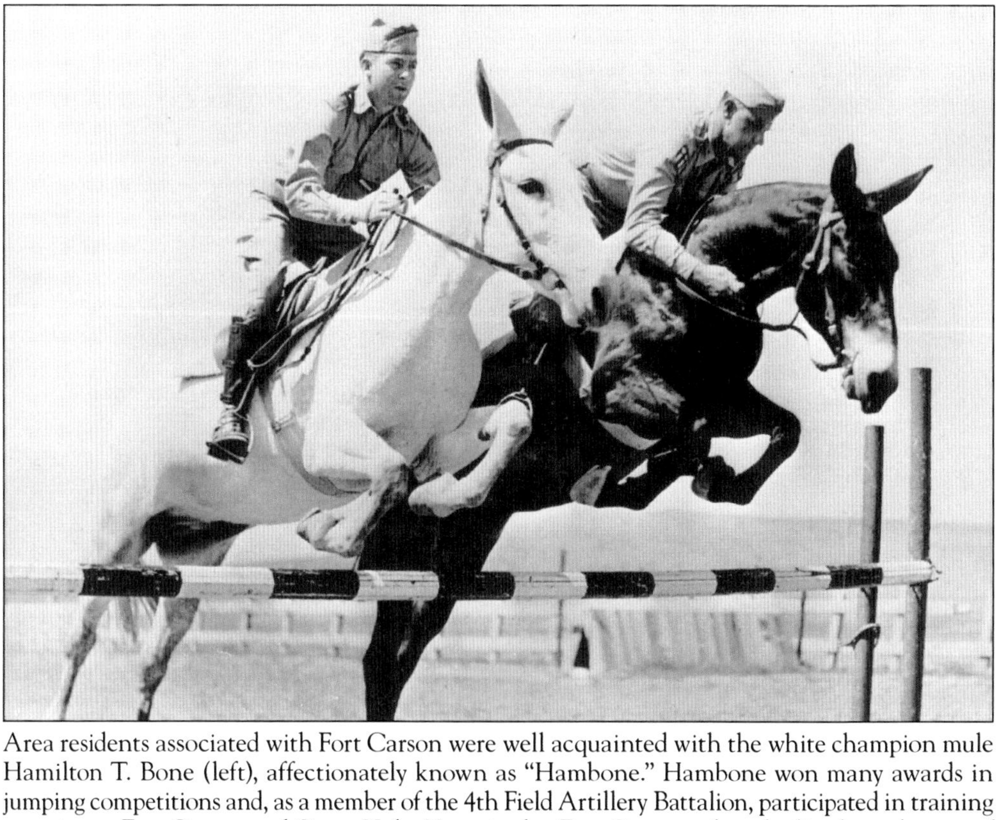

Area residents associated with Fort Carson were well acquainted with the white champion mule Hamilton T. Bone (left), affectionately known as "Hambone." Hambone won many awards in jumping competitions and, as a member of the 4th Field Artillery Battalion, participated in training exercises at Fort Carson and Camp Hale. He retired at Fort Carson, where he lived out the rest of his days and was buried with full military honors in front of the headquarters building. (FCM.)

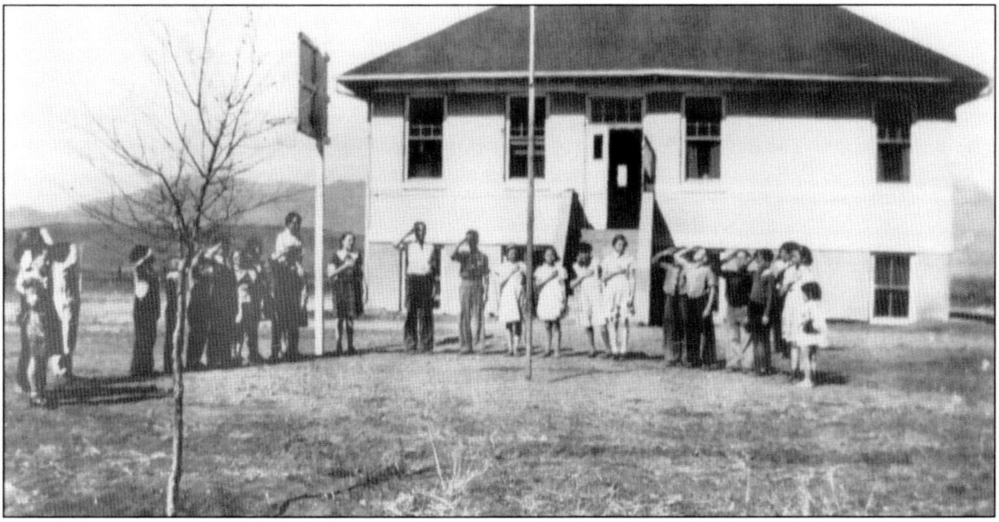

Children of all ages stand behind the Widefield School sometime in the 1940s to pledge allegiance to the flag of the United States. In 1973, the Widefield School was renamed the Kittie Paster School in honor of the woman who was a student and then a teacher in the first school built on this spot. This historic building now serves the senior citizens of the Fountain Valley. (FVSC.)

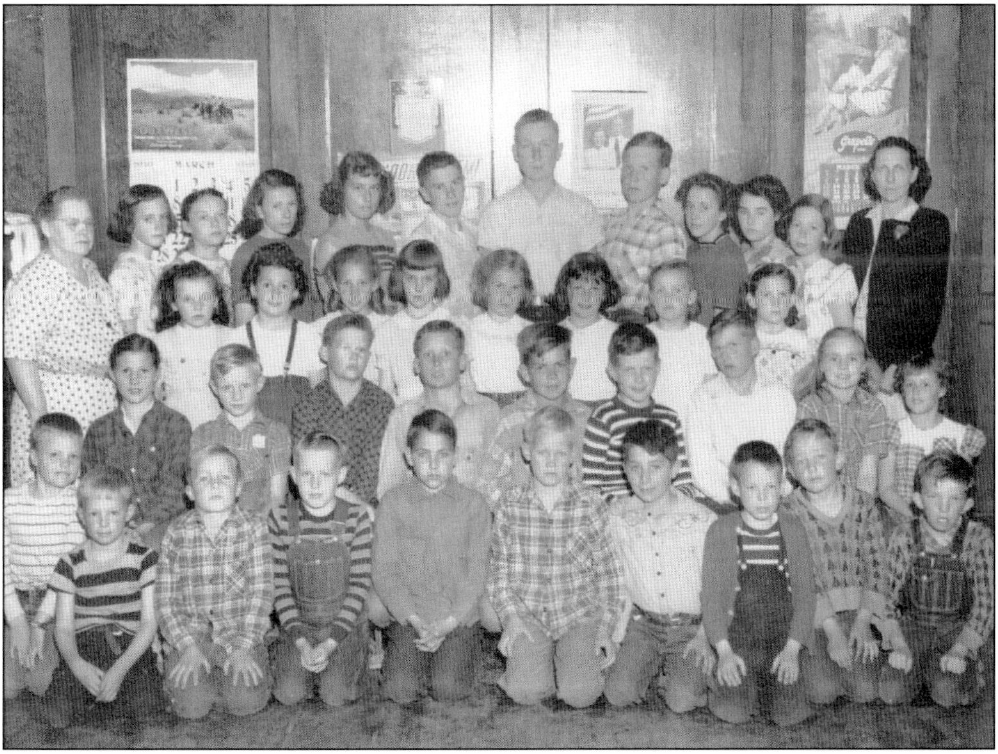

Students from the Widefield farming community gather for a group picture at Widefield School in March 1949. Included in this photograph are Chuck Wilson (first row, third from left), R.L. Pinello, (first row, fifth from left), Dave Wilson (first row, sixth from left), Phillip Pinello (first row, seventh from left), Mary Alice Janitell (third row, second from left), and Kay Sheldon (third row, seventh from left). (MAS.)

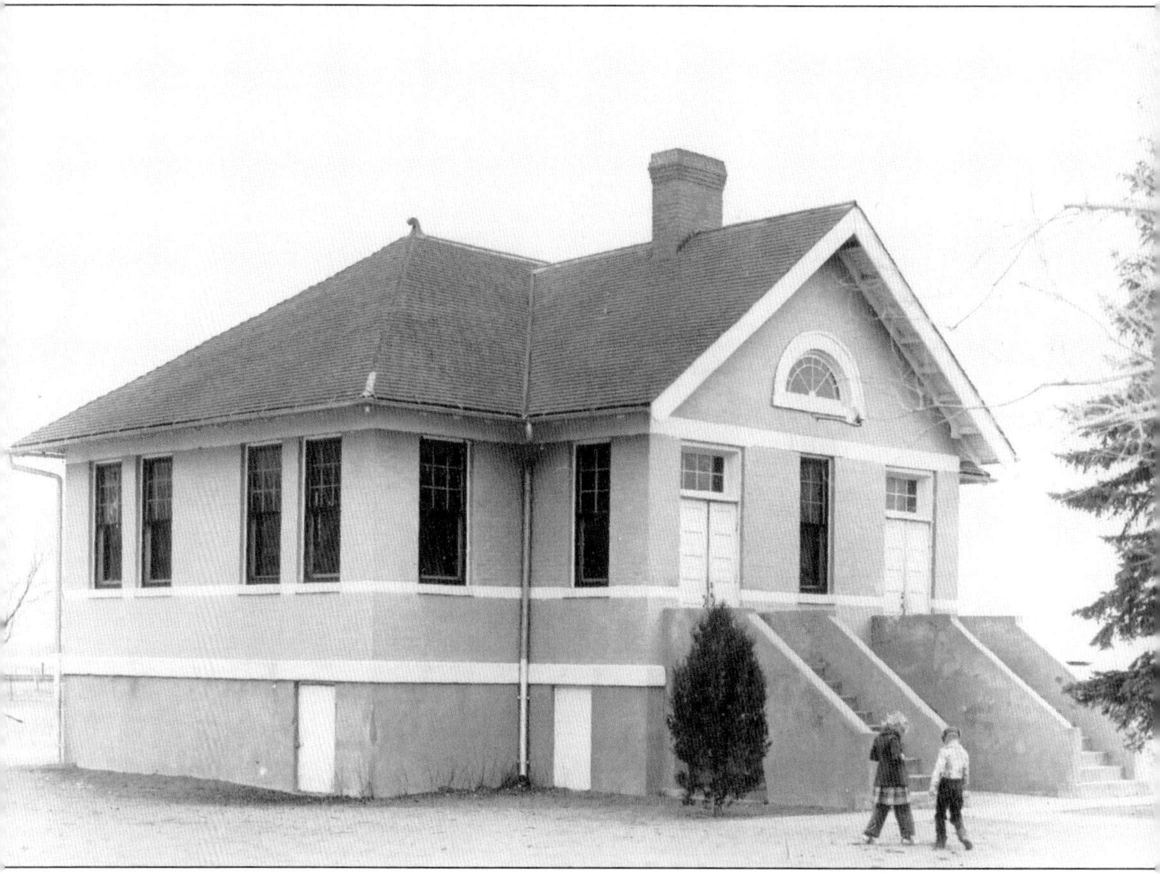

The Widefield School appears here in the 1950s. The local children often referred to this building as the "yellow schoolhouse." A tall blue spruce towers above the children in front of the building. Local legend relates that Louie Pinello planted this specimen of Colorado's state tree when he attended school there. He would have been about eight years old when the school was built. (SW.)

Two

Hard Work and a Little Luck

Very few relics remain among the streets and structures in Security-Widefield to evidence the prior farming activity in the area. However, the old Janitell place sits quietly between two busy roads, now reduced to a ghost farm where a few boarded horses graze in the neglected fields next to a run-down barn and a farmhouse, obscured by mature shade trees. Farther north, the rooftops of Pinello buildings peek above the creek bottom. Motorists on the highway can catch a glimpse of the deer that frequent the meadows of the old farm, which has been set aside as a wildlife refuge. Early residents delighted in the cinnamon rolls and large loaves of fresh Italian bread that were baked in an outdoor oven on the Pinello place and sold in their Brick Oven Bakery. Meanwhile, the Wilson dairy farm was transformed into one of the most desirable middle-class neighborhoods in the country. Representatives from all three pioneering families made a lasting impact on the community when they served on the local school board, and each was honored with a school bearing his name.

Even Walter Belveal's fishing ponds continue to benefit the residents of Security-Widefield and beyond. Belveal's former farm has been set aside as a shady wetlands habitat, in which visitors can stroll, jog, or cycle. Birds and animals, of which Belveal was so fond, find peaceful refuge in the park.

Nick Venetucci, the area's most influential farmer, operated a successful farm on the highway for an admirable 70 years. Boys from the new housing development across the road anxiously waited for the asparagus to get tall enough so they could begin the spring season working for Venetucci. He put money in the pockets of hardworking boys in exchange for picking vegetables, hoeing corn, filling gas tanks, and pulling accumulated debris from the ditches. He doled out more work than he really needed just to keep the young men busy until autumn. This is how he taught them the value of a good work ethic, integrity, and generosity. Venetucci often demonstrated this generosity when he had his boys throw more corn in the bag than was paid for by the customer. Similarly, anyone who visited the Venetucci home was offered a glass of his homemade wine in true Italian hospitality.

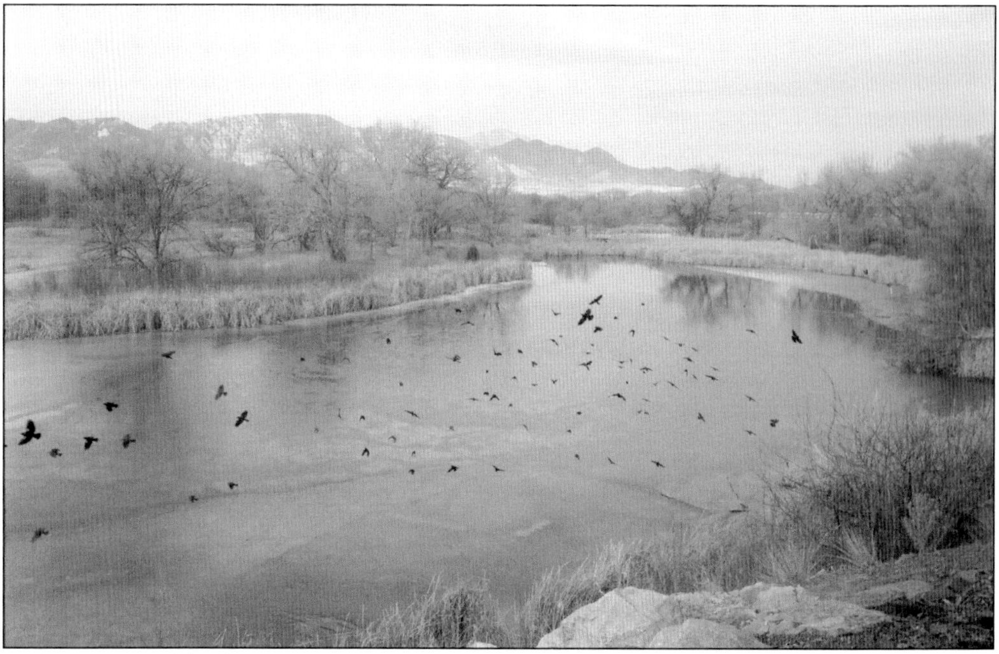

Red-winged blackbirds, along with waterfowl and wildlife, live in the wetlands created by ponds and springs now owned by the Fountain Creek Nature Center. Fish culturalist Walter Belveal, who owned these ponds from the 1920s to the 1960s, stocked them with trout, catfish, bass, and bluegill and made them available to fishermen. (ATH.)

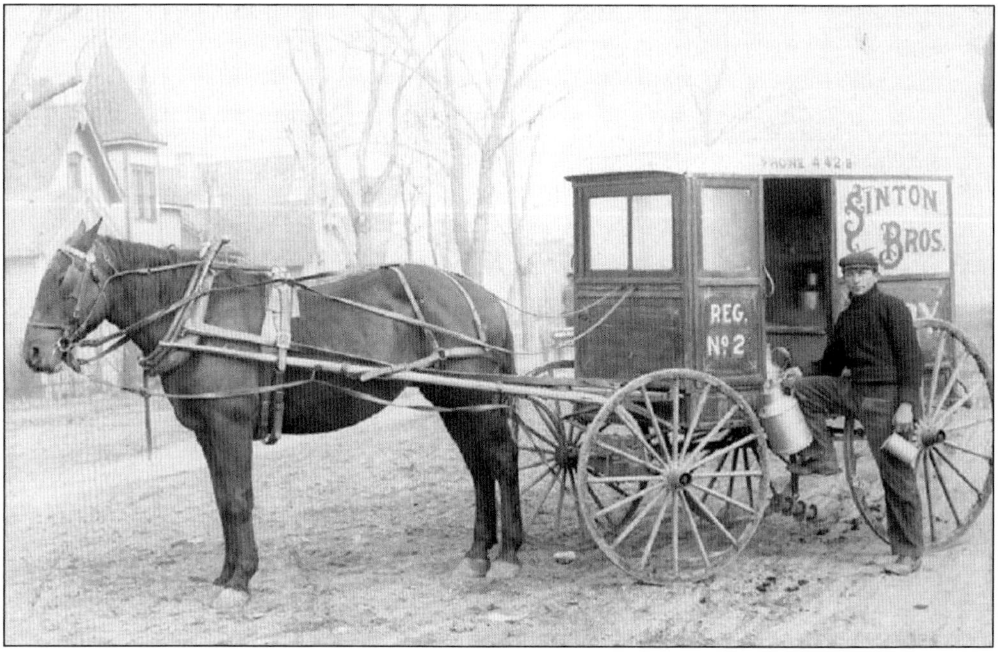

An employee of Sinton Dairy stands next to his delivery wagon in Colorado Springs in the early 1900s. As the business grew, George and Melvin Sinton found it necessary to find more pastureland for their cows. Consequently, in 1928, they acquired land in the rolling hills west of rancher Alphonso Pinello's property, which provided excellent grazing for dairy cattle. (SD.)

Little Howard Wilson sits atop his father's steel-wheeled John Deere tractor in about 1937 on the Wilson dairy farm in Widefield. With a hitch attached to the back of the tractor, these machines helped the farmer accomplish many tasks. (SW.)

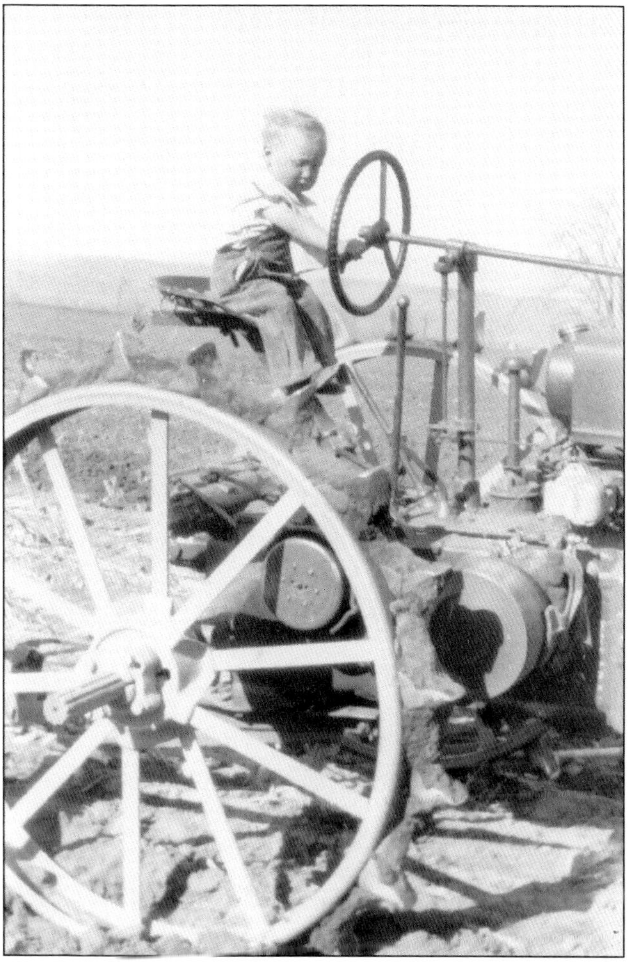

Florence Wilson stands outside her chicken coop in the 1930s. This large coop accommodated scores of chickens, which provided Wilson with many eggs to sell. Typically, farmwives saved their egg money to purchase a luxury later. The tower in the background supported a windmill, which pumped water from a well. Wilson lived with her husband, Seward, on a dairy farm south of Widefield on the east side of the highway. (SW.)

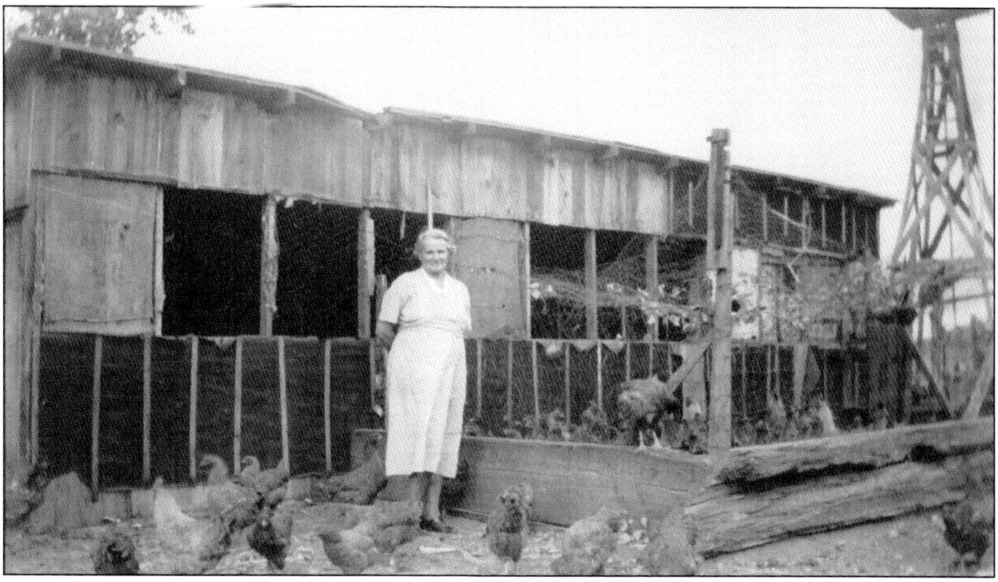

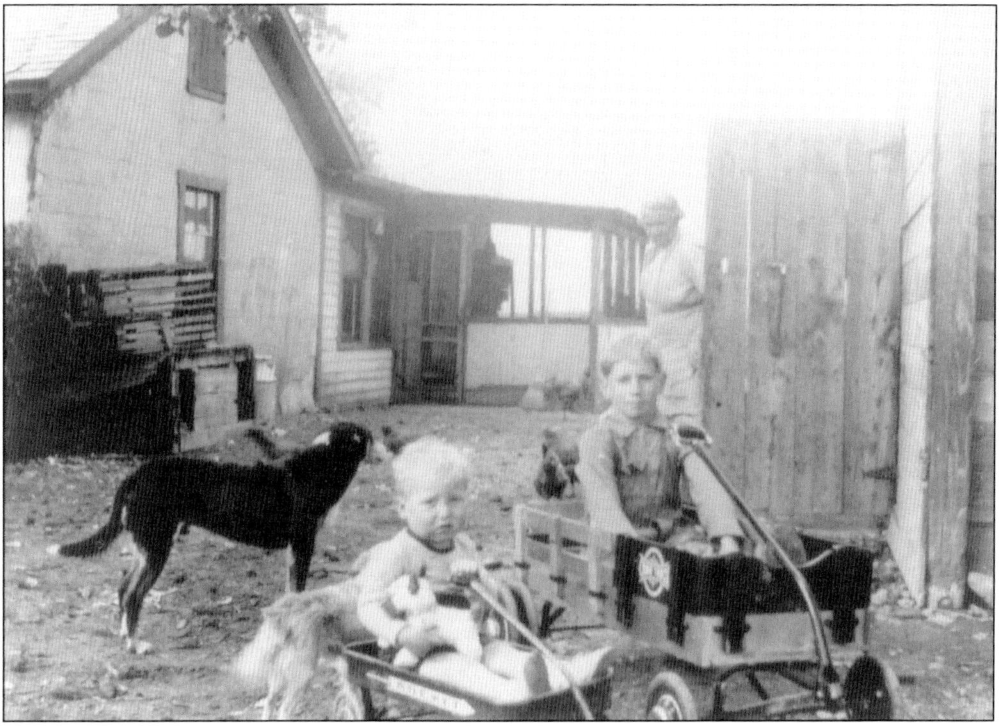

Florence Wilson emerges from the milk shed in which 10-gallon cans of fresh milk were cooled. Her grandchildren sit in the wagons in the foreground. Chickens and dogs roam the yard at the Wilson home, which was once located near present-day Jersey Lane in lower Widefield. (MC.)

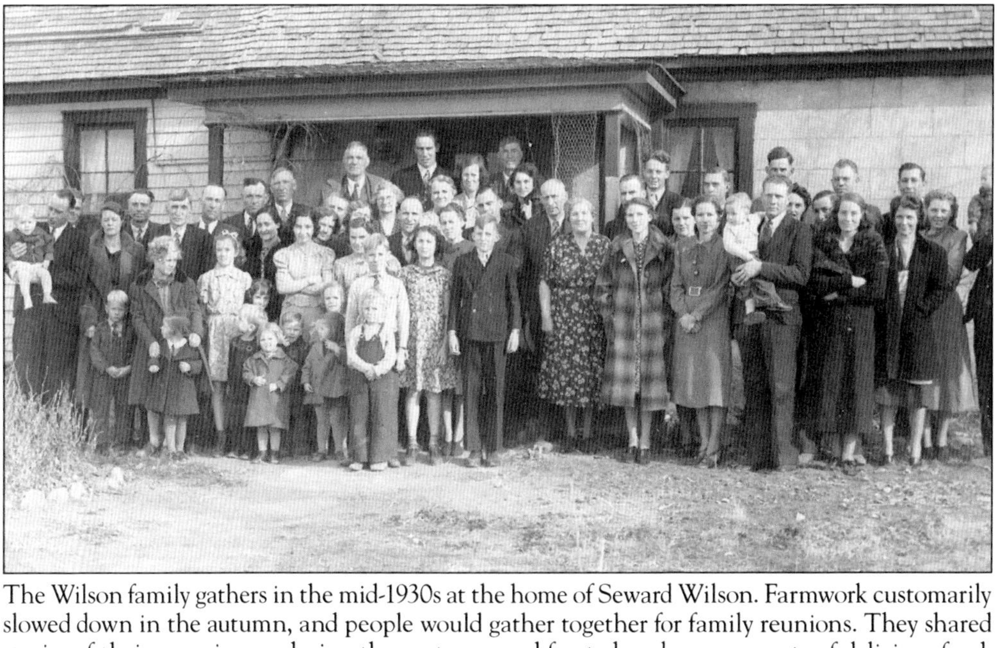

The Wilson family gathers in the mid-1930s at the home of Seward Wilson. Farmwork customarily slowed down in the autumn, and people would gather together for family reunions. They shared stories of their experiences during the past year and feasted on large amounts of delicious food. Wilson, his four brothers, and their wives, children, and grandchildren attended this reunion, which was reported to be the largest family gathering ever held in the Pikes Peak region. (SW.)

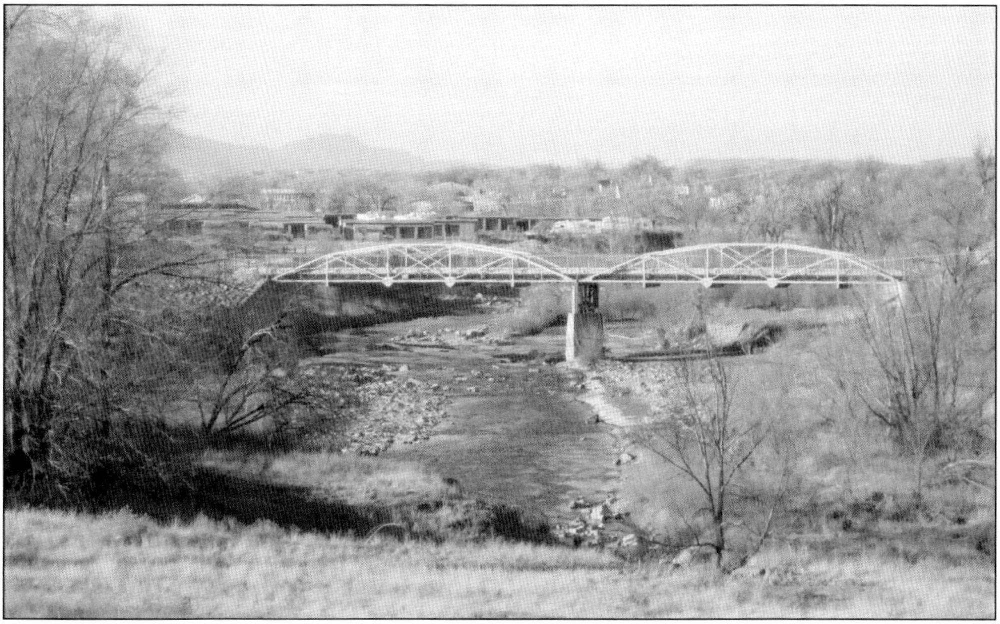

The Carson Road Bridge once spanned the river at Fountain. It was later placed across the river farther north when a road was built from the highway at Widefield to Camp Carson for access during its construction. After the subdivisions of Security-Widefield sprang into existence, this one-lane steel bridge saw a steady stream of vehicles carrying soldiers and their families back and forth until the mid-1970s. (ATH.)

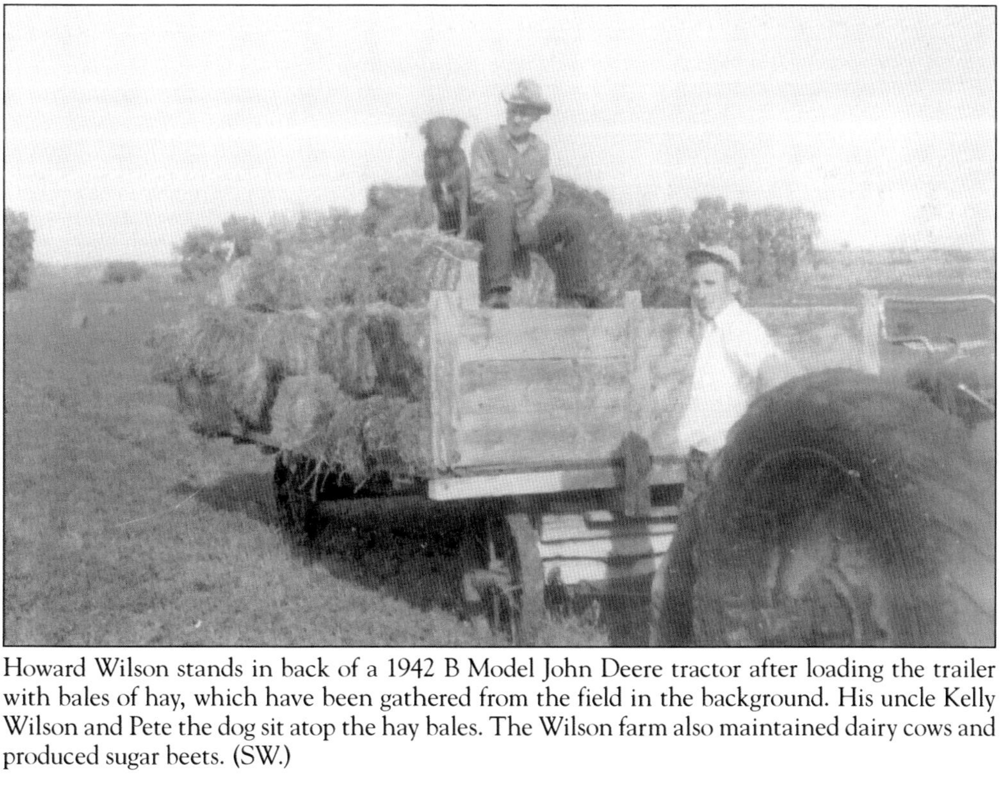

Howard Wilson stands in back of a 1942 B Model John Deere tractor after loading the trailer with bales of hay, which have been gathered from the field in the background. His uncle Kelly Wilson and Pete the dog sit atop the hay bales. The Wilson farm also maintained dairy cows and produced sugar beets. (SW.)

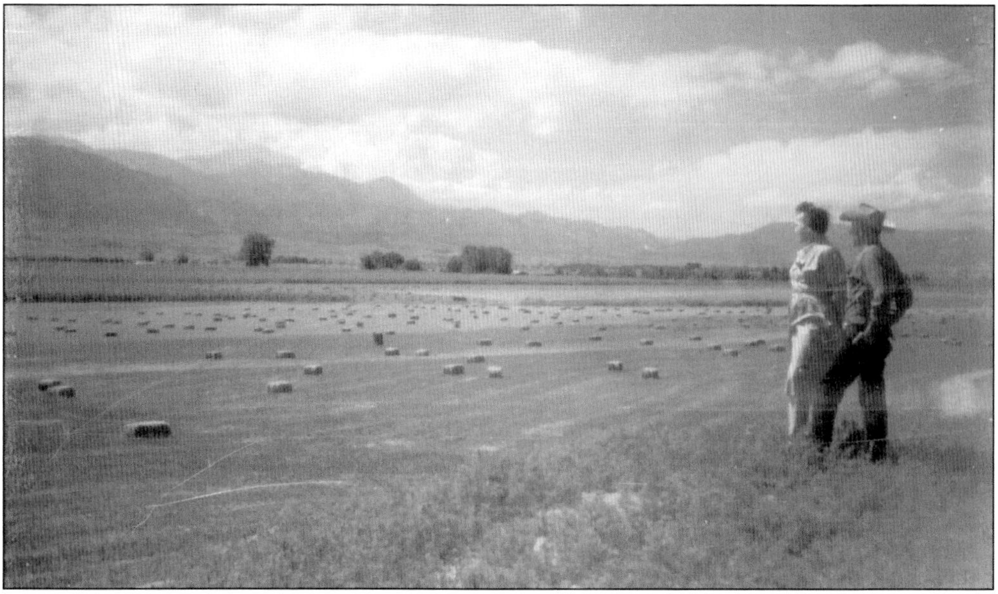

Mary (Wilson) Sample and her brother Kelly Wilson, both children of Seward Wilson, stand near the future site of Webster Elementary School as they survey the hay field on the southern portion of the Wilson dairy farm. The farm was situated between present-day Widefield Boulevard and Mesa Ridge Parkway. Water from Crews Gulch irrigated some of the fields, and the hay was fed to the farm's 85 Holstein cows. (SW.)

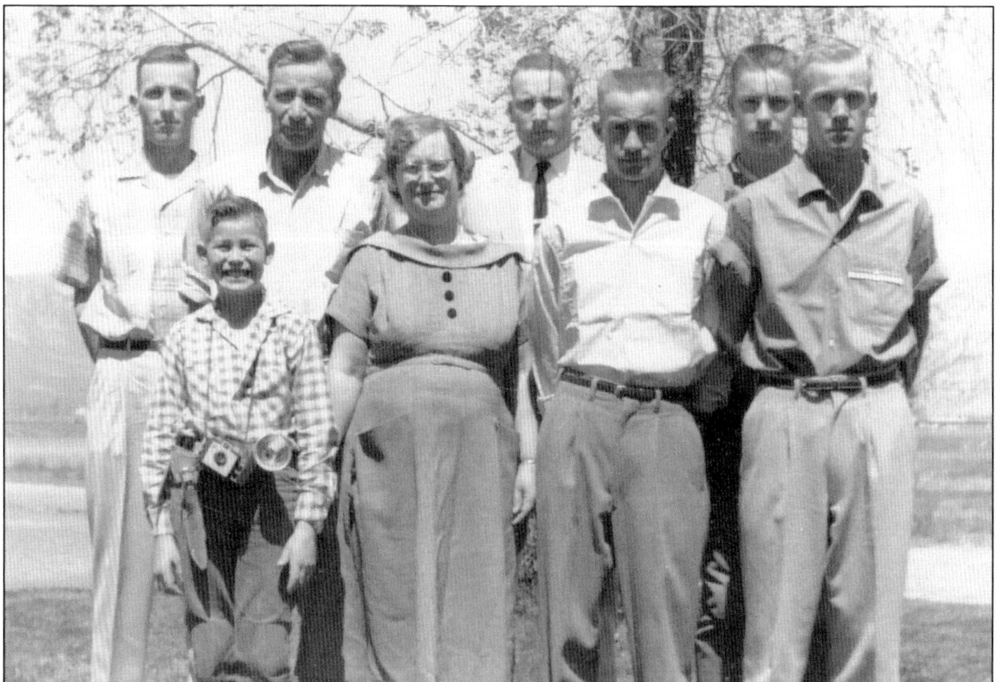

Jack Wilson's family poses for a picture in the 1960s. From left to right are (first row) Mike, Mildred, Sam, and Dave; (second row) Howard, Jack, Jim, and Chuck. Jack operated the Wilson dairy farm, which was established by his father, Seward, before 1900. (SW.)

The caption for this 1950s magazine advertisement for Purina states, "Jack Wilson, a dairyman since 1927, and his son [Howard] are shown at their Fountain, Colorado, dairy, ten miles south of Colorado Springs." It goes on to explain how Wilson's milk production increased with the Purina feeding program. (SW.)

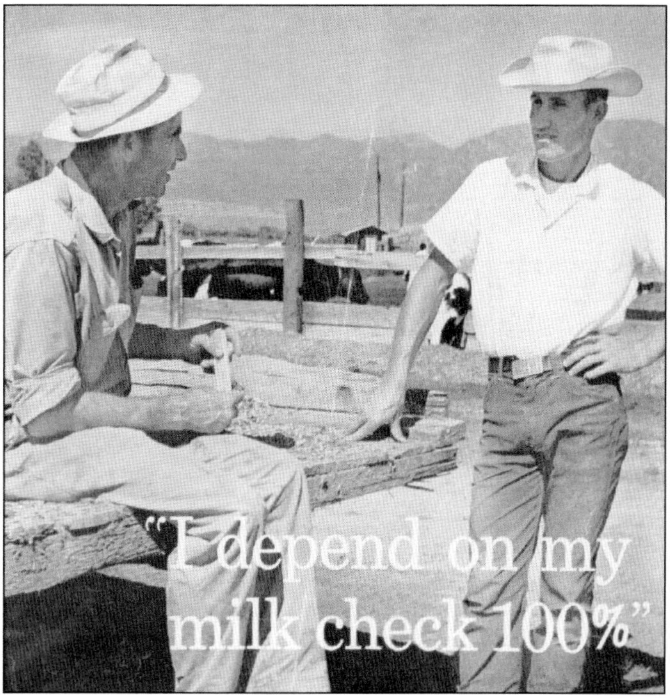

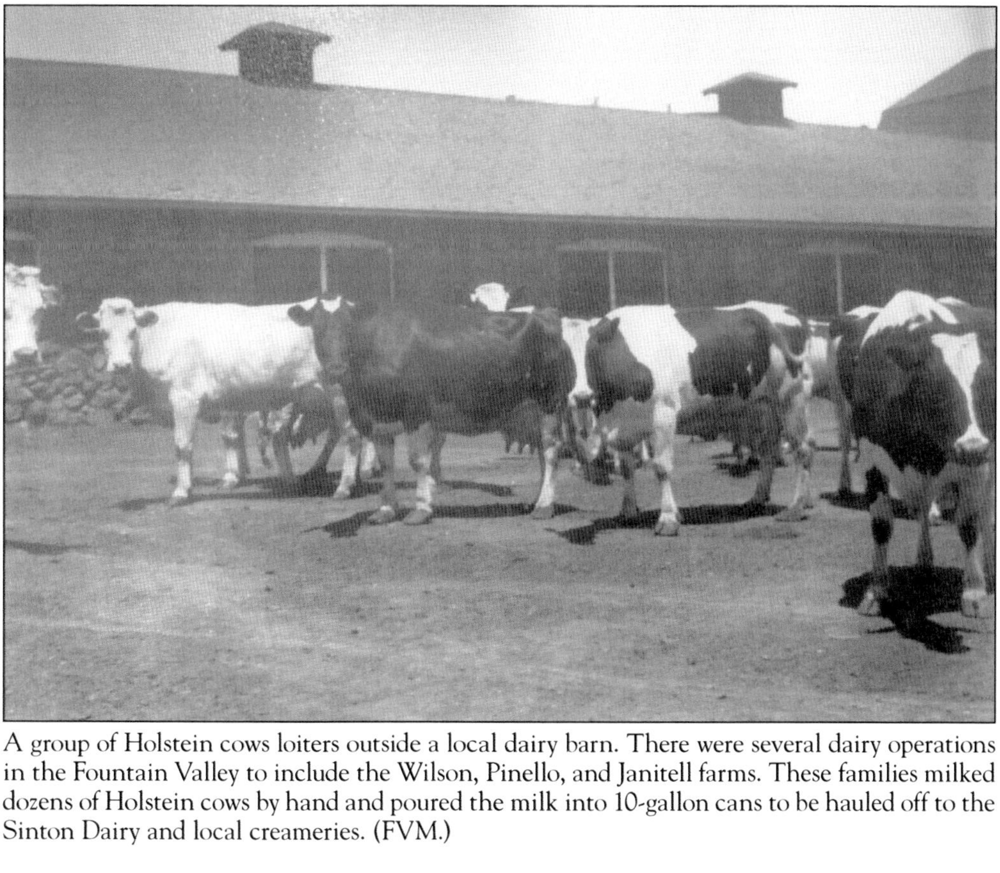

A group of Holstein cows loiters outside a local dairy barn. There were several dairy operations in the Fountain Valley to include the Wilson, Pinello, and Janitell farms. These families milked dozens of Holstein cows by hand and poured the milk into 10-gallon cans to be hauled off to the Sinton Dairy and local creameries. (FVM.)

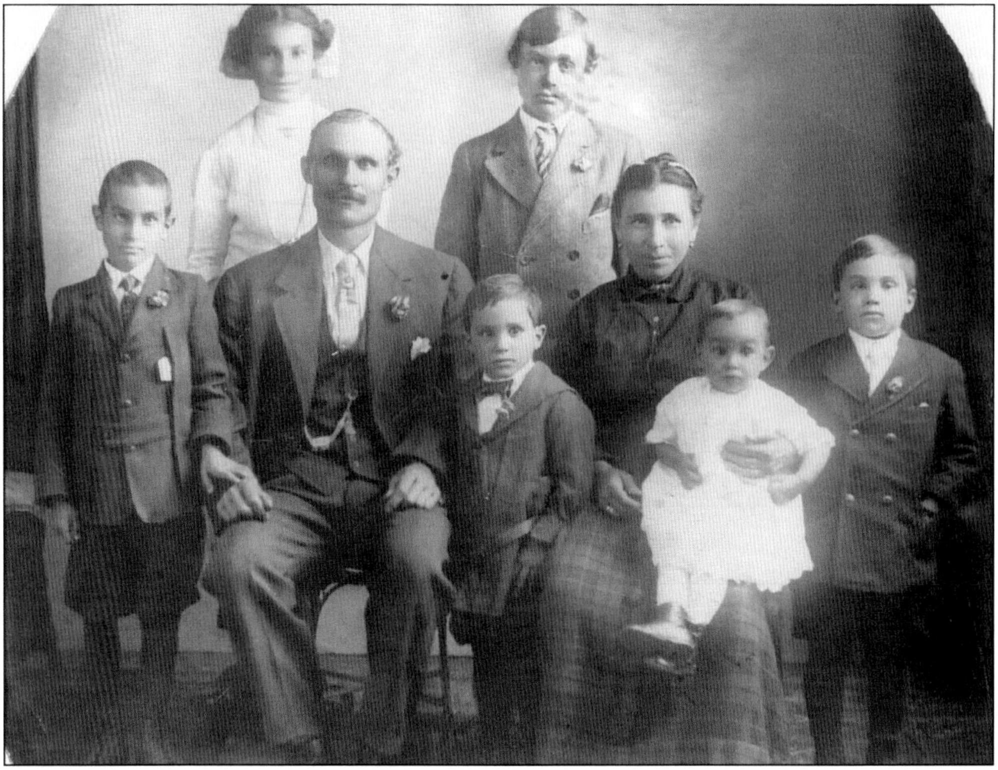

Nicholas and Marguerita (Carella) Venetucci immigrated to the Colorado coal mines from Picerno, Italy. They pose with their family for this portrait in 1916, when they lived in the Italian American colony in the coal-mining town of Papeton. The area is now known as Venetian Village in Colorado Springs. From left to right are (first row) Mike, Nicholas, Dominic, Marguerita, Rocco, and Joseph; (second row) Nina and Antonio. The youngest daughter, Mary, was born later. (MAS.)

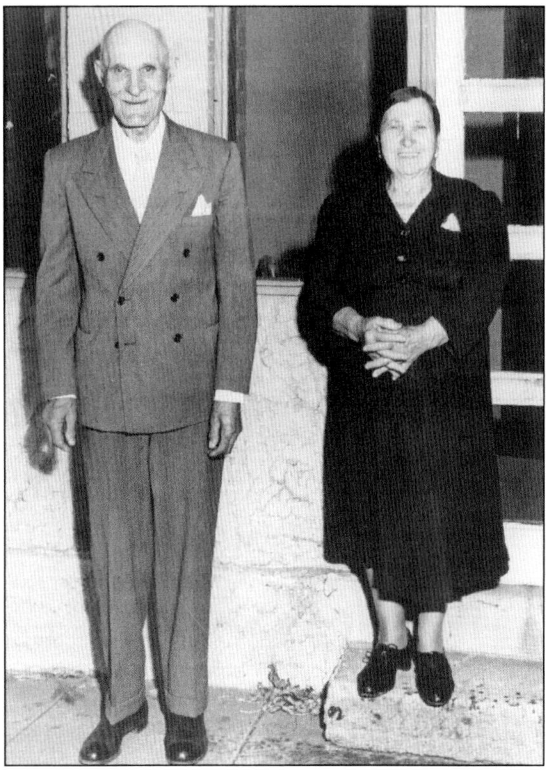

Nicholas (left) and Marguerita (Carella) Venetucci appear here outside their farmhouse located on Highway 85. Nicholas immigrated with his family at the age of six to Louisville, Colorado, where his father worked in the coal mines. Nicholas later worked the mines in Papeton, where his children were born. In 1936, the Venetucci family left the mines and bought the farm south of his sister Blanche (Venetucci) Pinello. (MAS.)

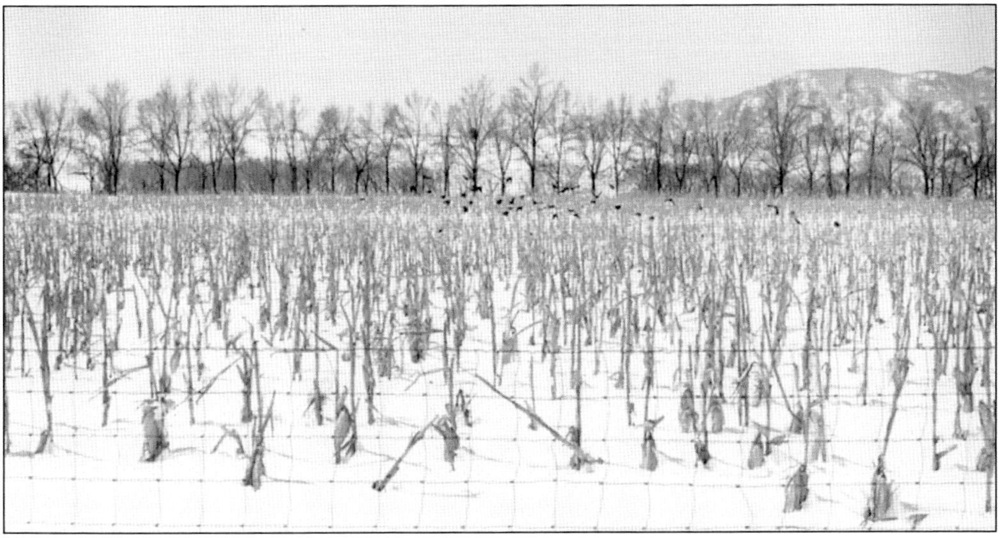

The Venetucci corn field rests during the winter of 1957. The original 1,000 acres extended across Fountain Creek to the hills beyond. Nicholas Venetucci, with the help of his sons Antonio, Joseph, and Dominic, developed a high-quality sweet corn for which the farm became famous. They also grew asparagus and pumpkins and were some of the valley's first to develop the use of well water. (PPCF.)

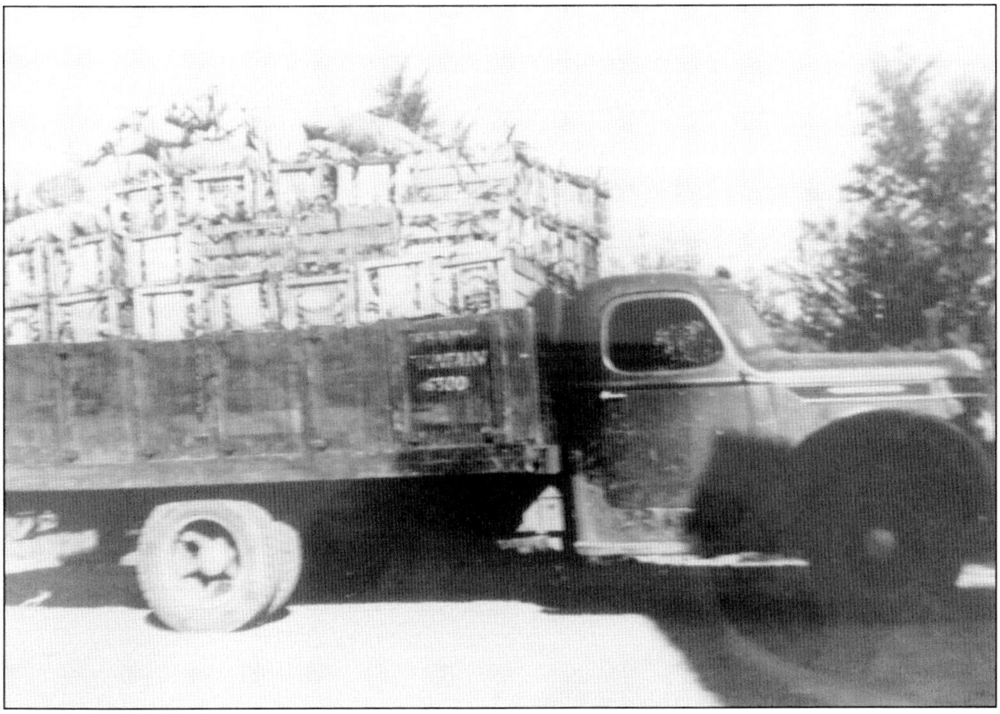

Nick Venetucci's farm truck is loaded with wooden crates filled with freshly picked sweet corn. During the 1960s, Venetucci hired local teenage boys to work on his farm. One of the tasks involved picking ripened corn and stacking the ears, four at a time, into wooden crates, which were then driven to Colorado Springs grocery stores and markets along Tejon Street and Colorado Avenue. (FVM.)

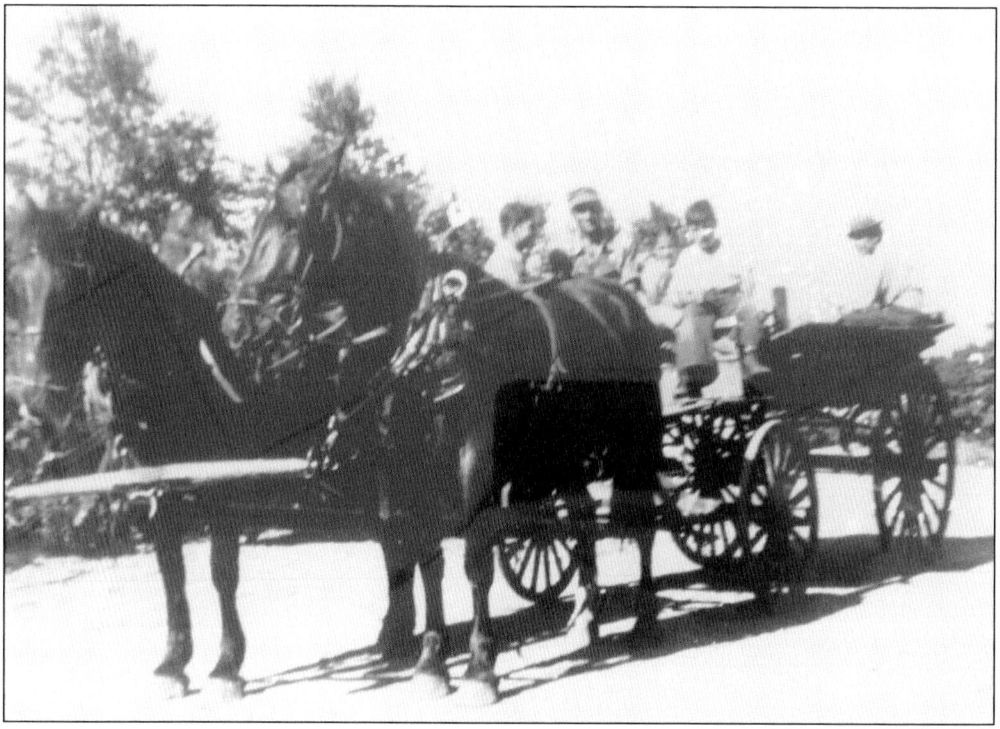

Nick Venetucci takes children for a ride in his wagon sometime in the 1950s. He had no children of his own but loved having them around. He had several nieces, nephews, and young cousins. Eventually, he would have thousands of schoolchildren visiting his farm annually. (FVM.)

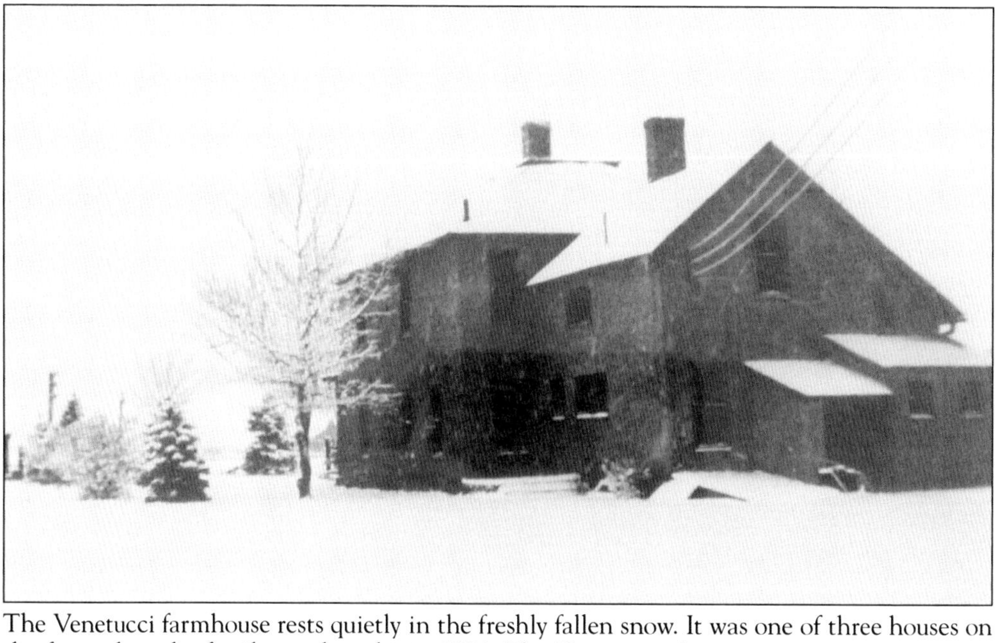

The Venetucci farmhouse rests quietly in the freshly fallen snow. It was one of three houses on the farm when the family purchased it in 1936. The Venetucci place continues to operate as a working farm that grows organic vegetables and raises grass-fed livestock. Schoolchildren visit the farm and the neighboring Pinello Ranch to learn about agricultural sustainability. (MAS.)

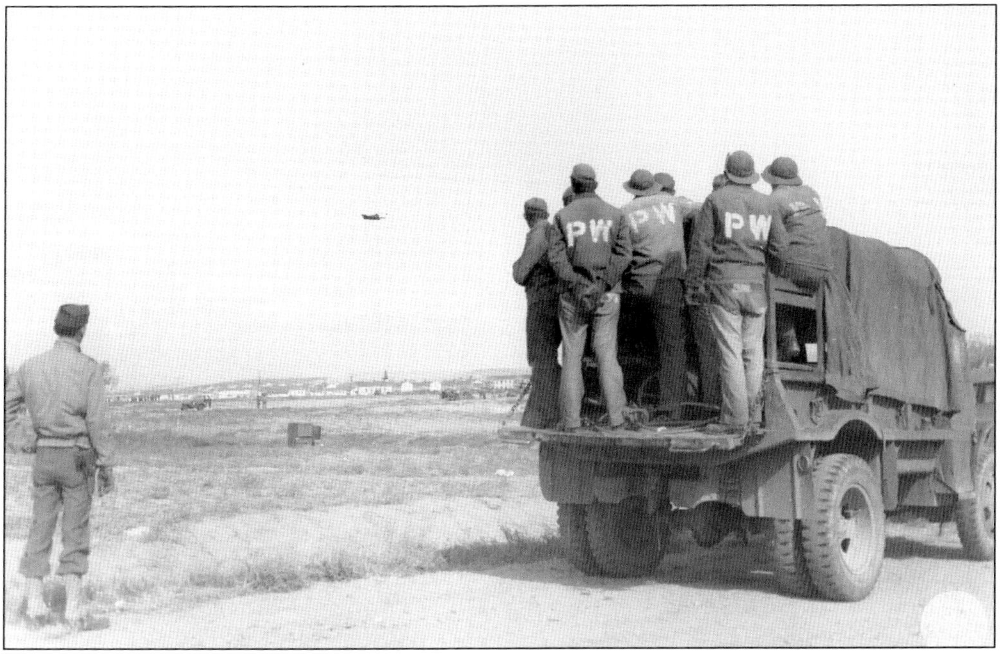

Fort Carson kept German and Italian prisoners of war during World War II. They alleviated Colorado's labor shortage by doing general farmwork around the region, earning 80¢ each day. They were taken out to the Venetucci farm to clear fields for planting and to the Wilson farm to labor in the beet field. (FCM.)

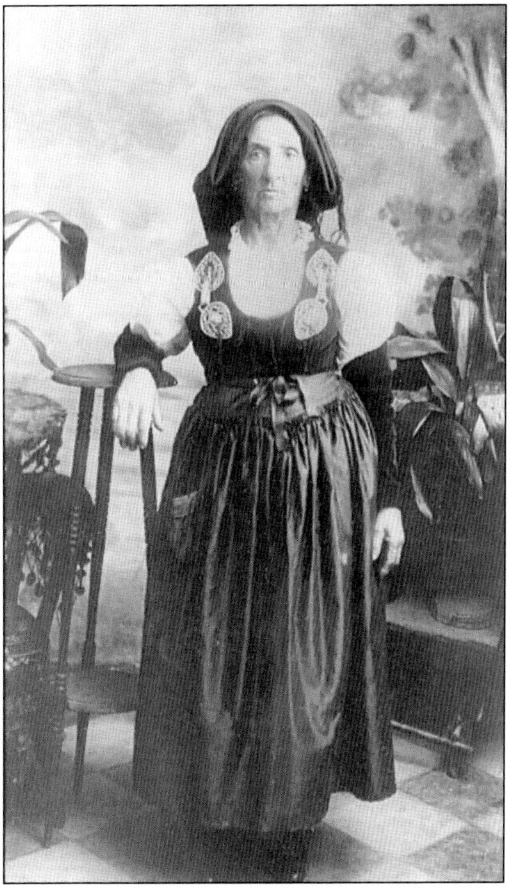

Maria Domenica (Ciallella) Janitell, grandmother of John Janitell, poses here in about 1930, dressed in her native costuming of Roccamandolfi, Italy. The words of miner Dan Marcantonio, father of Bambina Venetucci, speak for most Italian immigrants: "I came for the future of my children. For them I wanted an education, a better life. In the old country there was no future. There were too many people and no work. I had to come. There was no other way." (MAS.)

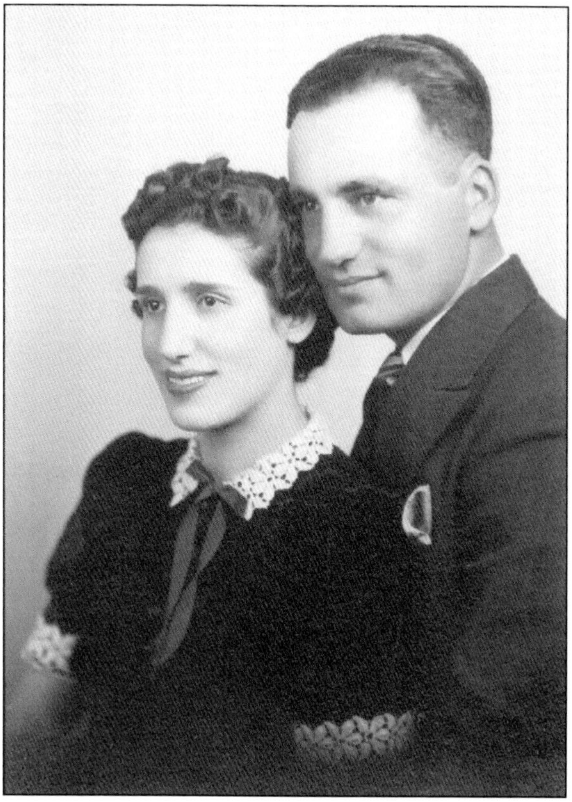

Pictured here are John Janitell and his lovely wife, Mae (Cuchares), both children of Italian immigrants. John grew up on his father's truck/dairy farm in an area that was known as Garden Valley, south of Colorado Springs, in the area of present-day South Circle Drive. This farm was purchased by John's father, who immigrated to America from Italy to work in Colorado's coal mines. (MAS.)

This aerial view shows John Janitell's farm as it appeared in the 1940s. It was located on the north side of Mesa Road. His acreage extended to include the present sites of Mesa Ridge High School and Janitell Middle School. Like his father, Janitell operated a truck farm and dairy. (MAS.)

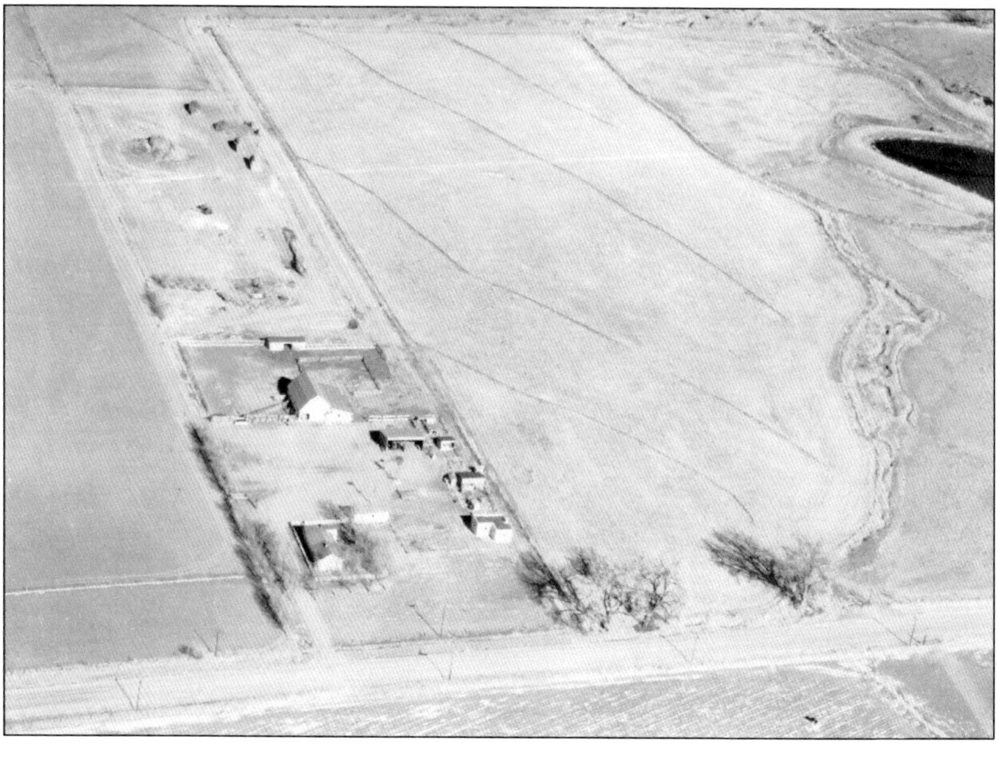

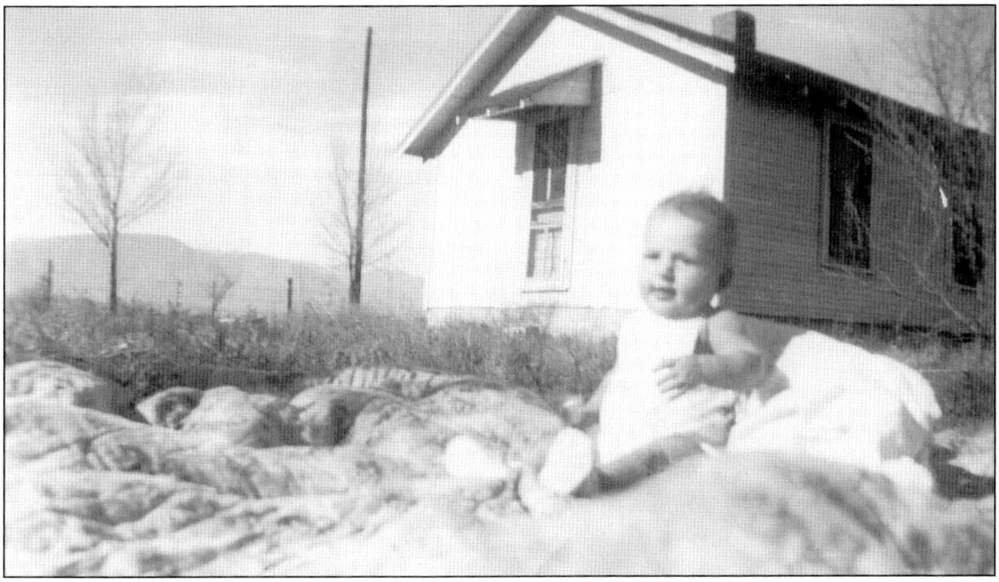

Mary Alice Janitell sits outside her family's farmhouse at the Janitell farm on Mesa Road in 1942. A white picket fence eventually surrounded the little white house. Mary Alice grew up doing all sorts of farmwork, including riding fences, but her favorite part of farm life involved caring for the horses. (MAS.)

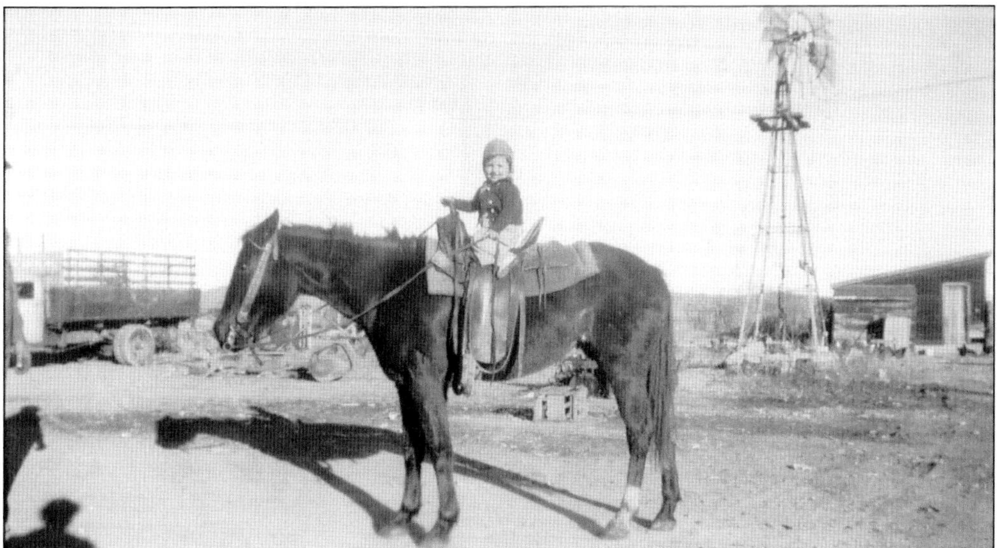

Little John Janitell sits astride a horse on his family farm in the 1940s. In the background, a windmill pumps water from a well. John Janitell Sr. later sold water from his wells to Widefield Homes for a housing subdivision. (MAS.)

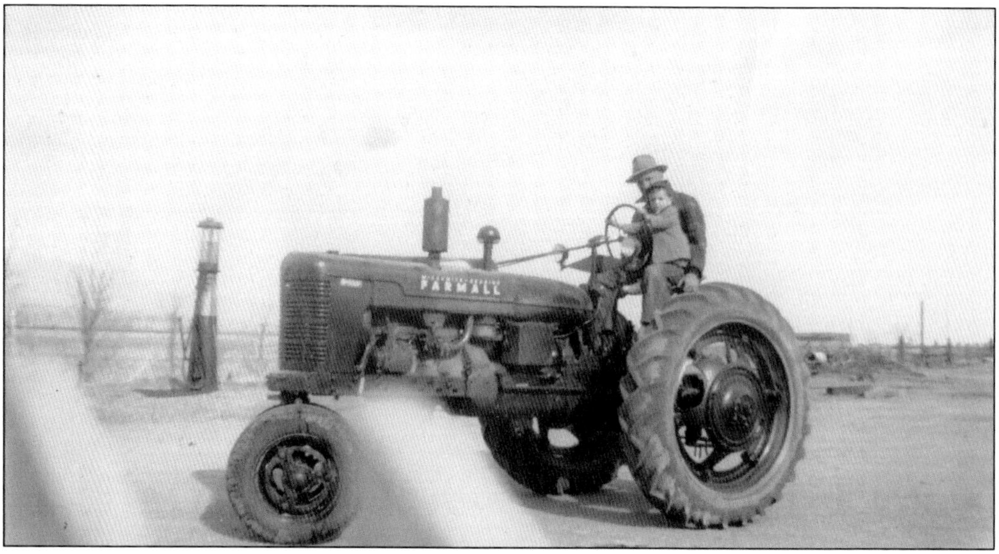

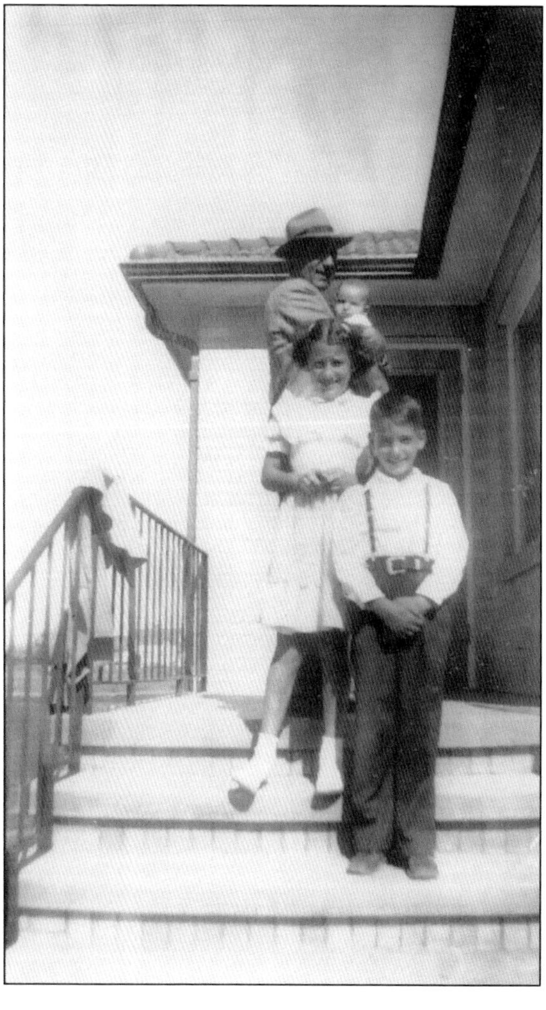

John Janitell Jr. sits on his father's lap as he steers the McCormick-Deering Farmall tractor sometime in the 1940s. One day, little John was allowed to drive the tractor by himself, and he alarmed his parents as he headed straight for the barn. The Janitell farm produced asparagus, corn, and cabbage. (MAS.)

The Janitell family moved across the road to this brick home on the hill about 1954. John Janitell stands on the steps of his new home while he holds his son Dick. His children Mary Alice and John join him. In addition to the truck farm and dairy, Janitell ran cattle and boarded horses. (MAS.)

In the 1950s, Mae (Cuchares) Janitell stands on the porch of her farmhouse on the south side of Mesa Road. With her are her son John and her aunt and uncle Marguerita and Nicholas Venetucci. People who knew Nicholas described him as a fine gentleman. (MAS.)

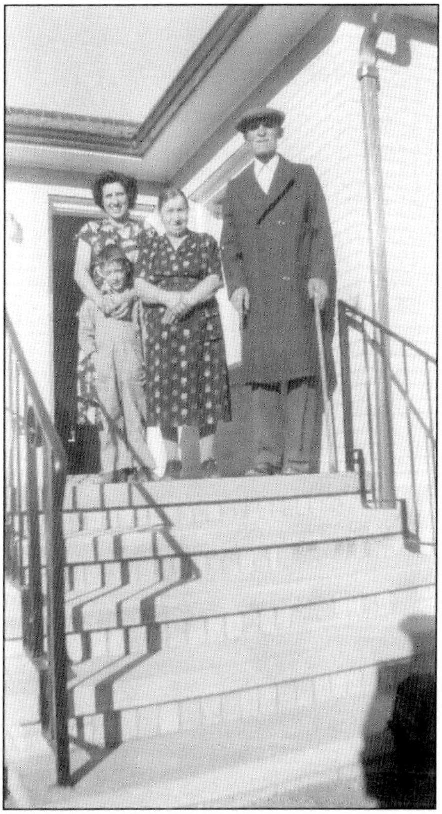

The Janitell family enjoys dinner while on vacation to California in 1957. From left to right are John Jr., John, Dick, Mae, and Mary Alice. The valley's Italian American farm families kept their ancestral culture alive through food. Farm children enjoyed stomping grapes that were put through a press and turned into homemade wine. Favorite homemade treats included gnocchi (soft dumplings) and pizzelle (a type of cookies). (MAS.)

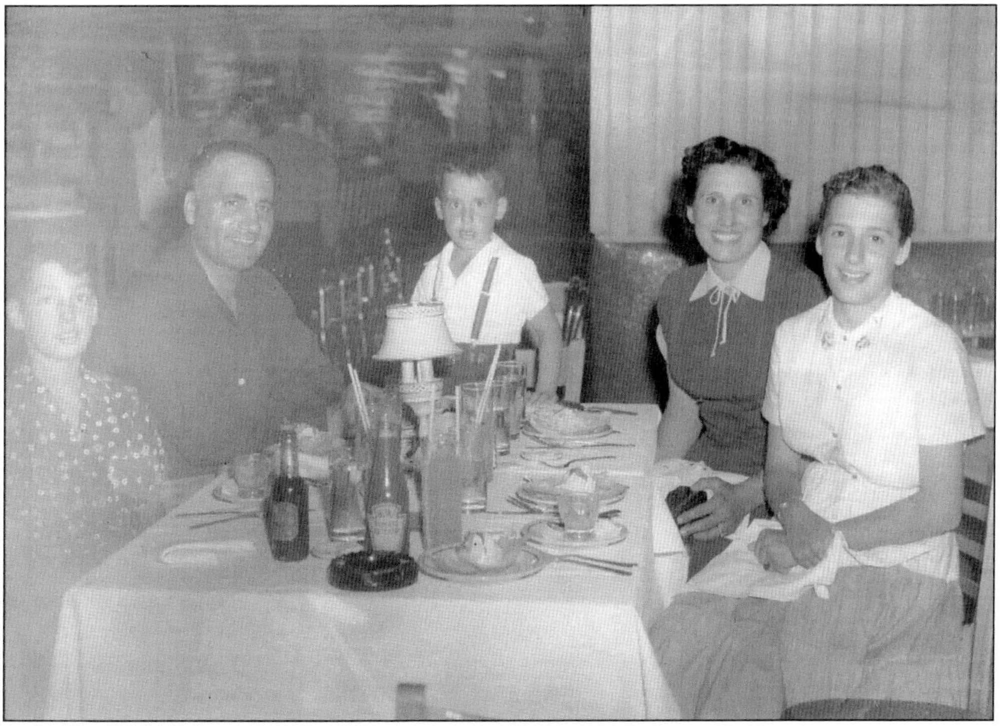

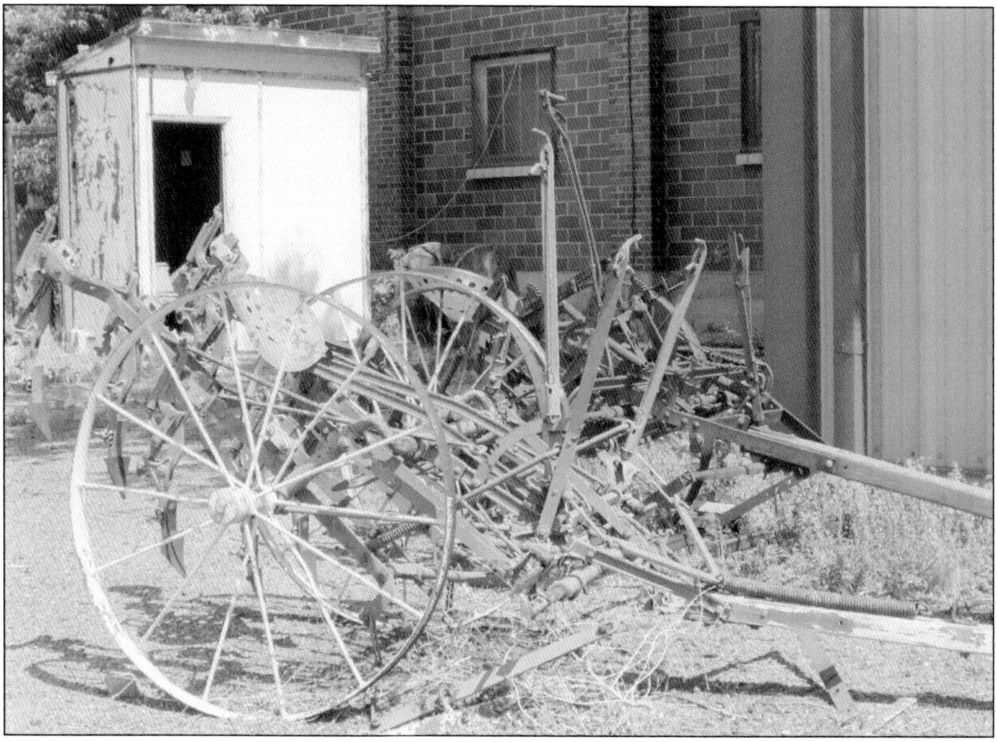

Antique farm machinery reminds the visitor of the agricultural activities that took place on the Pinello cattle ranch. The machinery rests outside the very large barn built into the side of a hill in 1947 from several shades of red brick under the direction of Louie Pinello. Legend has it that Pinello acquired the brick from a nearby train derailment. (ATH.)

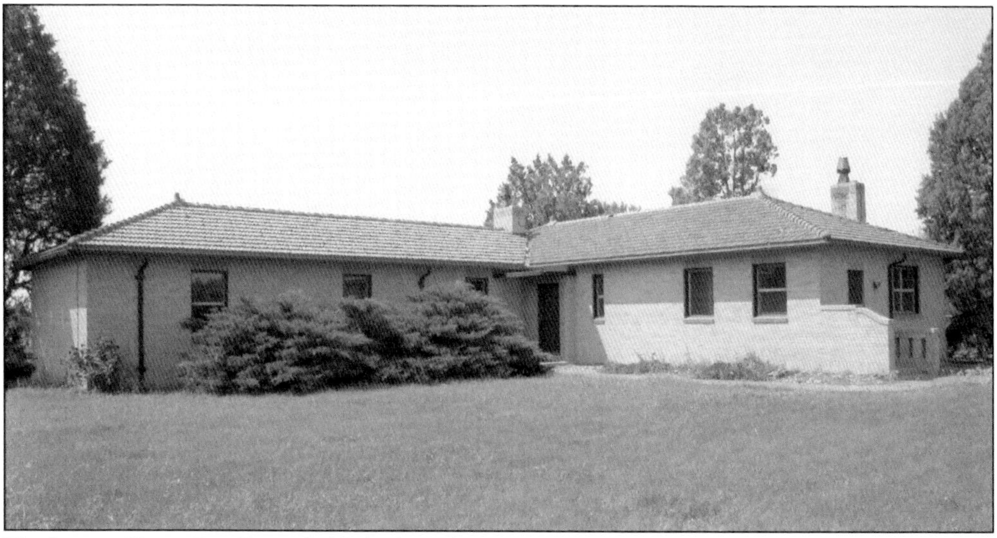

The home of Louie Pinello, probably built in the 1940s, lies hidden on low land between the highway and the river. Constructed of blonde brick and earthy terra-cotta roof tiles, it is reminiscent of Mediterranean architecture. Remnants of an intricate irrigation system surround the house and web across the property. Pinello's home and construction company headquarters were situated in the south end of his father's ranch. (ATH.)

Three

Living on Easy Street

The idea of security spilled over to Widefield families who could hope to send their children to good colleges with the money they saved by purchasing their affordable Widefield homes. The streets they lived on reminded them of this dream, for they were named for colleges, universities, and Ivy League schools. Simultaneously, Springs Southmoor Development Company began building Southmoor Estates west of Widefield in 1965, and it was predicted to be one of the nicest residential areas in the Fountain Valley.

However, living in Security was not always so easy. A flood that swept through the area in the summer of 1965 remains vivid in the memories of those who lived there. Roiling waters swept cars away and knocked houses off their foundations while dumping mud on lawns. Standing water soaked the vegetable fields along the creek. The dam across Carp Lake burst and spilled pond water downhill and into the basements of homes in lower Widefield. Some people found refuge in the schools and at the fire station, while firemen plucked stranded individuals from atop stalled cars. Mothers at home could not decide whether to take their children to the basement to hide from tornadoes or to high ground to escape the water.

Another disaster materialized in Security in 1987 when the metal-cleaning fluid known as perchloroethylene (PCE) was discovered on the grounds of the Schlage Lock facility. Many residents felt this was the cause of their mysterious health problems, and lawsuits followed. Subsequent investigations found worrisome amounts of PCE in the Widefield Aquifer supplying water to Security homes. Likewise, the poisonous chemical seeped its way underground to the Willow Springs Ponds, closing them off to fishing for 10 years. Schlage Lock immediately started cleanup efforts, which continue to this day.

In spite of these difficulties, most everyone who has spent time in Security-Widefield agrees it is has been, and still is, an extraordinary place in which to grow up and raise a family.

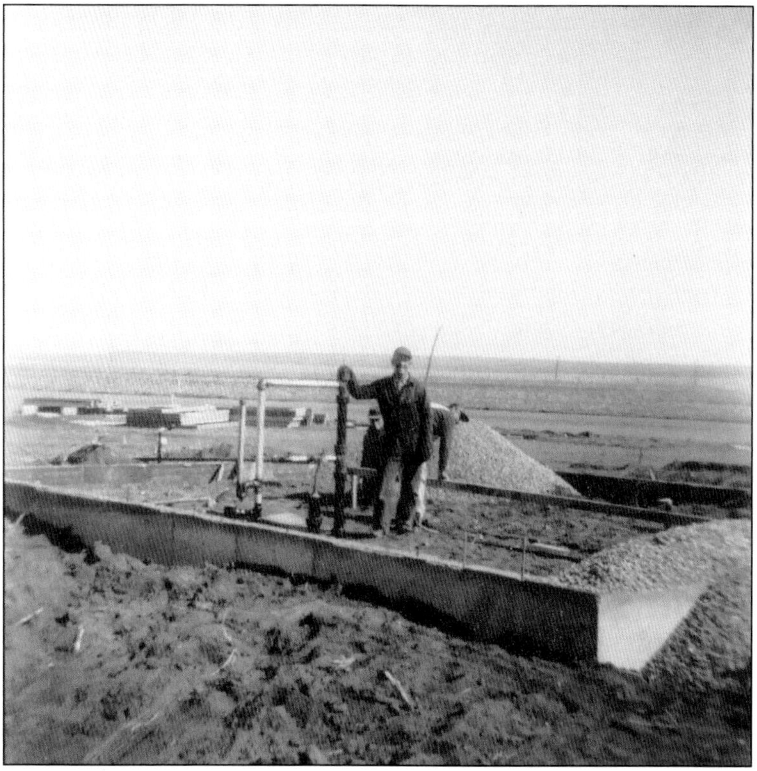

John Sinnes, an employee for Olson Plumbing & Heating, installs water pipes at one of the first 10 homes built along Security Boulevard in 1954. Sinnes eventually helped to put the plumbing in about 50 Security homes. He bought the 13th house built on Security Boulevard and continues to live there 60 years later. (JS.)

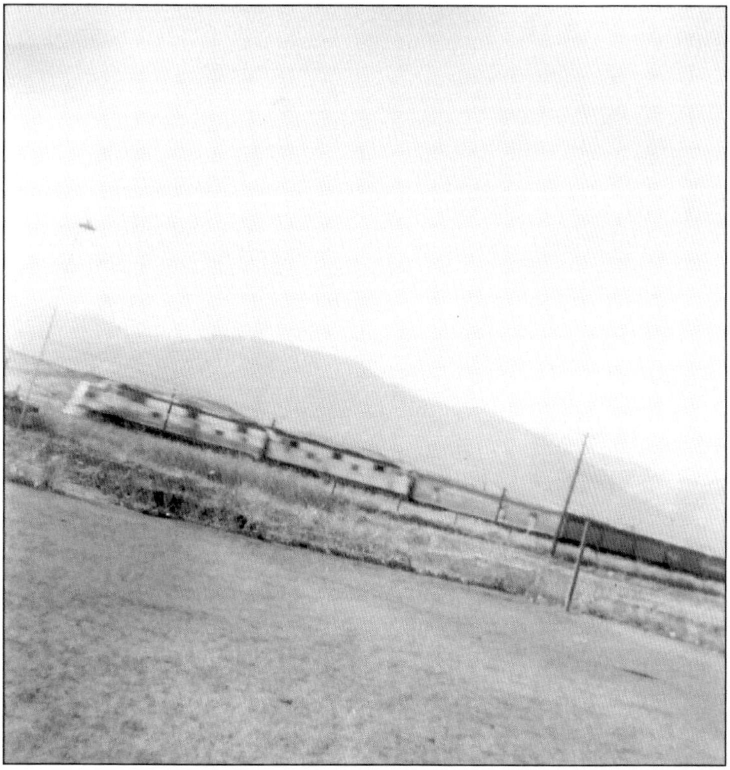

A train rumbles by on the southbound tracks behind the first homes built on Security Boulevard. The Denver & Rio Grande Railroad laid the first rails through the valley in 1871, connecting Denver and Pueblo. The Atchison, Topeka & Santa Fe Railway followed the same route with its own rails in 1887. Although the railroad came first, current homeowners have succeeded in silencing the whistles as the engines pass through the Security and Widefield intersections. (JS.)

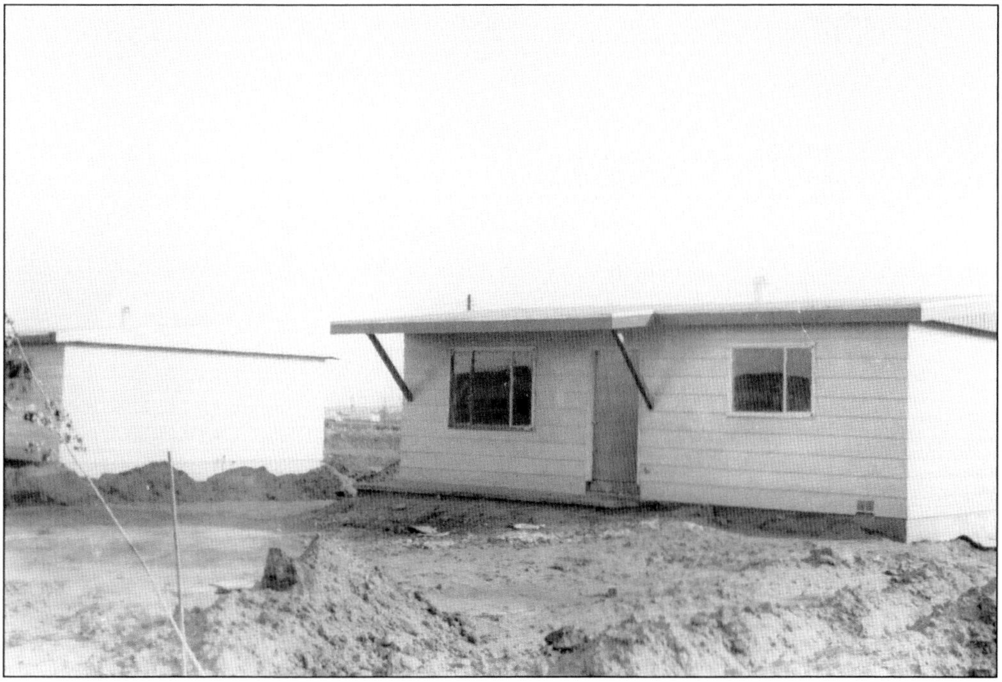

The Simon family moved into this little two-bedroom home in the fall of 1954. It was one of the first 10 houses built in the brand new suburb of Security. The little house, made affordable by the Security Development Corporation, functioned as a starter home for Simon's young family. (MS.)

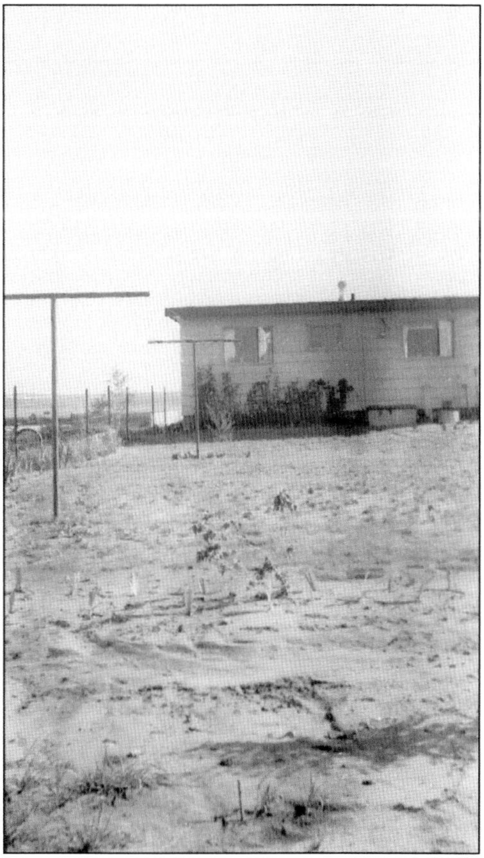

Martin Simon's home featured a deep backyard, typical of Security homes. It was the developer's idea that families could grow vegetable gardens and have real security. Having faith in the land that once grew corn, the Simon family did indeed grow a wide variety of vegetables. (MS.)

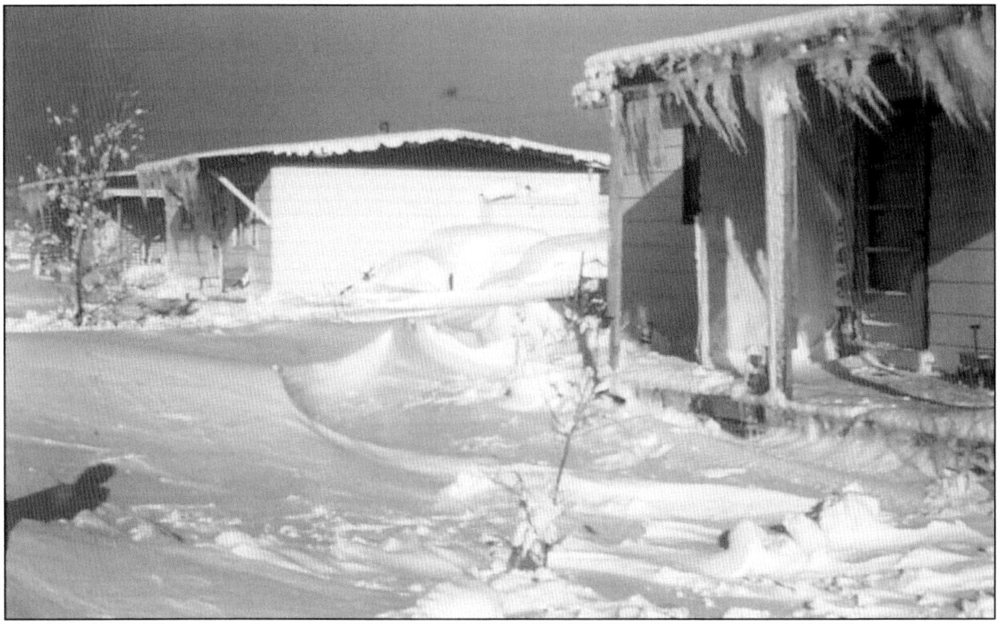

The Simons' yellow house (right) on Security Boulevard peeks cheerfully from 16 inches of snow that was dumped on April 2, 1957. District school buses, equipped with chains, rescued stranded motorists all day long. The next day, these buses transported Security residents from their homes to the grocery store. District employee Robert Poole organized a refugee effort at North Elementary School for families who found themselves without heat and electricity. (MS.)

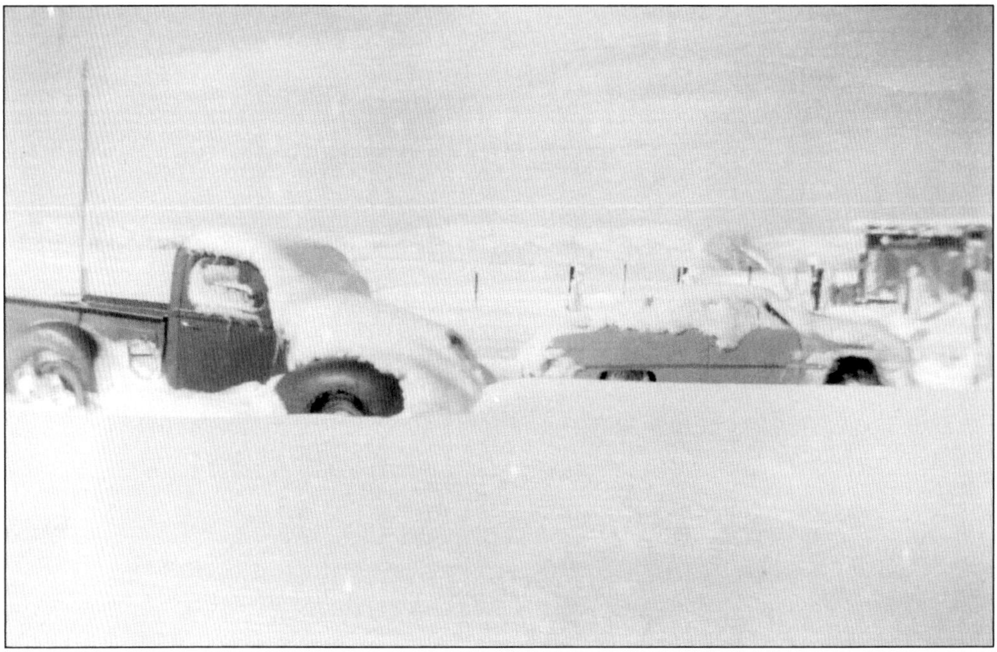

Vehicles at Seward Wilson's farm are almost buried in another big snow in 1959. This storm dumped enough snow for delighted children to dig snow tunnels, igloos, and forts. The region saw lots of snow that watered the fields and gardens, and melted snow seeped into underground aquifers and trickled its way down to the river. (MC.)

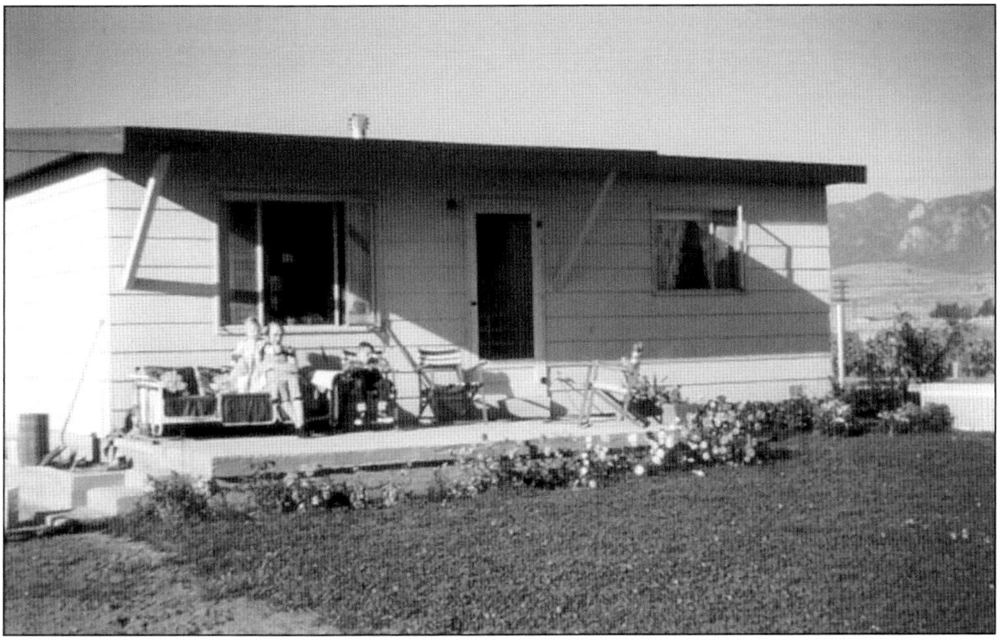

Martin and Esther Simon wasted no time in landscaping around their little yellow house with grass and flower beds. Many Security homeowners patronized Kenny's Nursery, which opened in the 1950s. Frilly curtains adorn a bedroom window, while summer breezes, fresh air, and the sound of children's laughter enter the home through the screen door. Esther's mother sits on the front porch with her grandchildren Karen (left) and Karl. (MS.)

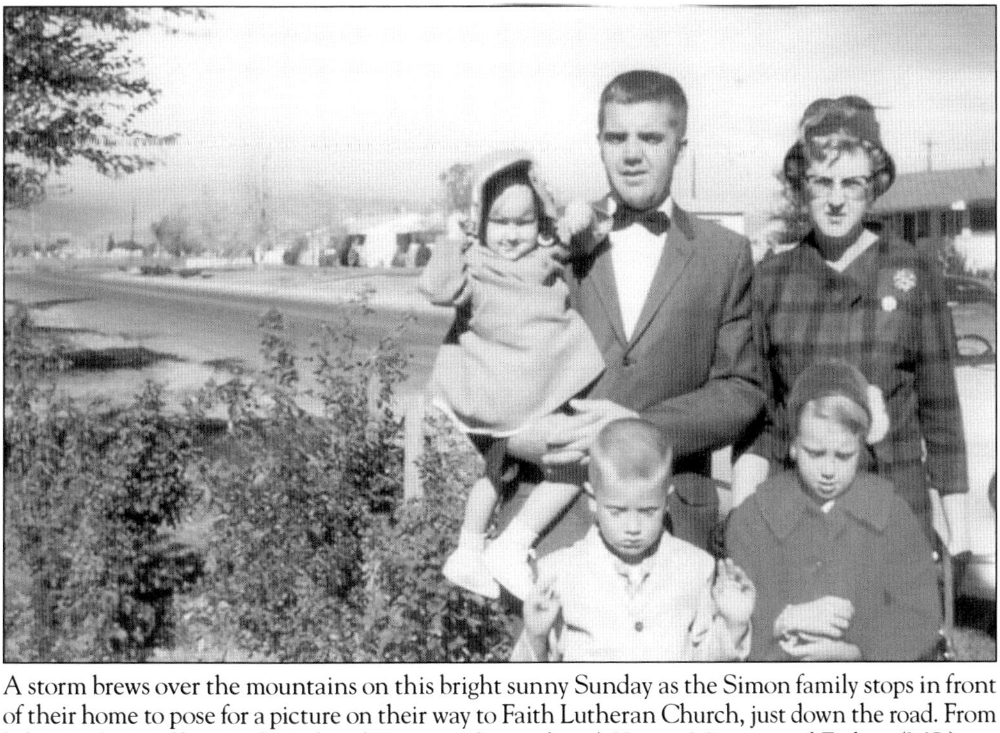

A storm brews over the mountains on this bright sunny Sunday as the Simon family stops in front of their home to pose for a picture on their way to Faith Lutheran Church, just down the road. From left to right are (first row) Karl and Kristine; (second row) Karen, Martin, and Esther. (MS.)

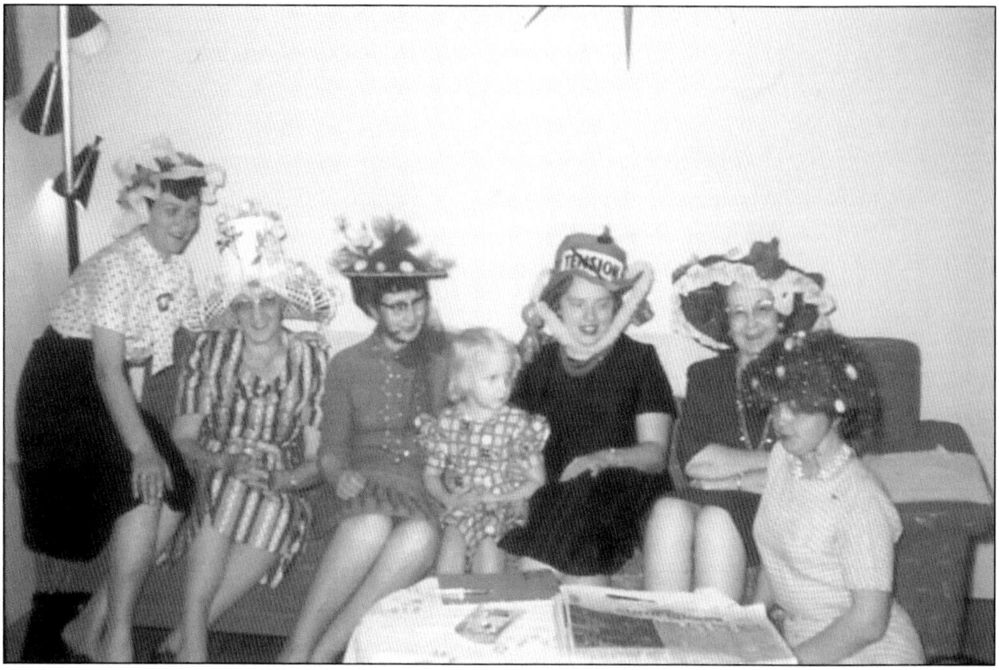

Esther Simon photographed her neighborhood friends as they displayed their colorful, crazy hat creations. Simon explains that in Security's early days, neighbors formed close friendships. Neighborhood mothers gathered together regularly in informal groups to discuss the various aspects and challenges of child rearing and homemaking and also to socialize and have fun. (MS.)

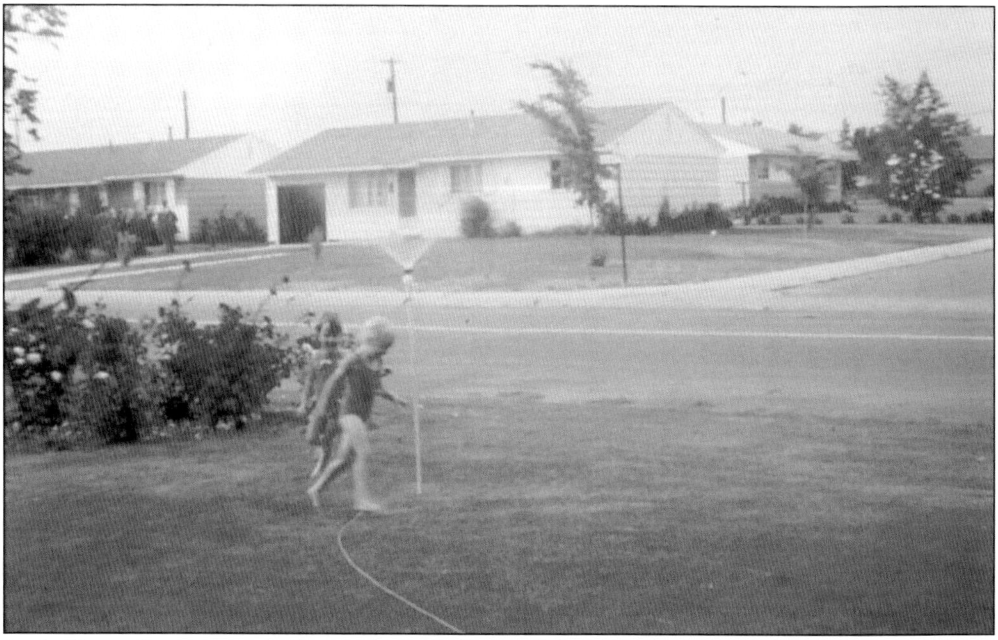

Little Karen Simon (right) plays in the sprinkler with her friend on a hot summer day in front of her home, which was located on Security Boulevard across from Zuni Drive. American Builders accessed water from a large underground aquifer and piped it to the subdivision. Homeowners had plenty of water to run through sprinklers for their beautiful lawns and flowers. (MS.)

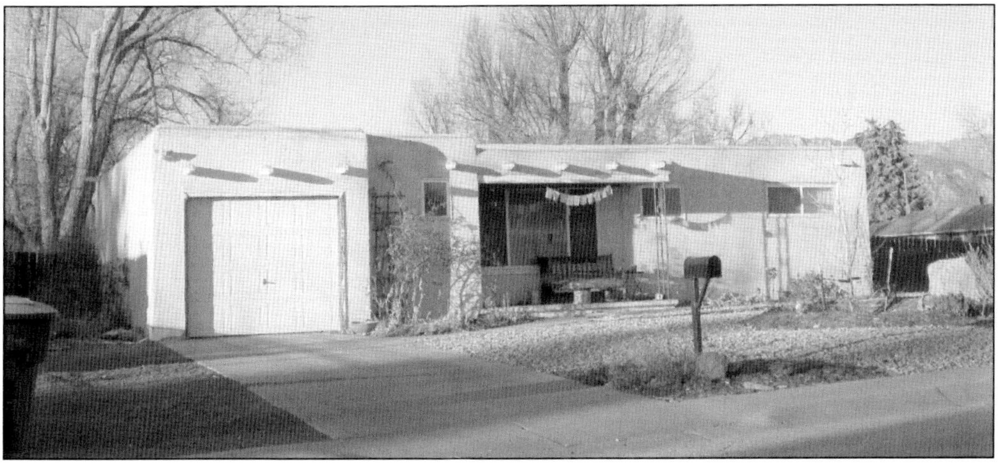

Fred Sproul, an Albuquerque developer, continued the construction that had already started in Security. One of his signature models resembled the adobe pueblos of the Old Southwest, with their stucco siding and faux vigas, made to look like the rough-hewn roofing timbers of traditional Southwestern architecture. The various contractors became quite practiced at their craft. For instance, a two-man roofing team could cover from three to five roofs per day. (ATH.)

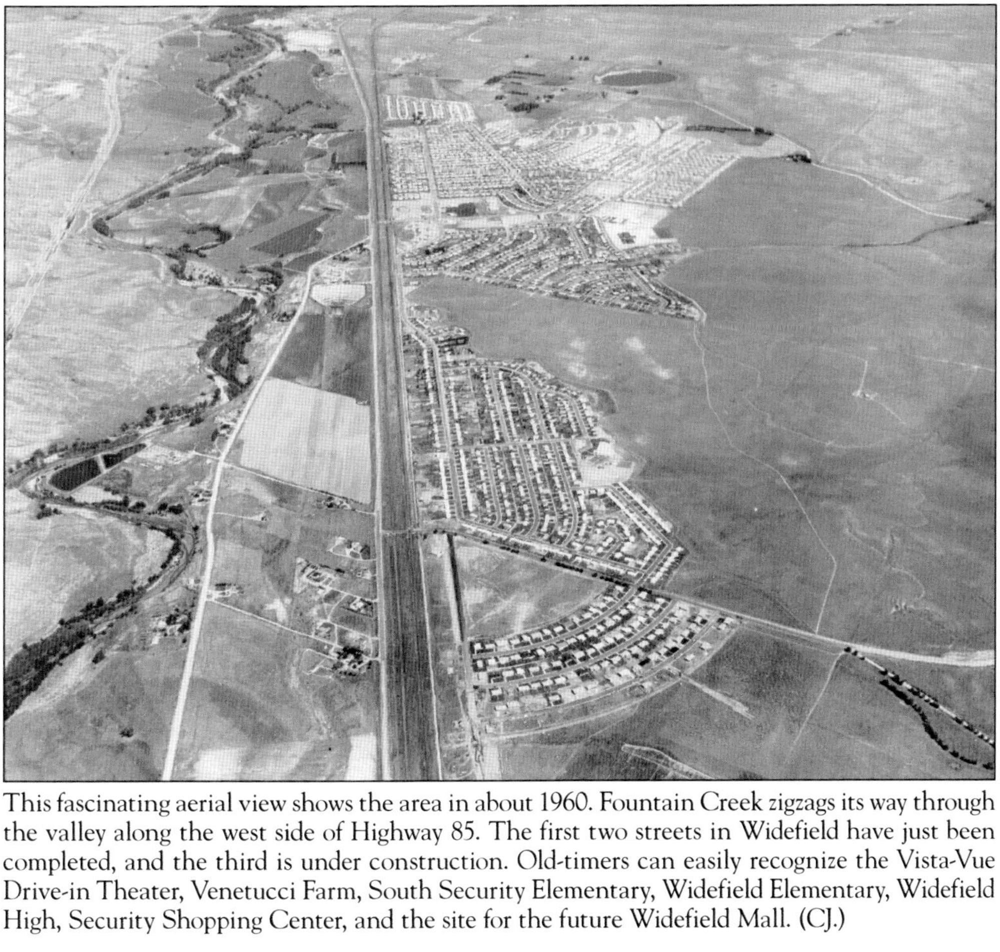

This fascinating aerial view shows the area in about 1960. Fountain Creek zigzags its way through the valley along the west side of Highway 85. The first two streets in Widefield have just been completed, and the third is under construction. Old-timers can easily recognize the Vista-Vue Drive-in Theater, Venetucci Farm, South Security Elementary, Widefield Elementary, Widefield High, Security Shopping Center, and the site for the future Widefield Mall. (CJ.)

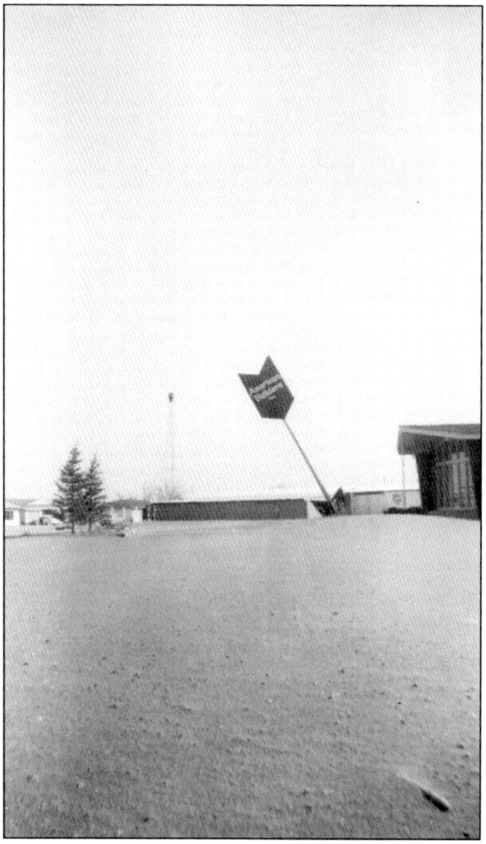

The big red arrow marks the location of the American Builders office, once located south of the Security intersection. This photograph was taken just after a windstorm like the one in 1961 that shifted large amounts of sand up against the buildings. The developers soon learned that the loose sand would be a problem without the right kind of grass to hold it in place. (RL.)

Trees line this unpaved county road, which was later named Fontaine Boulevard. The brick gateway marks the newly cut Amherst Street, where the first three model homes were built. Locally known as the alphabet streets, the first roads in Widefield started with each letter of the alphabet from *A* through *K*. (MW.)

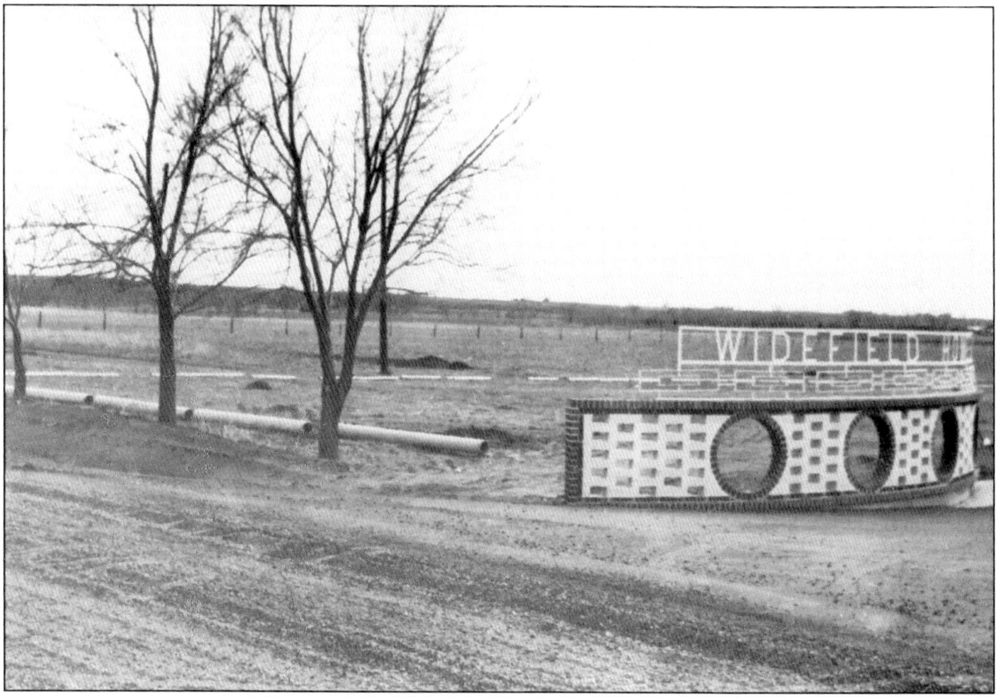

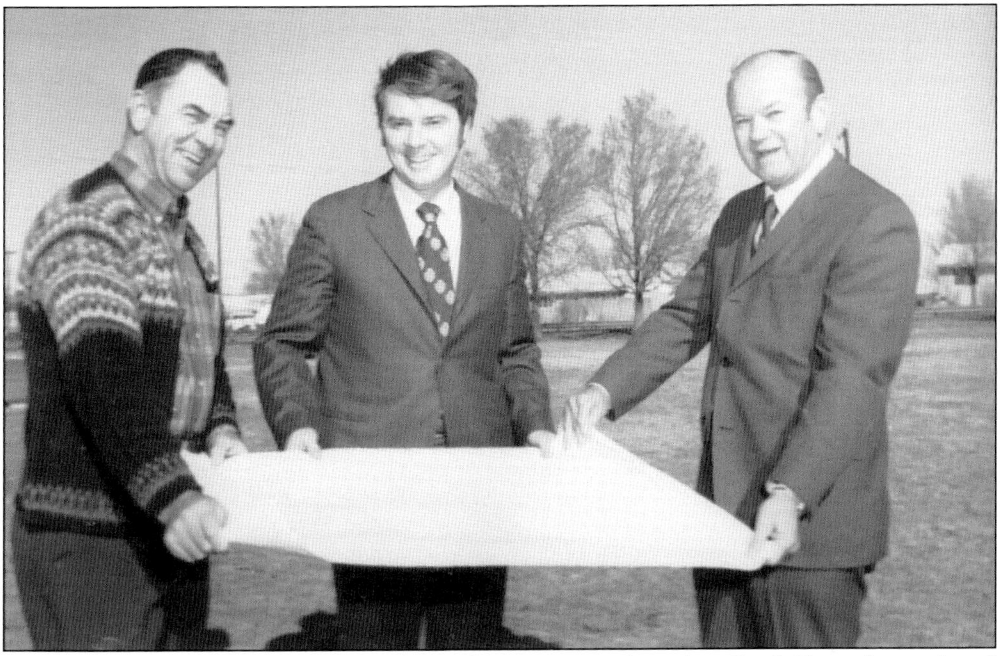

Developer Jules Watson (right) holds out blueprints with realtor Fred Short (center) and chief superintendent Ray Hunke as they contemplate the next phase of development. To secure water for the residents in his new homes, Watson created the Widefield Water & Sanitation Company. (MW.)

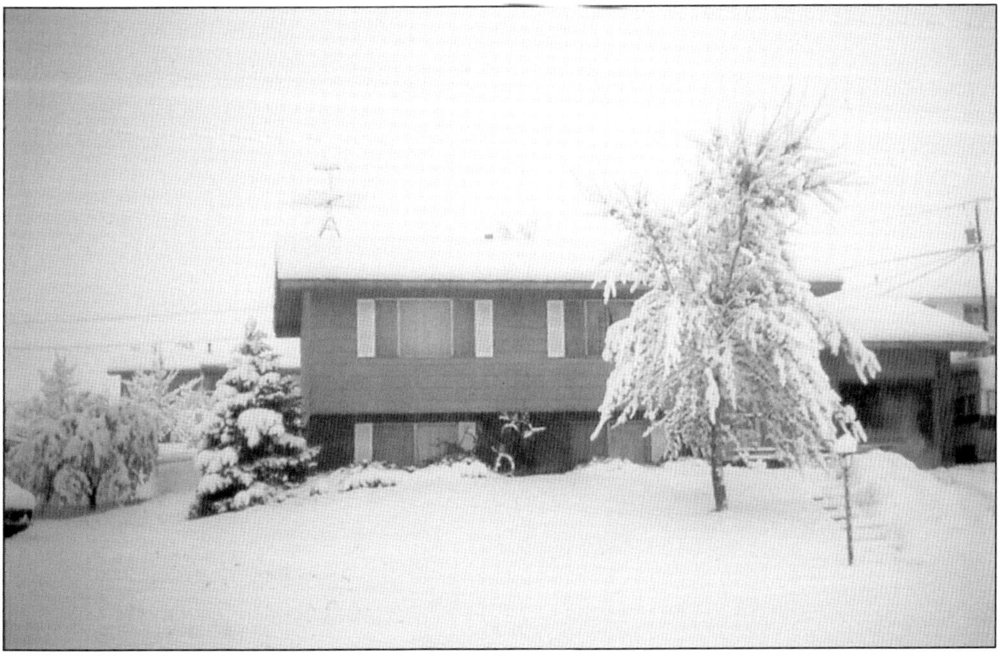

In 1965, Widefield Homes expanded to Widefield Heights, where this La Bonita model was built. The developer obtained this small tract of land from the Fountain Valley Boys School. It lies just east of the former South Security Elementary School and north of Fontaine Boulevard, placing the neighborhood in south Security. (NBT.)

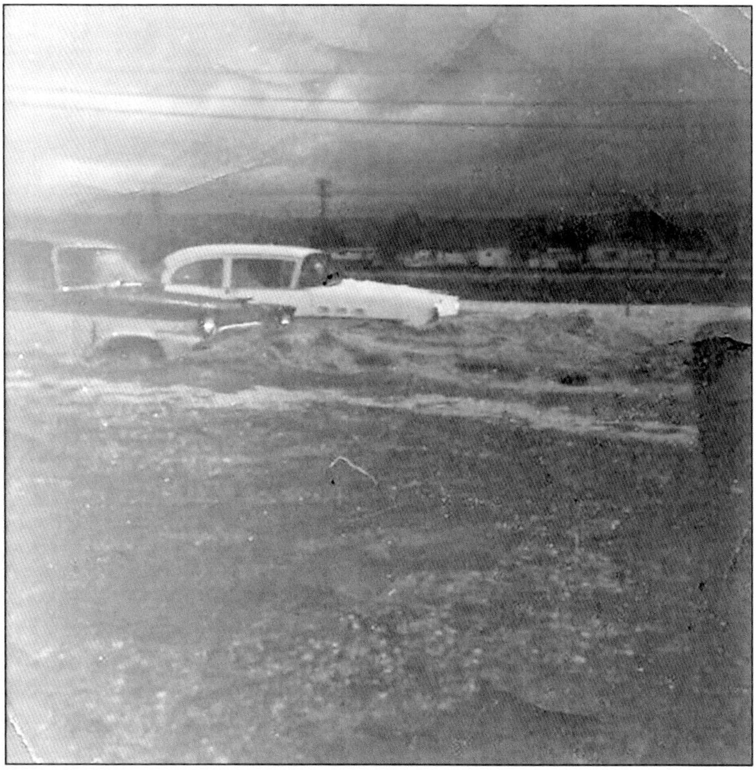

Stalled cars sit motionless as floodwaters swirl around them on Security Boulevard near Grand Boulevard. The flood of 1965 caught the residents of Security-Widefield by surprise. After four days of rain, hail, and tornadoes, the saturated ground could hold no more water, and the streets turned into rivers. Local gulches and lakes spilled over into the yards and basements of homes on lower ground. (DB.)

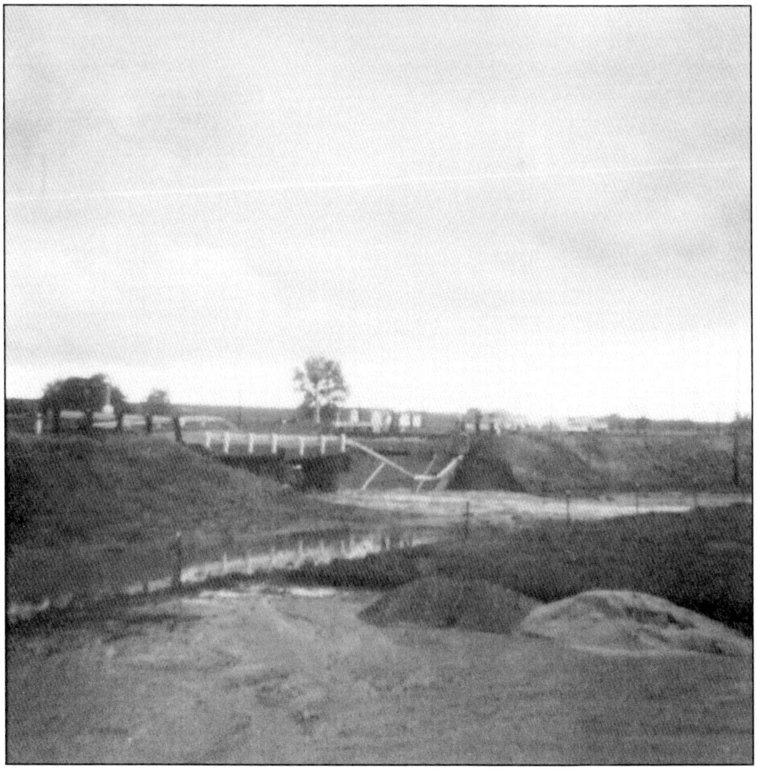

This bridge on the highway over Crews Gulch sustained damage during the 1965 flood, cutting off access to the town of Fountain farther south. The railroad bridge over Crews Gulch also had to be repaired. From June 14 to June 17, rainwater collected in the low-lying areas of Security-Widefield as it drained toward Fountain Creek. The flood destroyed the Widefield intersection at Highway 85. (MC.)

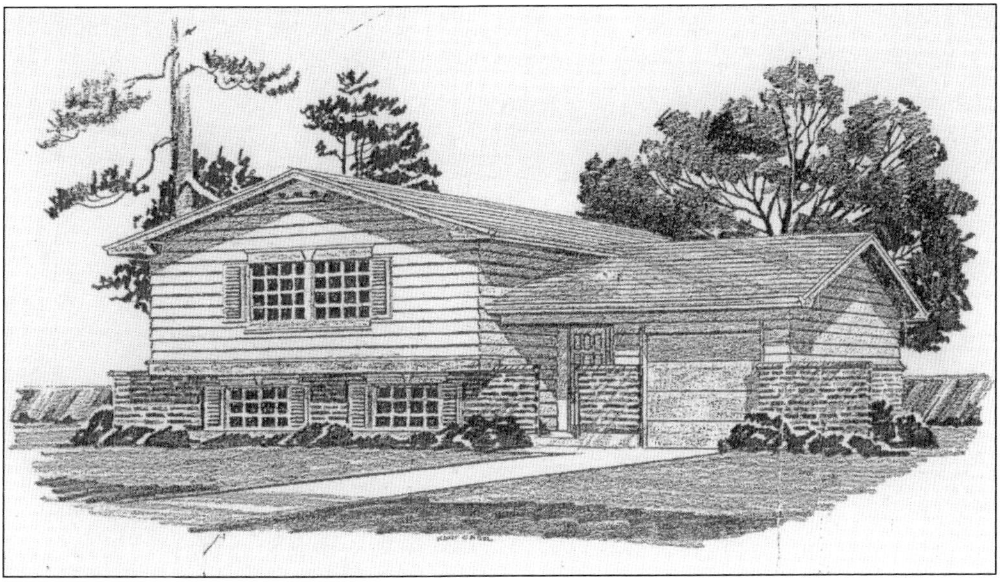

Widefield Homes advertised this Warwick model in 1966 for $16,450. All models featured brick construction, ceramic-tile windowsills, aluminum windows, two ceramic-tile baths, Formica countertops, birch kitchen cabinets, hardwood floors, mahogany doors, cement driveways, and a basement or lower level. Changes made yearly to the models gave each street in Widefield a different look. (MW.)

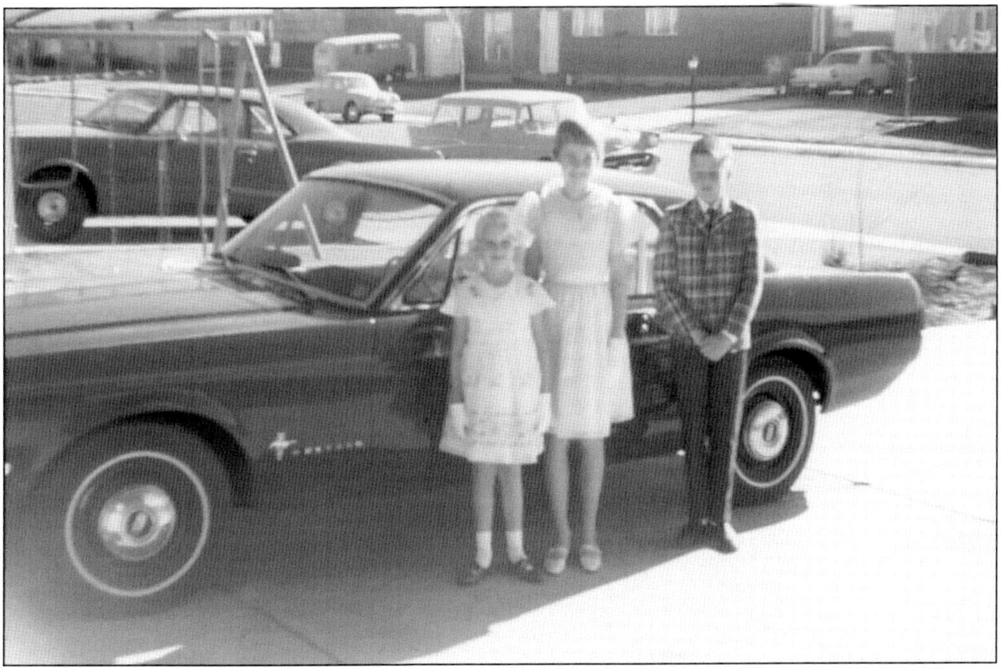

Siblings Karen (left), Kristine, and Karl Simon stand next to the family's maroon Mustang on Easter Sunday in the mid-1960s. In 1964, the family had outgrown their little house on Security Boulevard and had moved to a bigger home, the Buckingham model, on Judson Street in Widefield. (MS.)

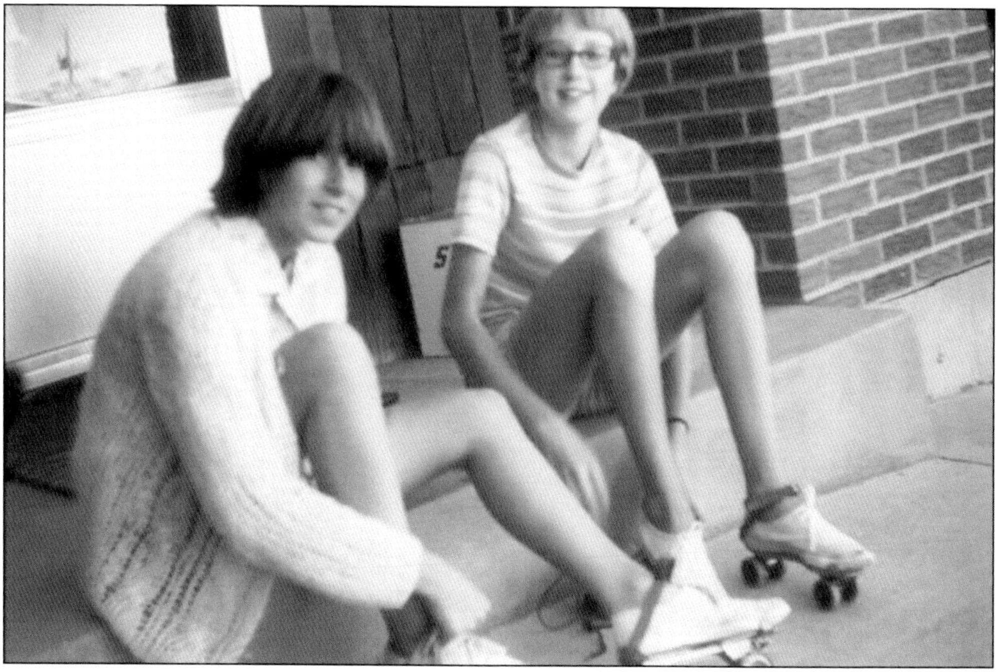

Kristine Simon (right) and her friend fasten roller skates to their shoes in preparation to skate down the sidewalks of their neighborhood on Judson Street in Widefield. These metal skates were adjustable and fitted to one's shoe with a unique skate key, most often worn around the neck on a string. This generation of children living in a blue-collar community remembers how they created their own fun. (MS.)

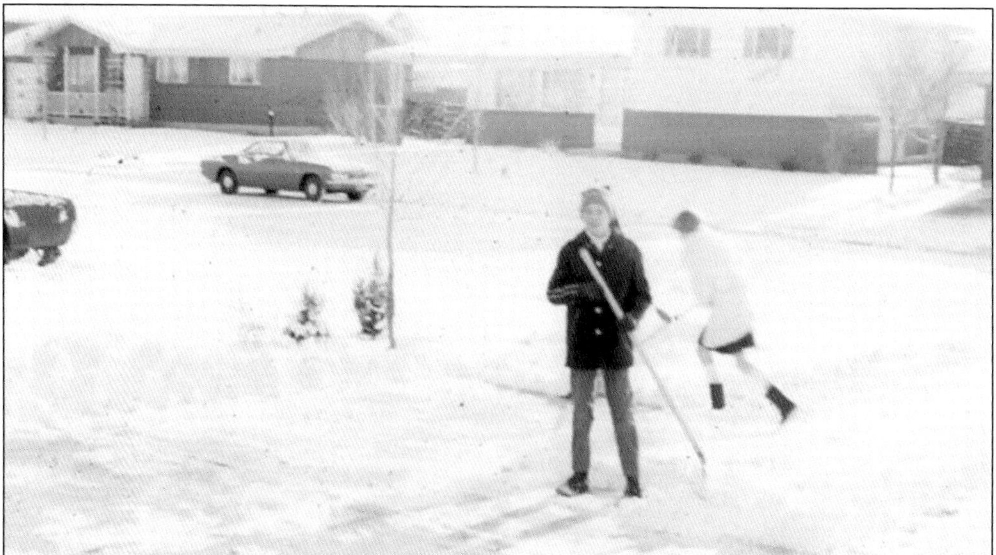

Karl Simon (left) and his sister Kristine work at clearing the snow from their driveway on Judson Street in the mid-1960s. This particular storm appears to have dumped about six inches of snow. Frequent snowstorms through the colder months commonly delivered several inches of snow. (MS.)

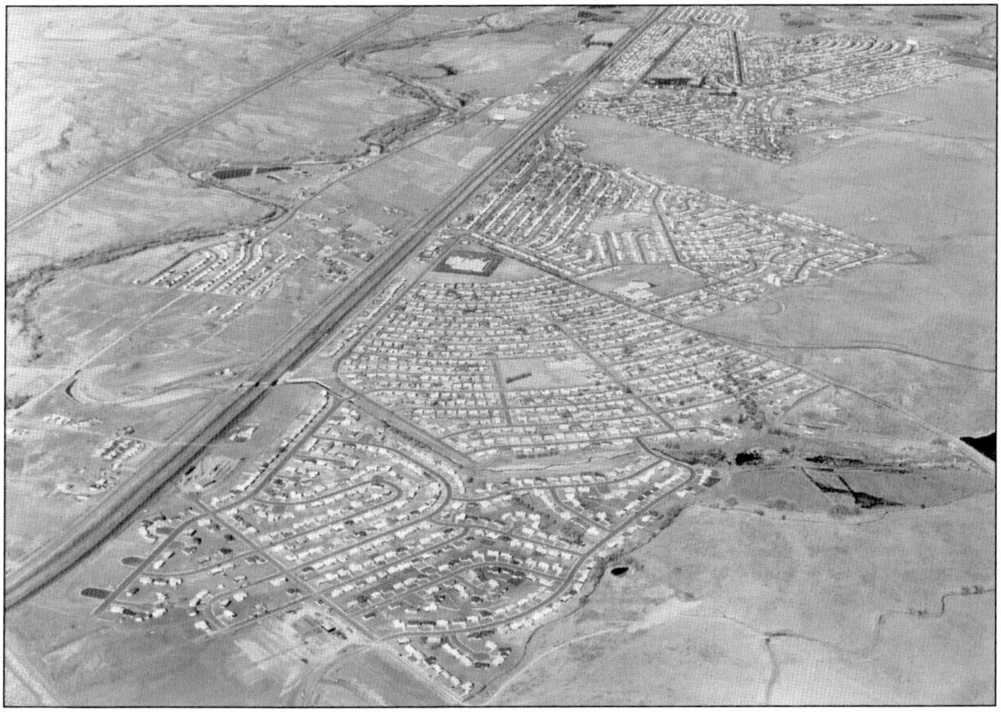

This aerial view shows growth in Widefield in the late 1960s, its southern portion once being the dairy farm of Jack Wilson and his father, Seward. Longtime residents will recognize the Widefield Mall, Watson Junior High, Talbott and Webster Elementary Schools, Carp Lake, the Fountain Ditch along present Metropolitan Street, and the first few streets in Southmoor. (RL.)

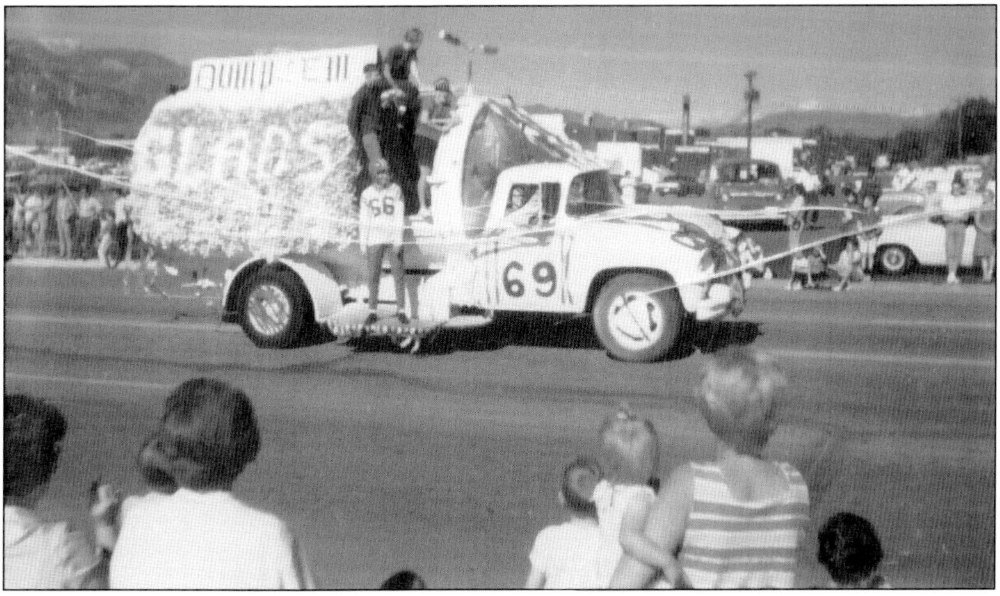

Unlike the typical big-city suburb, Security-Widefield has always held at least one parade per year. In 1969, the Security Garbage Company lent a trash truck for the Widefield High School float in the homecoming parade. The stark white truck, decorated in Gladiator blue, cleverly proclaims "Dump 'Em" as it heads up Main Street toward the high school. (JP.)

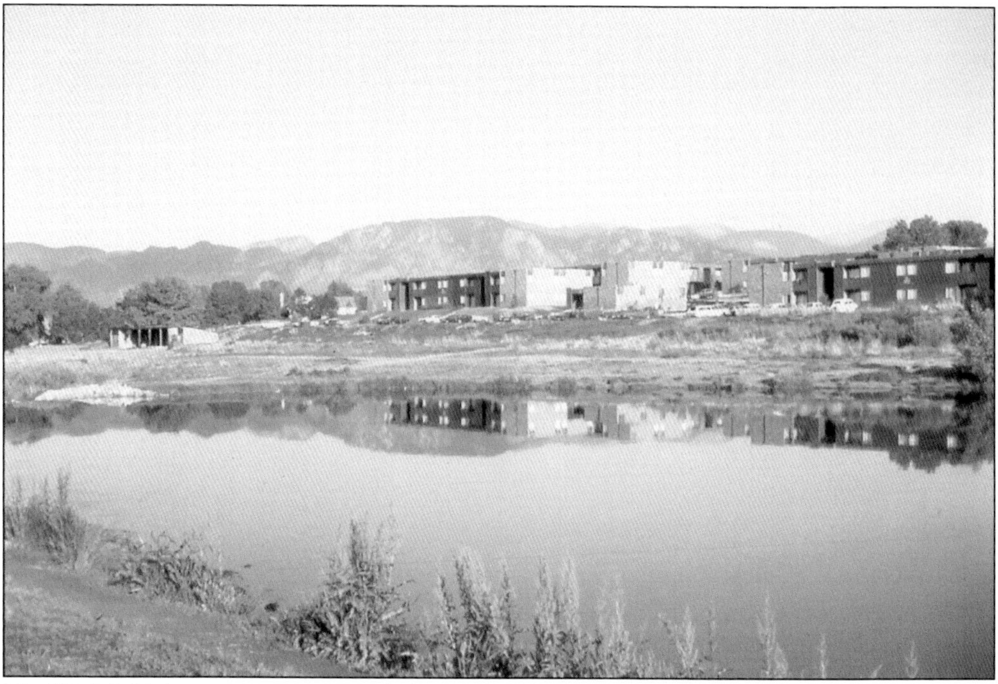

The Widefield Apartments, commonly known as the Kokomo Apartments, are reflected in this pond that once existed in Widefield Park. The water was the result of a spillway from Carp Lake under Fontaine Boulevard. (NBT.)

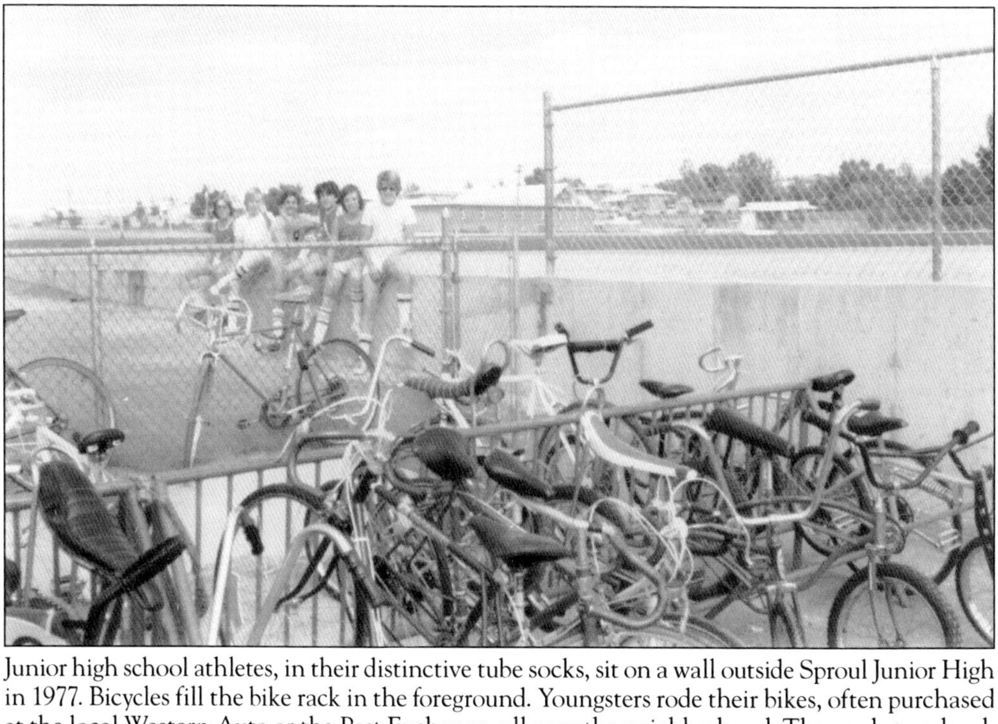

Junior high school athletes, in their distinctive tube socks, sit on a wall outside Sproul Junior High in 1977. Bicycles fill the bike rack in the foreground. Youngsters rode their bikes, often purchased at the local Western Auto or the Post Exchange, all over the neighborhood. They rode to school, to the store, to their friends' homes, and to Carp Lake with their fishing poles. (WSD.)

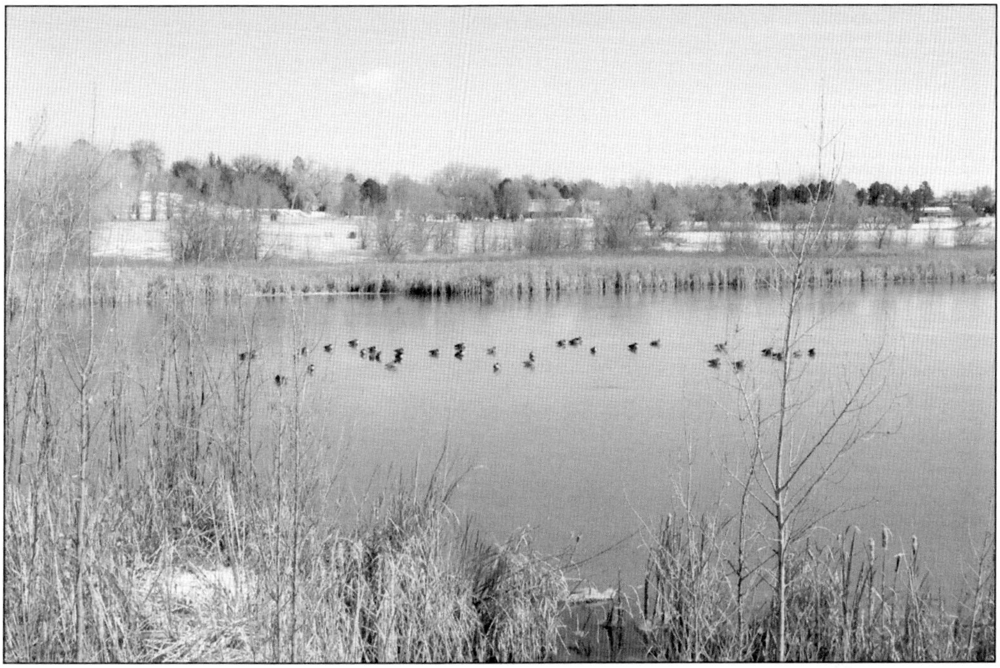

Carp Lake, officially known as McCray Reservoir, was the destination of many Security-Widefield children looking for a chance to go ice skating when it was frozen over. Members of the Widefield High School hockey team ventured to the lake on their own time to practice. (ATH.)

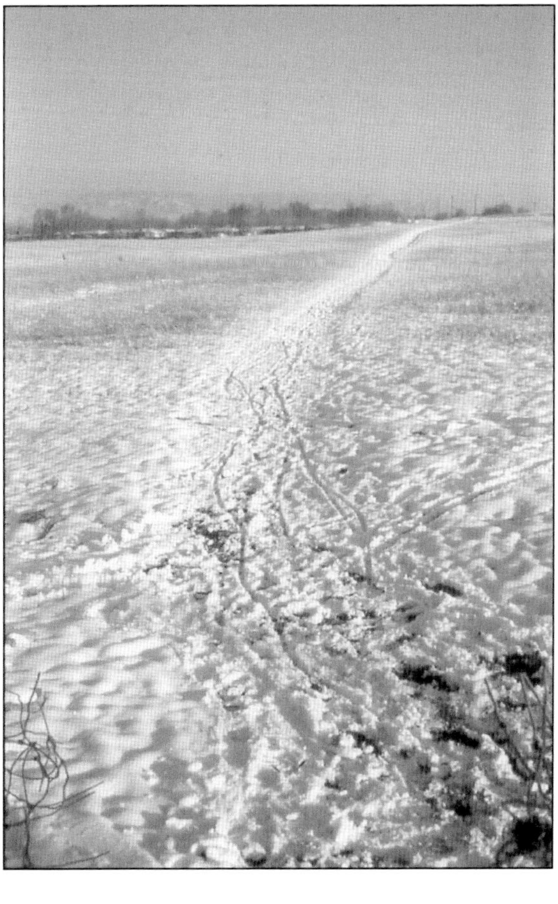

High school students living in Widefield Heights walked to and from school, in all kinds of weather, by stepping over a barbed wire fence at Monk Street and McBurney Boulevard, which provided them a shortcut across the field belonging to the Fountain Valley School. The school's cattle were often silent observers of the twice-daily treks. Flitting from post to post, meadowlarks sang loudly as they followed the students. (NBT.)

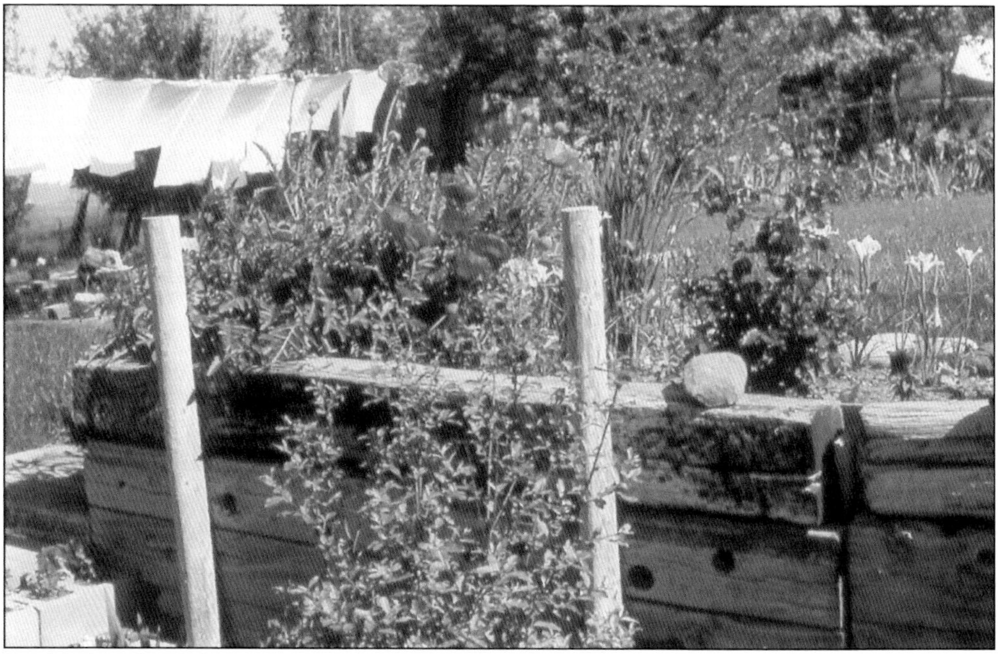

Freshly laundered diapers dry in the summer sunshine at the home of Les and Nancy Thaden. The diapers belonged to their grandchild. Indeed, the fourth generations of many of the first families are now growing up in Security-Widefield because it is such a desirable place to live and raise children. (NBT.)

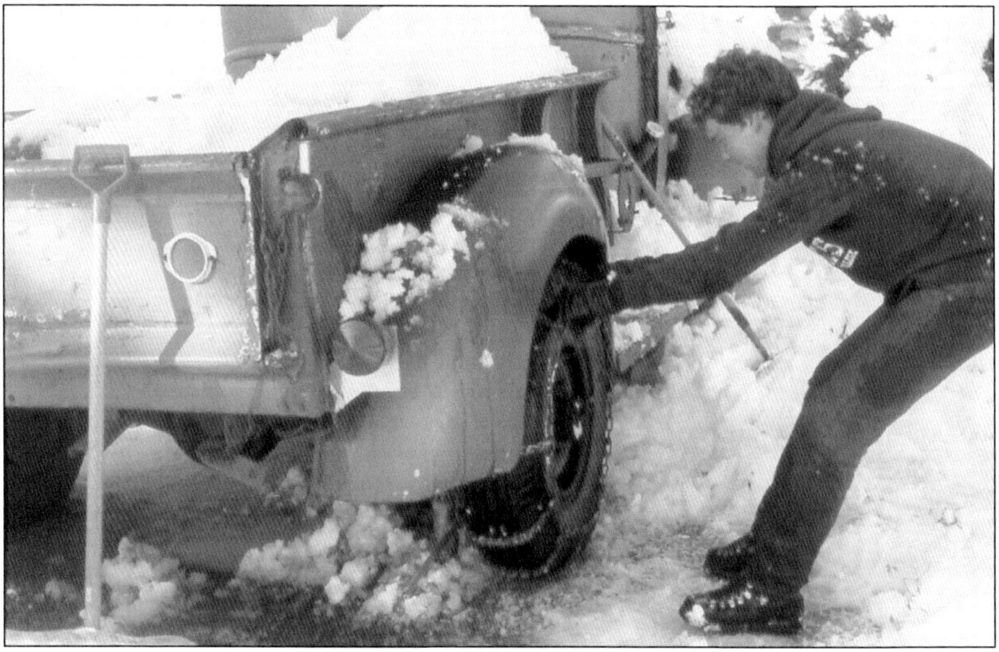

Fred Thaden attaches chains to his truck before driving on the snow-packed roads of Security. In 1985, this storm dumped a foot of snow in the Pikes Peak region. Because of frequent storms, many residents owned tire chains and used them to gain traction when the roads became slushy and icy. (NBT.)

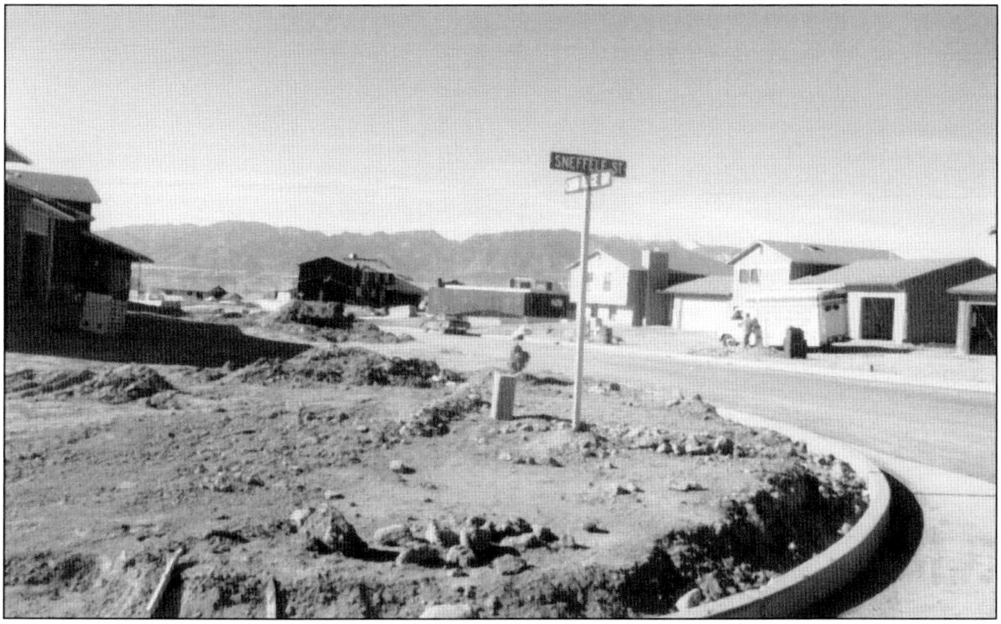

In this January 1986 image, construction continues at Sneffels Street and Cabin Ridge Drive in the Sunrise subdivision east of Widefield. By this time, Widefield Homes had purchased large acreages of land east of the Fountain Valley. The area continued to be an attractive place for prospective home buyers. (WSD.)

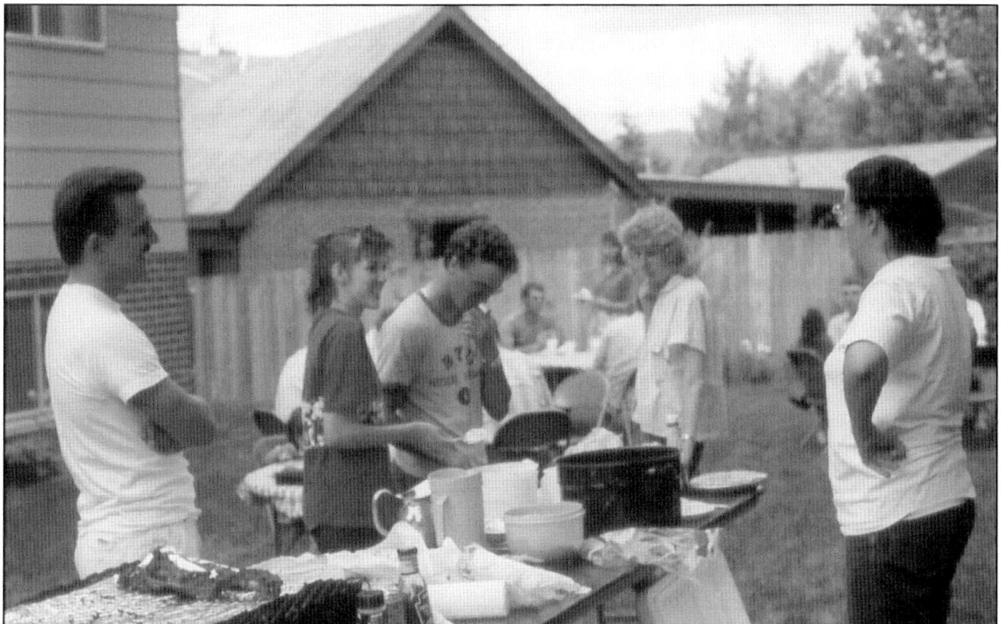

The smell of grilled meat drifts through the neighborhood while the Thaden family enjoys a backyard barbecue in the summer of 1988. From left to right are unidentified, Dee Dee Campbell, Fred Thaden, Ellen Campbell, and Angela Hahn. The occasion was a prewedding party for Dee Dee and Fred. Many guests attended and enjoyed the warm day under the shade provided by a large elm tree. (NBT.)

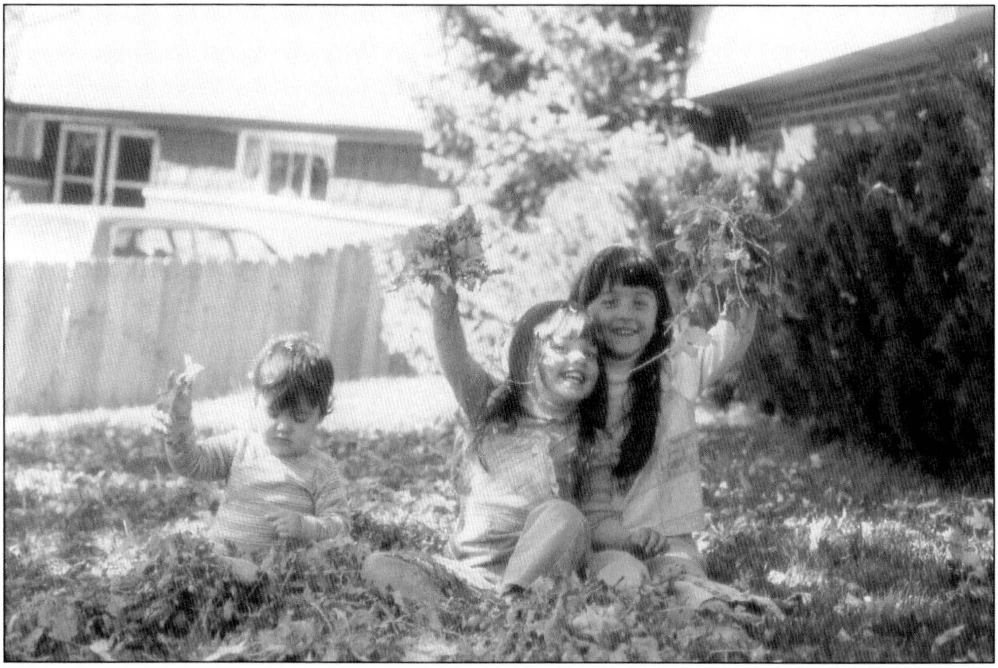

By the time the Thadens' grandchildren came along, the maple tree in their front yard on Byron Place shed enough leaves to make playing in them a delight. From left to right are sisters Melanie, Jennifer, and Maria Hahn in the autumn of 1988. The tradition continues with great-grandchildren raking the leaves and then jumping in them before stuffing them into lawn bags to be used as winter bedding for the flower beds and shrubs. (NBT.)

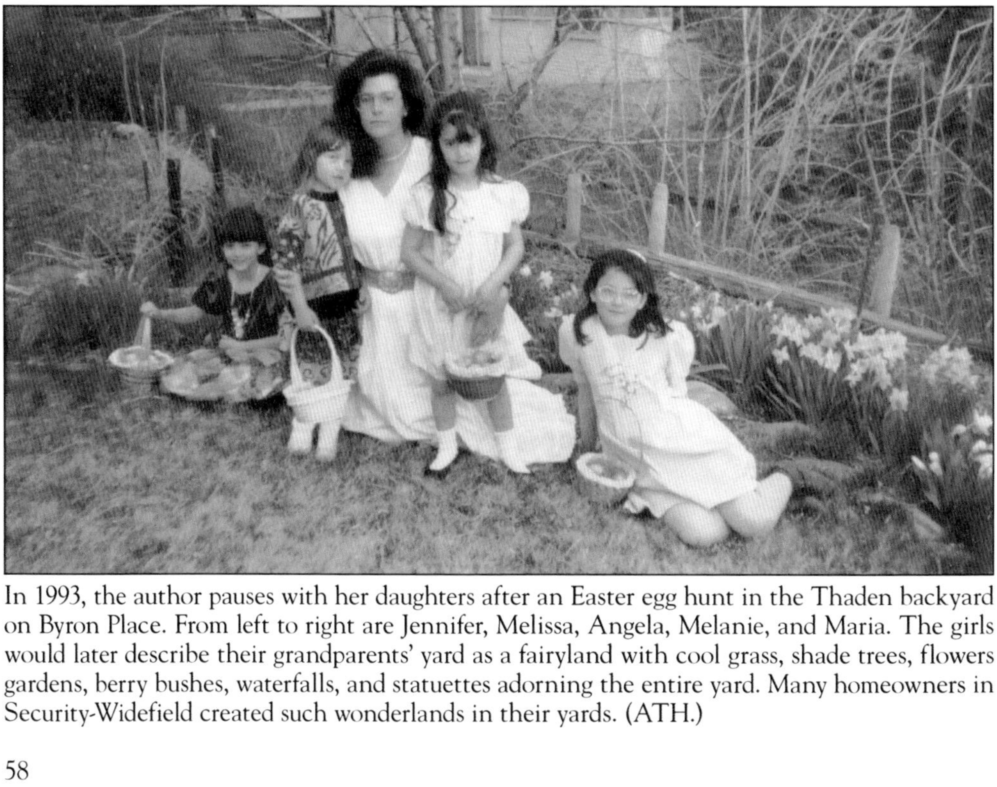

In 1993, the author pauses with her daughters after an Easter egg hunt in the Thaden backyard on Byron Place. From left to right are Jennifer, Melissa, Angela, Melanie, and Maria. The girls would later describe their grandparents' yard as a fairyland with cool grass, shade trees, flowers gardens, berry bushes, waterfalls, and statuettes adorning the entire yard. Many homeowners in Security-Widefield created such wonderlands in their yards. (ATH.)

Four

The Tie That Binds

The Security-Widefield community is tied together through the support of Widefield School District. The schools have historically been the home away from home in which students have spent many of their waking hours. They have developed close relationships with teachers and administrators who have followed their progress from kindergarten to graduation. Memories of living in Security-Widefield undoubtedly include time spent in school and participation in after-school activities. Furthermore, the school district is one of the community's biggest employers, welcoming alumni back to teach the next generation of Widefield District children.

Notably, the school district is responsible for the local library, swimming pool, and community center. Most residents have patronized the library to borrow books or participate in the summer-reading program. The community pool has satisfied the residents with open swims and swimming lessons. There has been something for everyone at the community center, including preschool; athletic programs for all ages; and classes in art, dance, exercise, and first aid.

The school district brings the community together, regardless of school involvement, when it invites all residents to the Community Day parade and football game. Some will recall when this was Widefield High School's annual homecoming. Some will also remember when the school district partnered with the fire department to offer Fourth of July fireworks at the high school stadium, to which the entire community was invited.

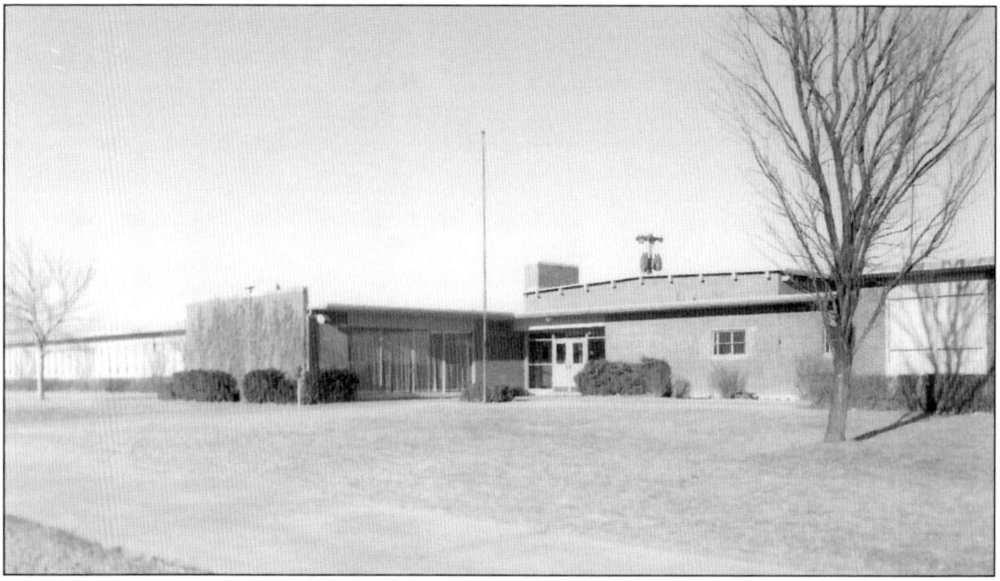

Widefield Grade School, built on Widefield Drive in Security, was completed in 1955 for Security's first through eighth graders. Students outside of the Security area continued to attend the old two-room school on the other side of the highway, and Security's secondary students attended Fountain High School. (WSD.)

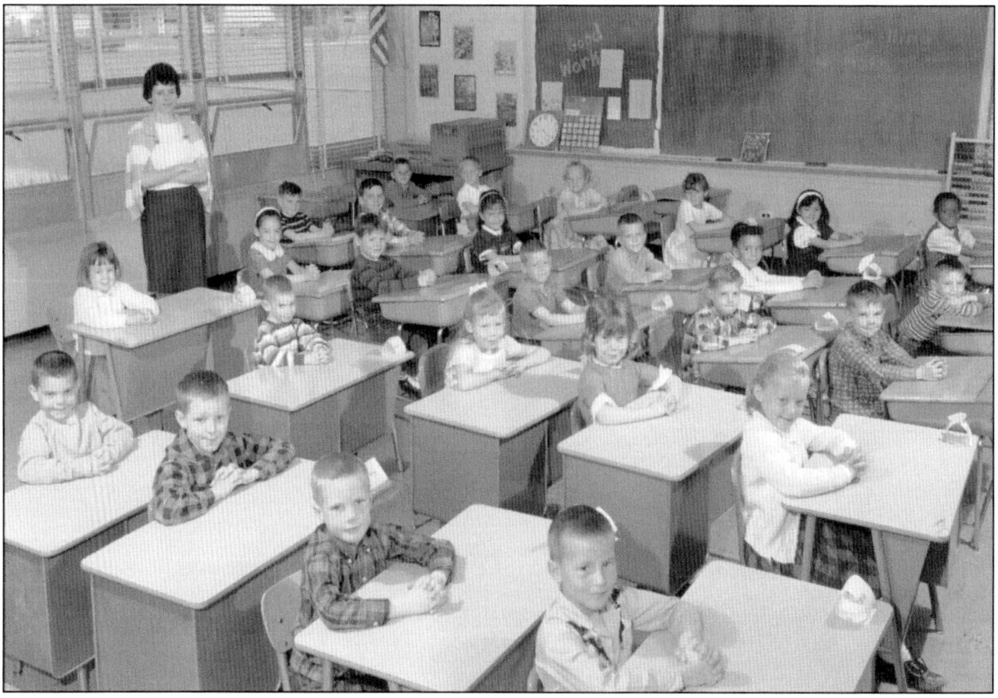

Teacher Jo Brown's first-grade class sits nicely for this group photograph at Widefield Elementary School in 1963. Boys put on button-up shirts for school, and girls wore dresses. In 1961, a fourth-grade female student was disciplined at South Security Elementary for wearing pants to school and was taken home by the principal. Exceptions were made during the cold months when girls were allowed to wear leotards or pants under their dresses for warmth. (WSD.)

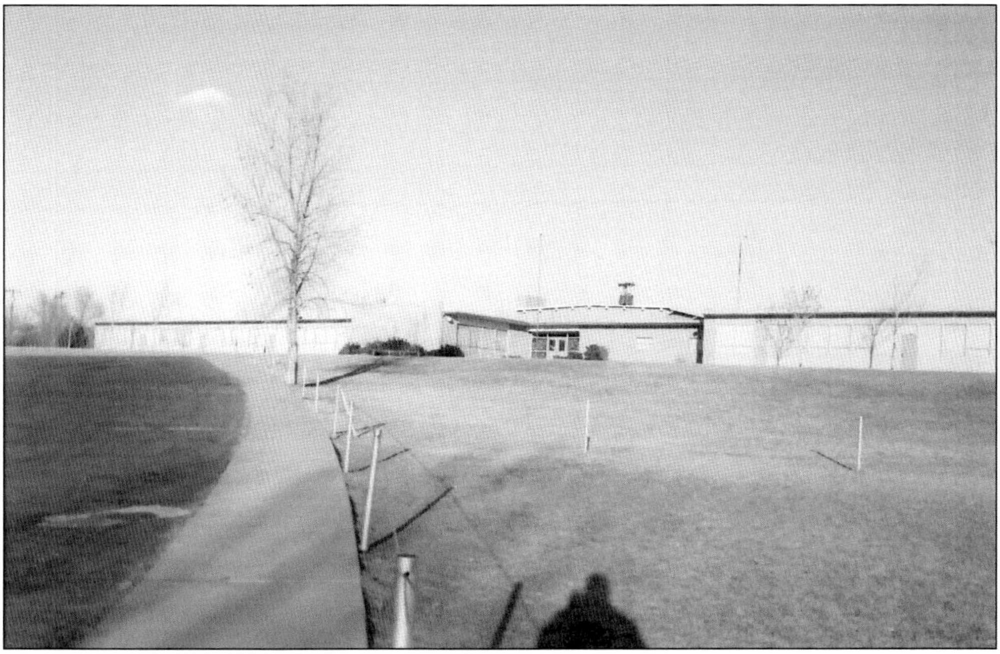

North Elementary School opened for students in October 1956, just a year after the completion of Security's first school. Located in the north end of Security on Leta Drive, North Elementary followed the same architecture as its predecessor, with the main offices in the middle of the building and two wings of classrooms stretched out on either side. (WSD.)

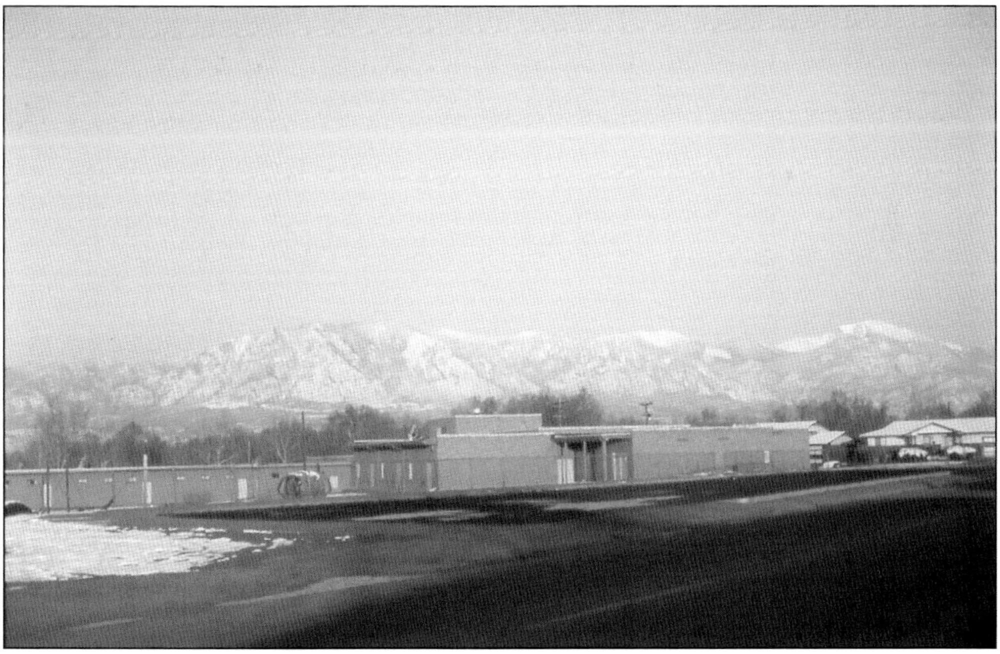

The author and her brother both attended sixth grade with a Mr. Sciortino at South Security Elementary School in the 1970s. They walked a block every day and approached the school from the east side, as shown here. This building was erected in 1957 and named for its location in the southern end of Security on Willis Drive. (NBT.)

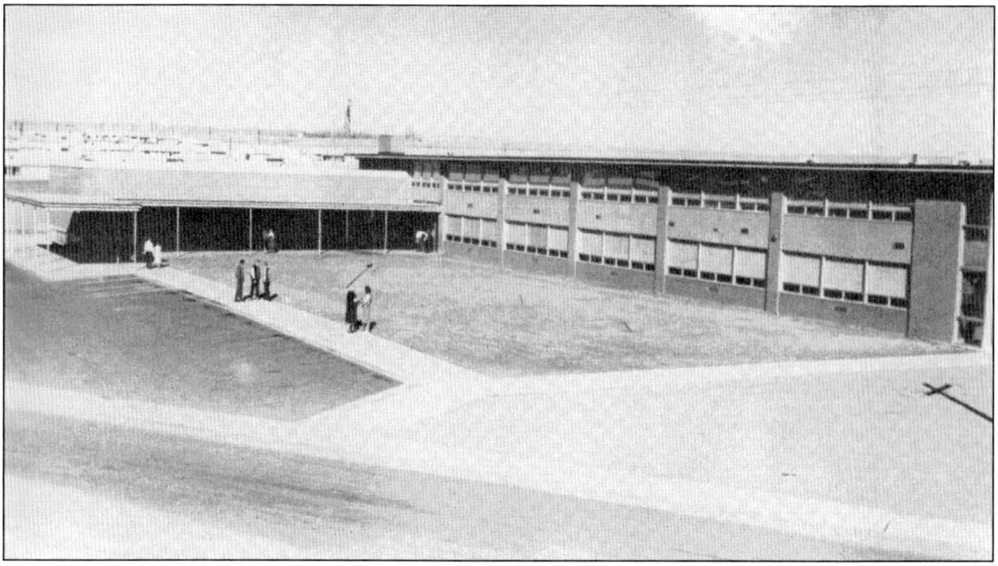

The very modern, two-story Widefield High School opened its doors in 1958. It was built on 10 acres previously owned by the Fountain Valley Boys School. While waiting on the completion of their new school, the underclassmen of young Gladiators, affectionately known as "Wee Gees," had attended classes next door in Widefield Elementary. In addition to basic high school subjects, the students were offered home economics, typing, band, journalism, photography, shop, and rifle club. (WSD.)

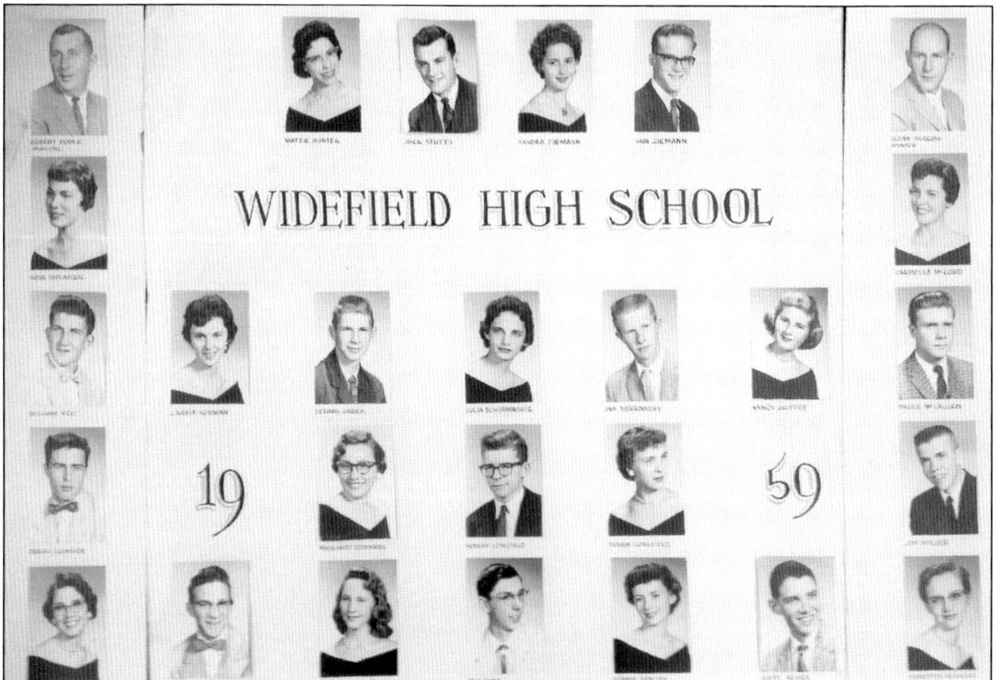

Widefield High School's first class of seniors graduated in 1959. Principal Robert Poole and senior-class sponsor Glenn Driscoll served the school district for many years. Poole also participated outside the school district in community clubs and organizations. (WSD.)

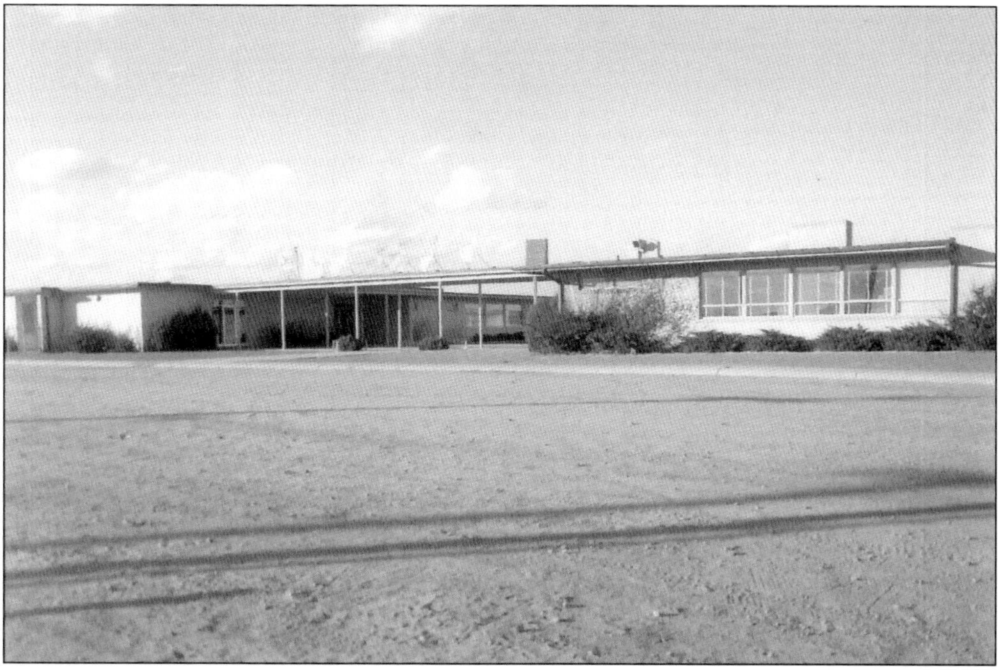

S.A. Wilson Elementary, located on Leta Drive in the north end of Security, was completed in 1959. An addition two years later included a kindergarten room, which featured alphabet letters and nursery rhyme characters inlaid in the floor tiles. The completed architectural plan of this building featured three wings of classrooms built around a large courtyard. (WSD.)

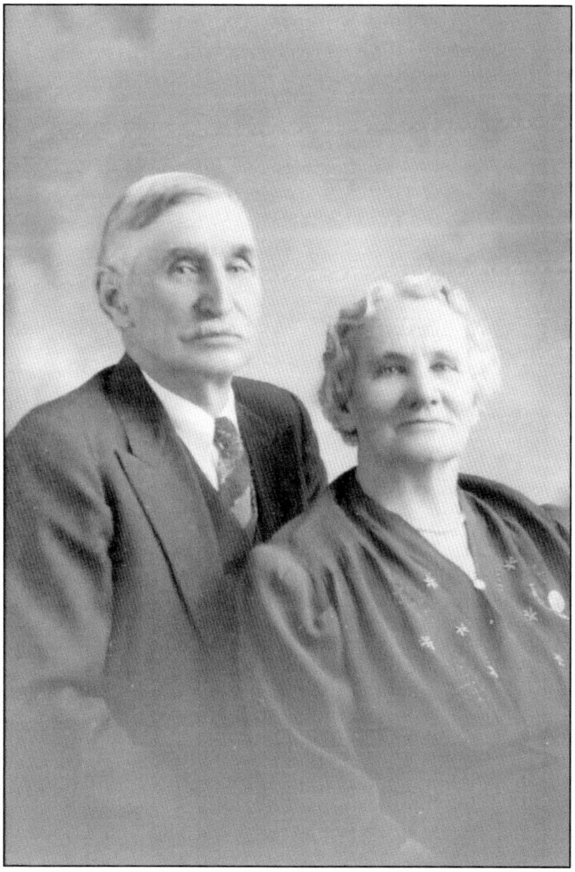

S.A. Wilson Elementary was named for Seward A. Wilson, pictured here with his wife, Florence. He operated a dairy farm for many decades south of Widefield. He served a number of years on Widefield School District's board of education when it was still a rural district, and he also participated in the Fountain Valley Grange and the Woodmen of the World. He attended the Baptist church in Fountain, and his hobbies included fishing and reading. (SW.)

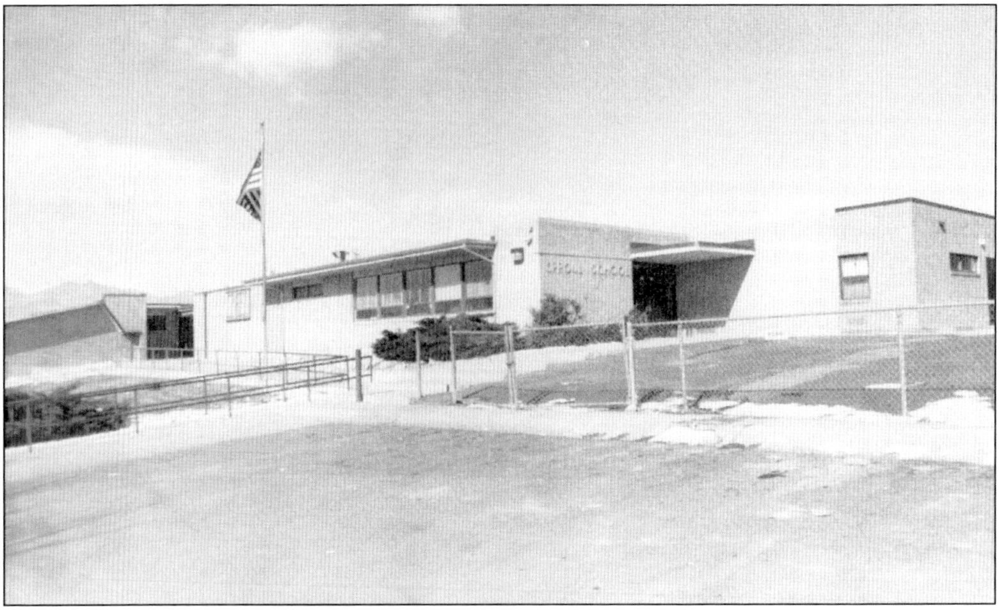

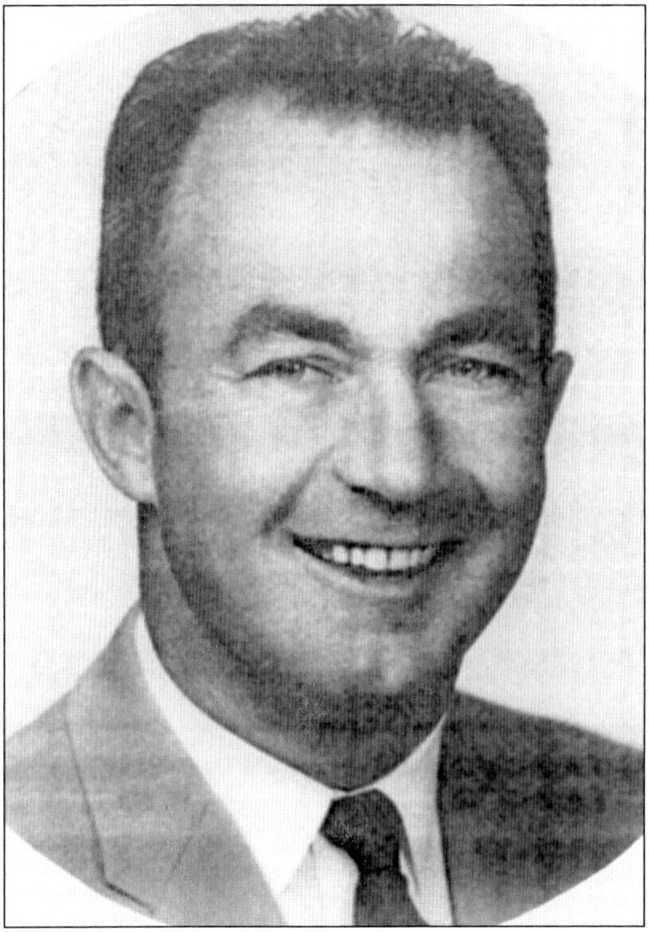

Sproul Junior High School, now a middle school and home of the Spartans, perches atop a hill on Sumac Drive in a tight little neighborhood in north Security. It shares the same courtyard layout as Wilson school. While waiting for the completion of this school in 1959, students temporarily attended classes at Widefield High School. (WSD.)

Sproul Junior High was named for Security developer Fred Sproul Jr., who donated land for the school. After serving in the Army Air Forces during World War II, Sproul partnered with his brother Elmer and established the land-development company known as American Builders. They constructed homes all over the Southwest, including Security Village in Colorado. Some local business owners remember Sproul's willingness to give them a helping hand. (BK.)

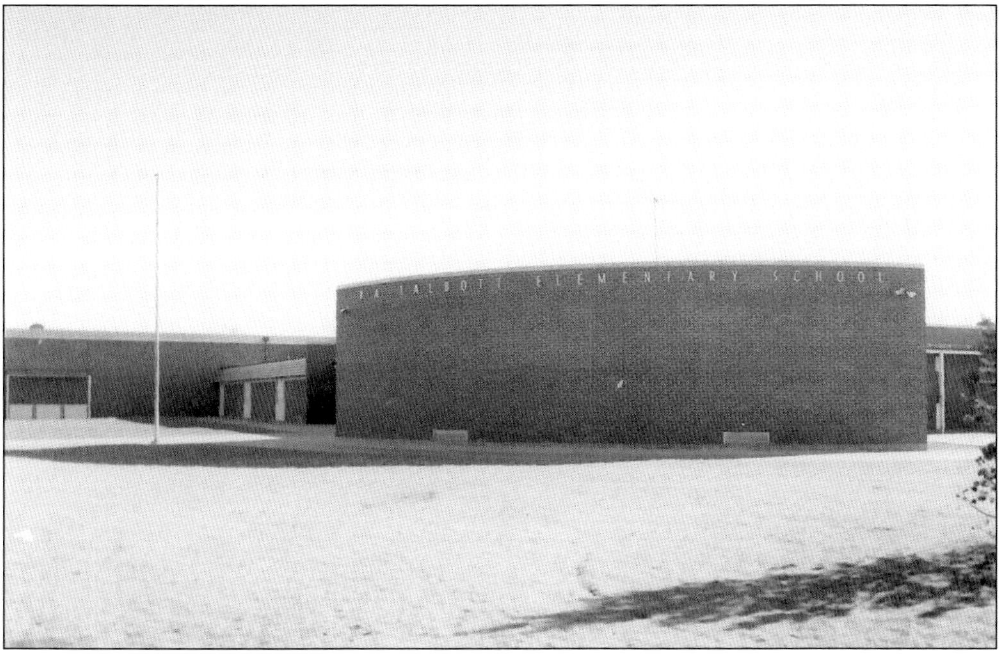

James A. Talbott Elementary School was named for Widefield School District's first superintendent, who died unexpectedly at the age of 33. Completed in 1963, it was the first school built in the new Widefield subdivision. The curved portion of the building housed a group-teaching room. (WSD.)

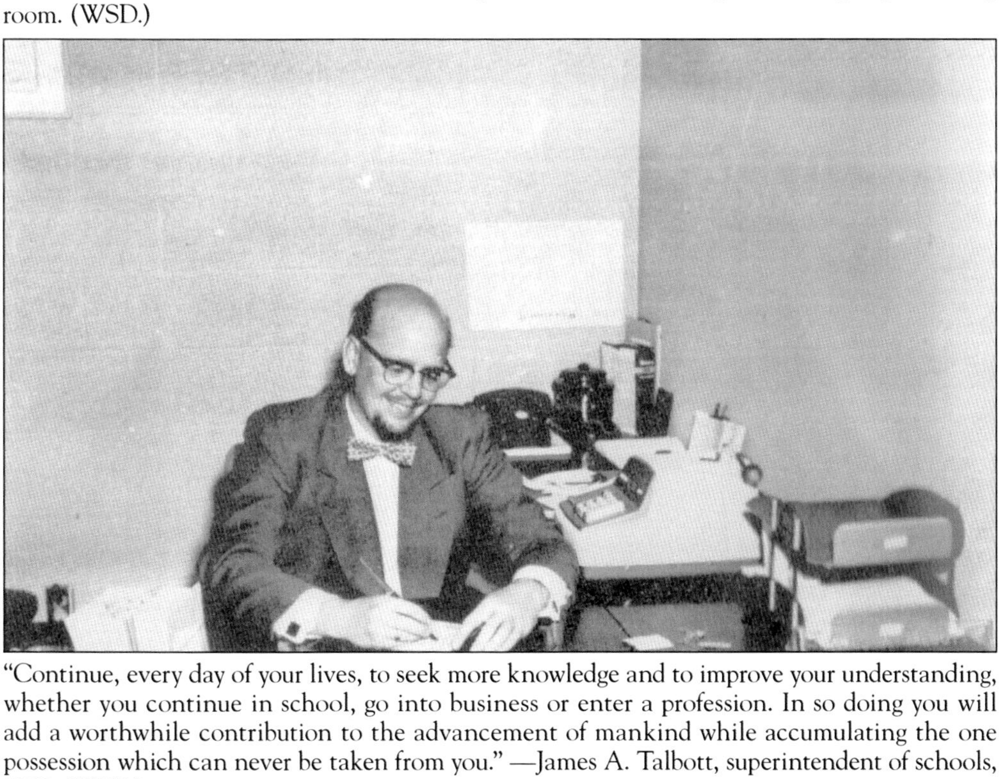

"Continue, every day of your lives, to seek more knowledge and to improve your understanding, whether you continue in school, go into business or enter a profession. In so doing you will add a worthwhile contribution to the advancement of mankind while accumulating the one possession which can never be taken from you." —James A. Talbott, superintendent of schools, 1959. (WSD.)

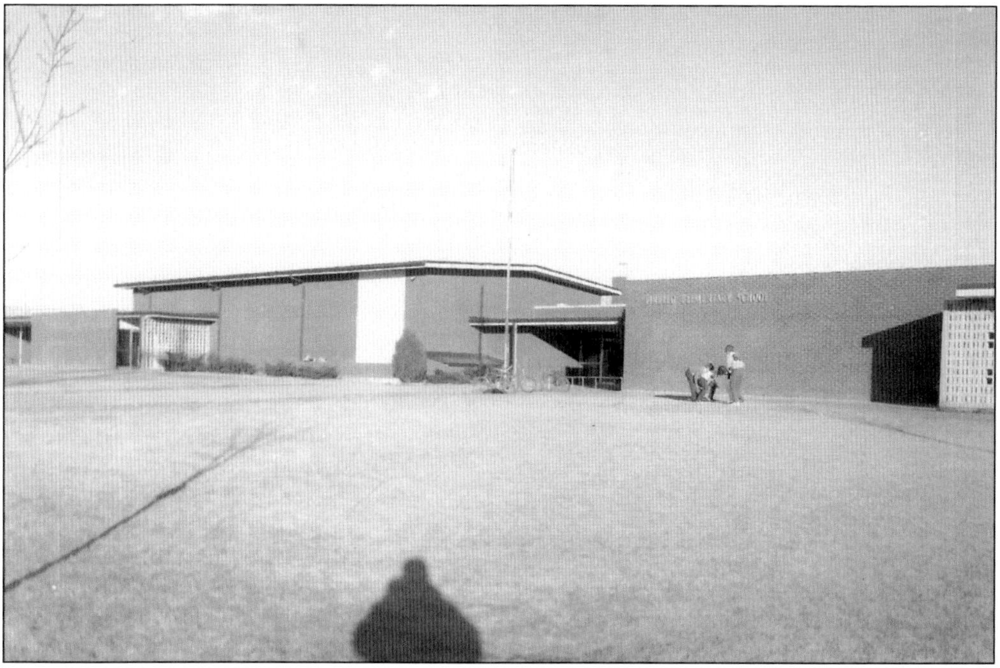

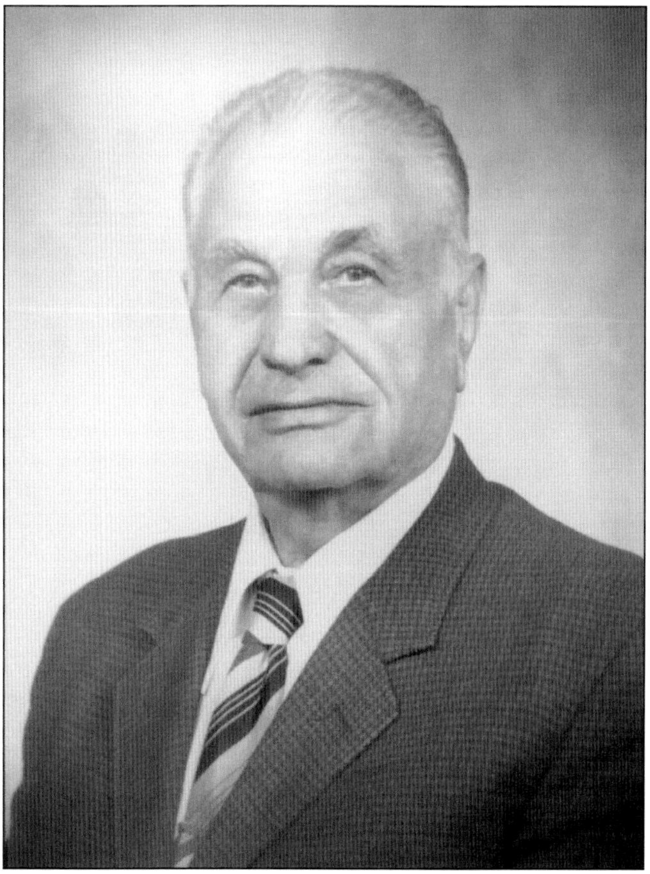

Pinello Elementary School was one of two schools opened to students in 1964. The school is located on Cody Drive at the extreme north end of Security. It was named for Louie Pinello, who served on the board of education during the school district's rapid growth in the 1950s. (WSD.)

Louie Pinello was the son of Italian immigrants Alphonso and Blanche (Venetucci) Pinello. He was born in the coal-mining town of Pikeview, located northwest of Colorado Springs. He moved with his large family to a farm near Skinner, just north of Widefield. Pinello later owned a construction business with his brothers and served on the board of the Widefield School District for many years. (WSD.)

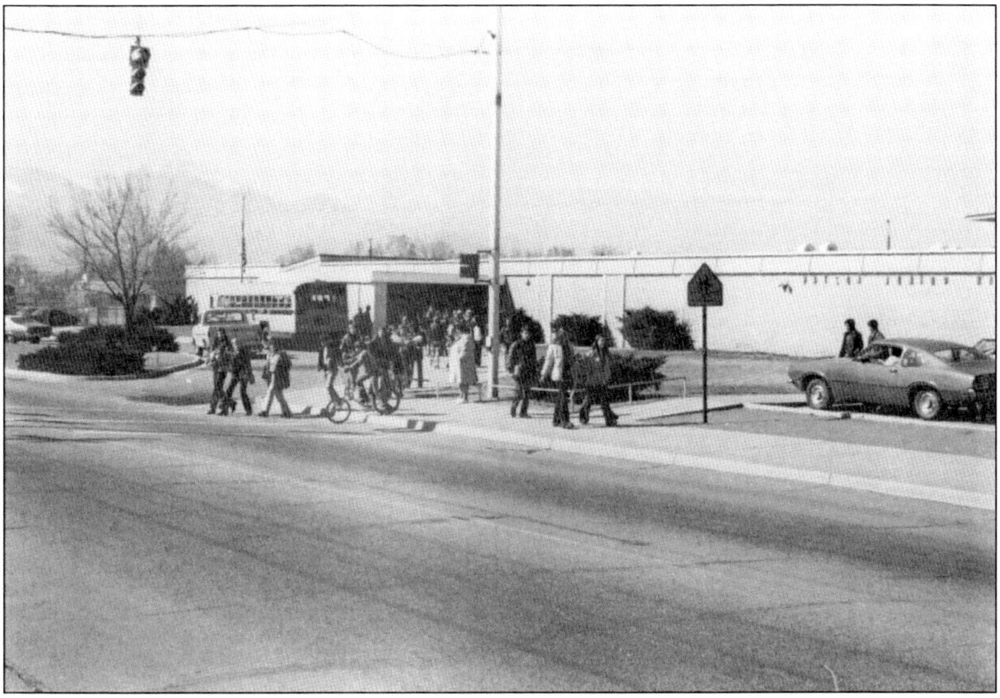

Watson Junior High is pictured in 1975 on Fontaine Boulevard. It opened in 1964 as the home of the Rebels but now operates as a middle school. It was named for Jules Watson, president and owner of Widefield Homes, who donated the land for the school. The fact that he was from Louisiana may have had some bearing on the selection of the rebel soldier for the school's mascot. (WSD.)

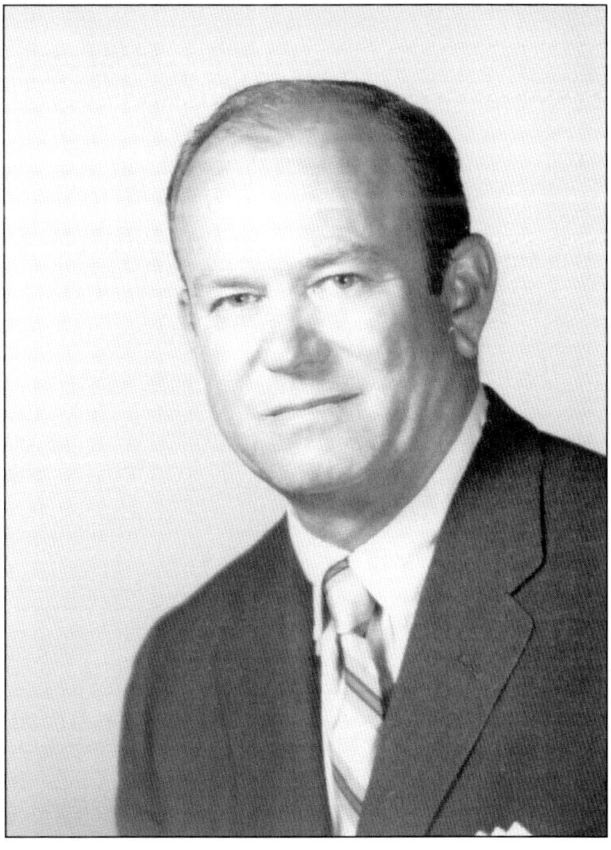

While living in Shanghai in the 1940s, Jules Watson flew 400 missions over the Hump, an extremely dangerous flight zone over the Himalayas between China and India. Next, he flew for Flying Tiger Line, carrying freight for the US military. He entered the home-building business in Arizona and later moved his interests to the Colorado Springs area. Watson is remembered for his fairness, compassion, and genuine concern for the individual. (MW.)

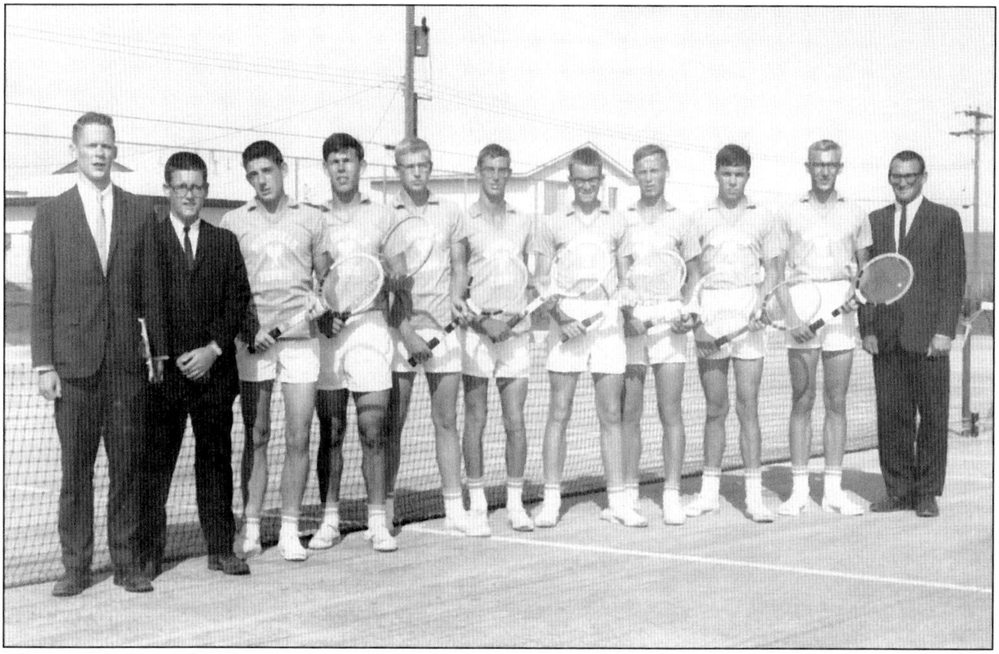

The Widefield High School tennis team appears here in about 1965. Pictured are, from left to right, manager Dave Larsen, Gary Galyardt, Bob Duhon, Dave Sharp, Terry Hoffmann, Lary Shelton, Warren Knight, Lonis Brown, Steve Williams, Rich Hoffman, and coach Don Jorgenson. Knight later became a member of the band Flash Cadillac and the Continental Kids. (LB.)

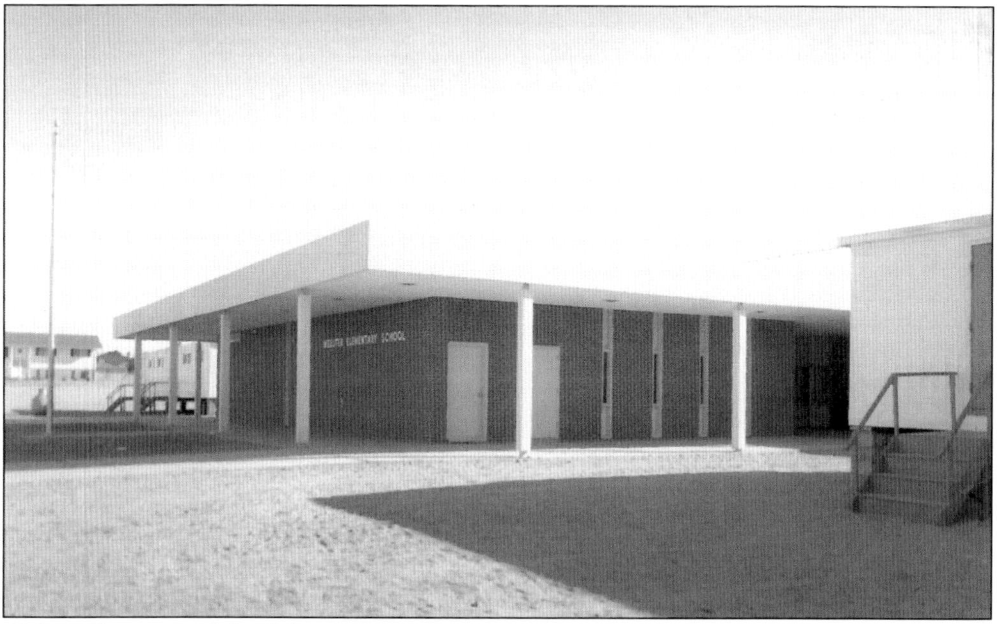

Webster Elementary School, located on Jersey Lane, was completed in 1969. This school was named for Noah Webster, who has been called the "Father of American Scholarship and Education." Modular classrooms sit on either side of the building. In many cases, these temporary classrooms were hauled onto school lots to provide additional space for the ever-increasing number of students. (WSD.)

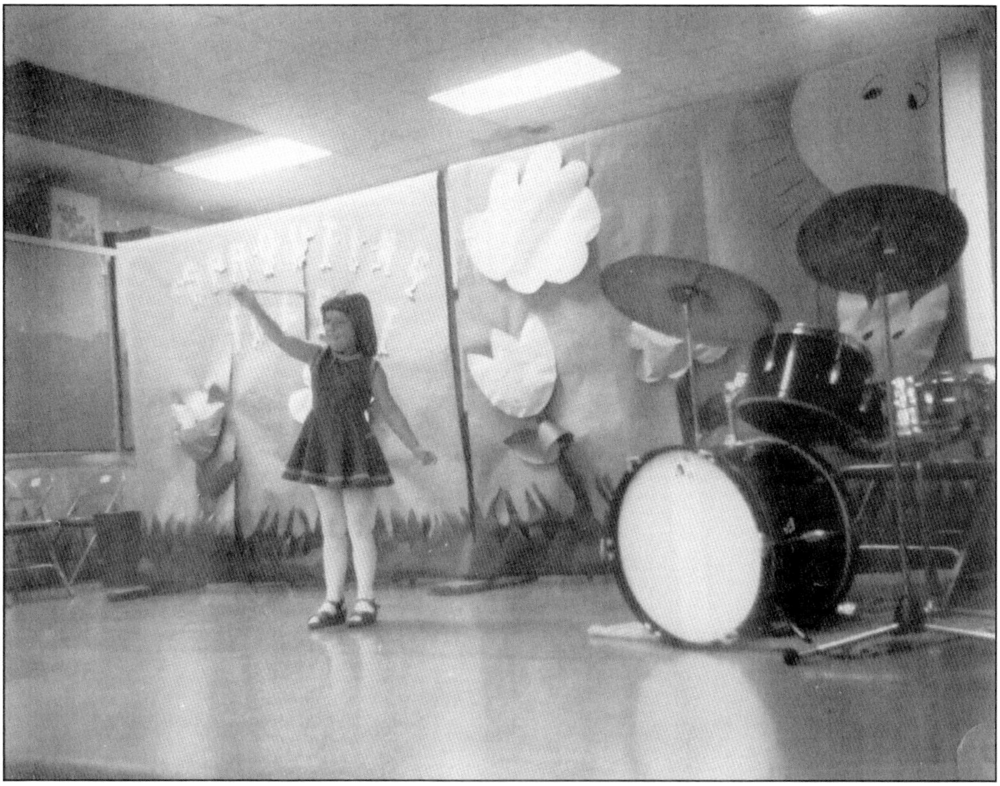

A young performer waves to the audience at Webster Elementary School's springtime talent show sometime in the early 1970s. School talent shows, where students perform in a wide variety of ways on stage in front of an audience, have been popular for many years. (WSD.)

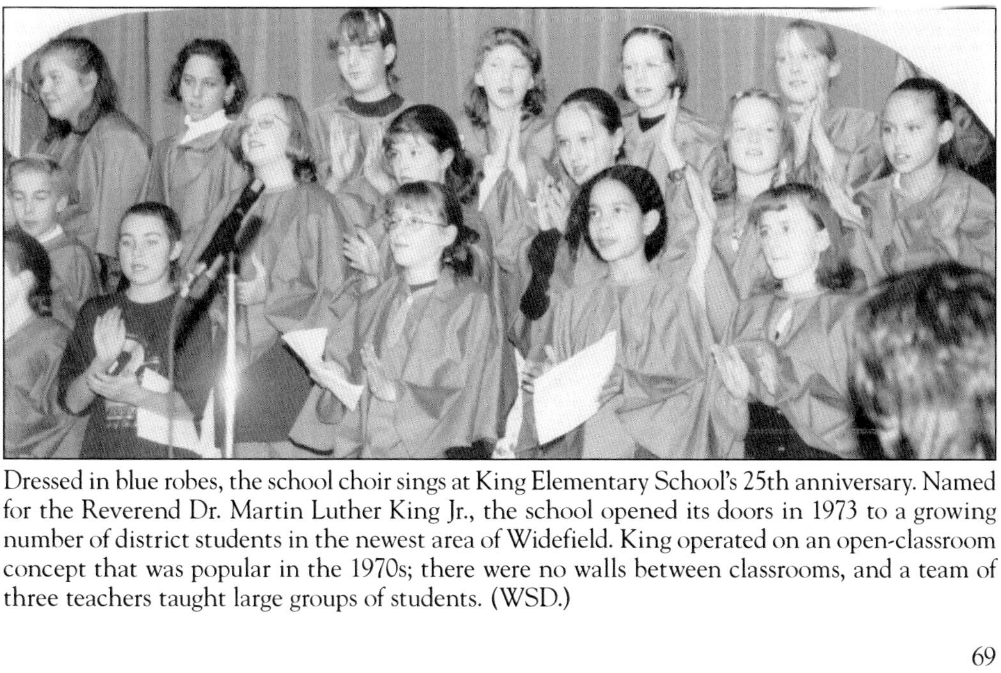

Dressed in blue robes, the school choir sings at King Elementary School's 25th anniversary. Named for the Reverend Dr. Martin Luther King Jr., the school opened its doors in 1973 to a growing number of district students in the newest area of Widefield. King operated on an open-classroom concept that was popular in the 1970s; there were no walls between classrooms, and a team of three teachers taught large groups of students. (WSD.)

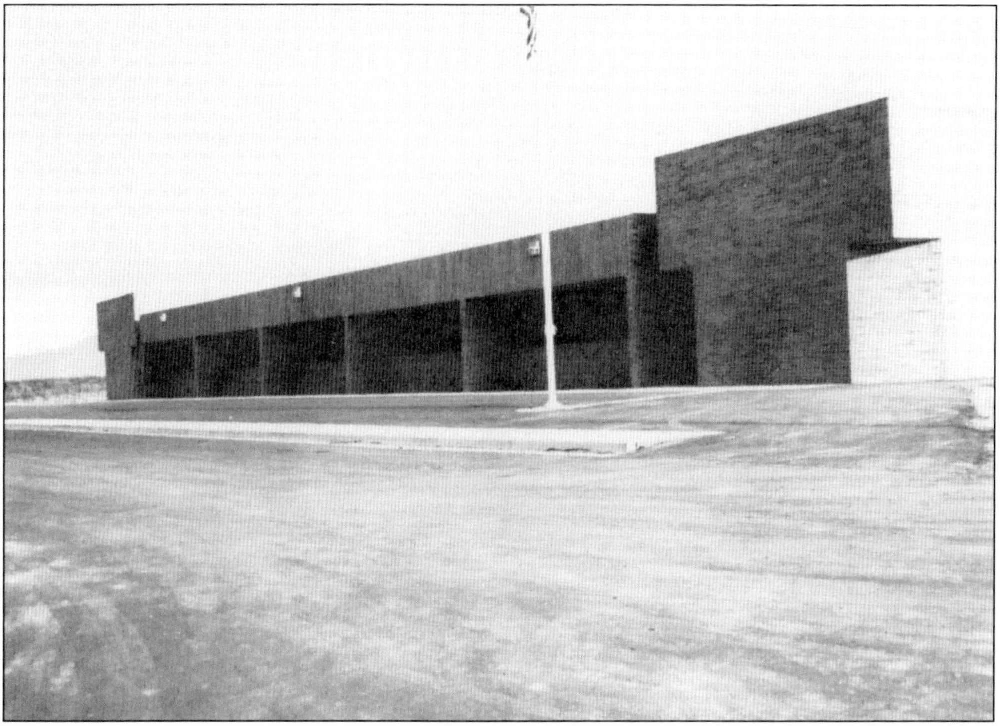

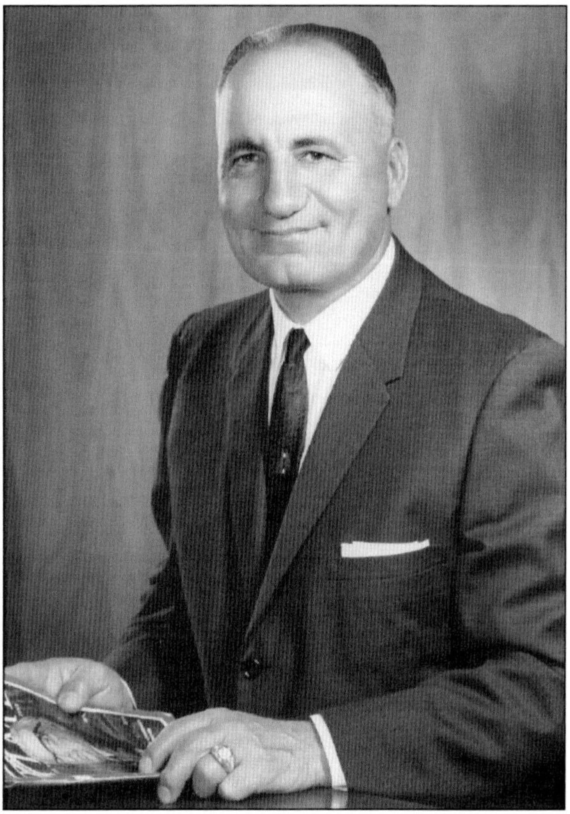

Janitell Junior High School, now a middle school and home of the Jaguars, is located on Fountain Mesa Road. It opened to students in 1974 even though it was not yet completed. Without a functioning cafeteria, the children walked around the building on plywood walkways to access the gym, where they ate their sack lunches. (WSD.)

Janitell Junior High was named for John Janitell, who once owned the land on which the school was built. Janitell was a rancher specializing in Hereford cattle. As a member of the school board, he was instrumental in redrawing the district boundaries in 1951 in anticipation of the population explosion. He also served as a member of the Fountain Valley Soil Conservation District and the Fountain Mutual Irrigation Company. (MAS.)

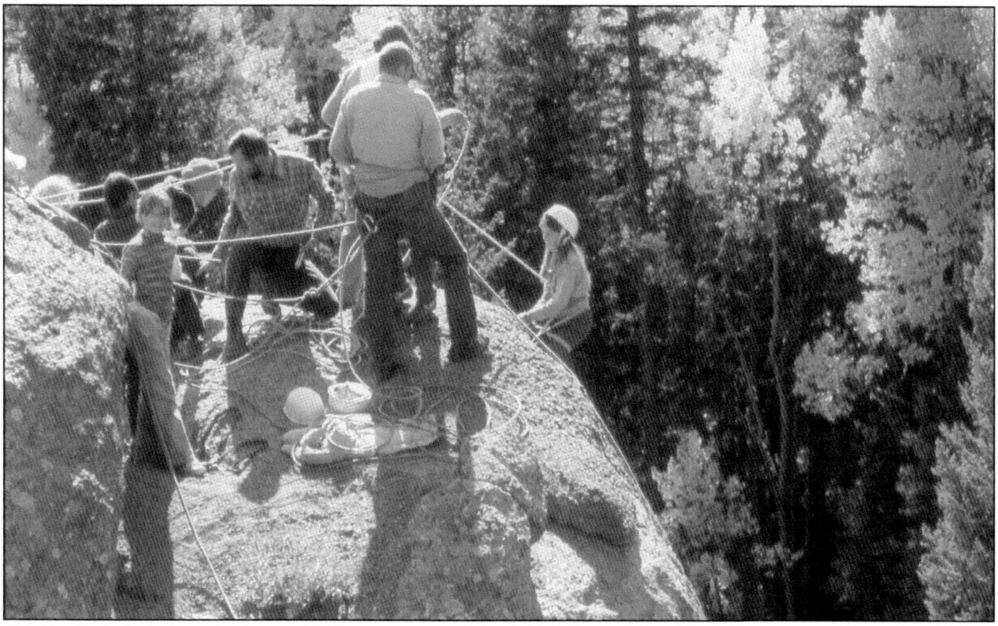

A Pinello Elementary sixth-grade student prepares to rappel down a mountainside at Bear Trap Ranch on an October day in 1978. Keeping up with many schools across the country, David Fussell organized this outdoor education program for Widefield's sixth-grade curriculum in the mid-1970s. The program helped students develop trust in their teachers and peers and to bond together as a class. (WSD.)

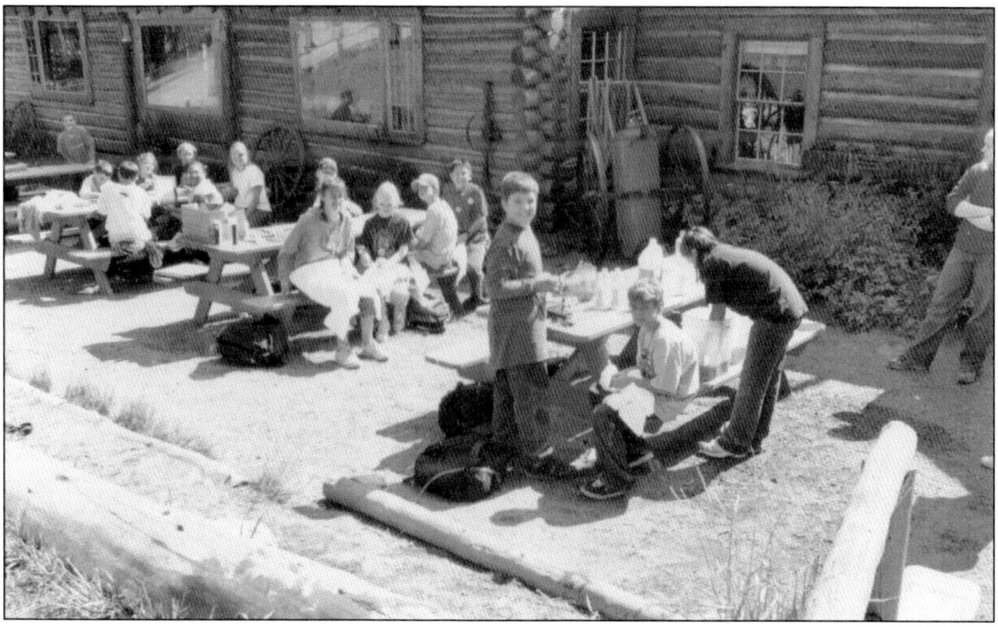

Excited sixth graders from Venetucci Elementary School gather in 2003 by the cabins at Bear Trap Ranch, located on Old Stage Road in the mountains west of Colorado Springs. For three days and two nights, the students participated in activities with their sixth-grade teachers and with camp assistants recruited from the district's two high schools. The students learned team-building skills that would help them transition from elementary to junior high school. (WSD.)

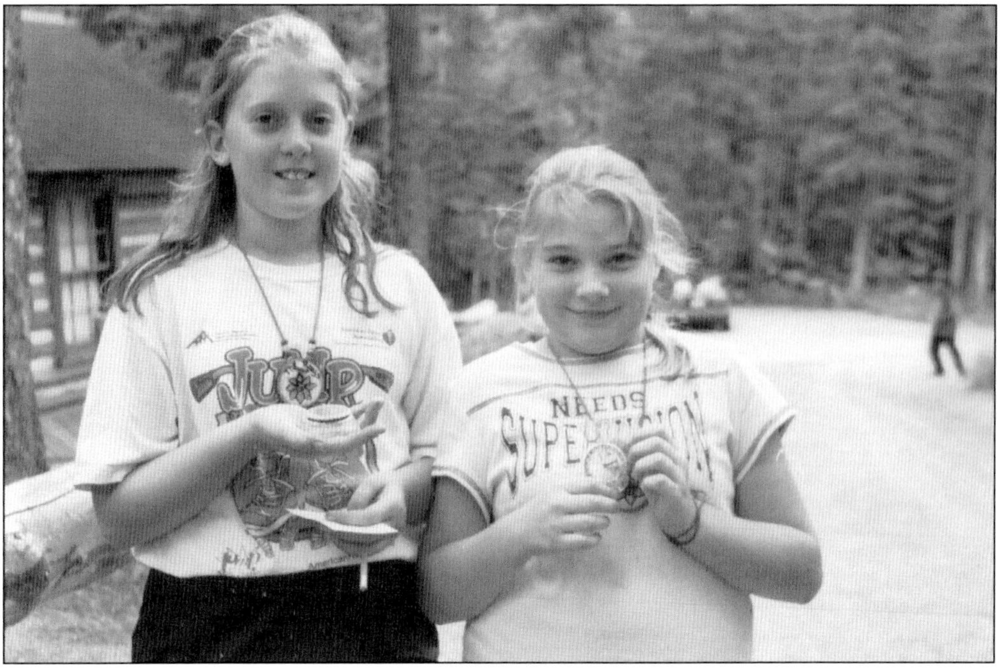

In this 2003 photograph, these Venetucci Elementary sixth-grade students display the compasses they will use in their orienteering activity at Bear Trap Ranch. Schoolchildren looked forward to the time when they would be old enough to leave their parents for two nights and experience nature and the outdoors. Children had to leave candy and electronics at home, and they had to eat everything on their plates before they could have seconds. (WSD.)

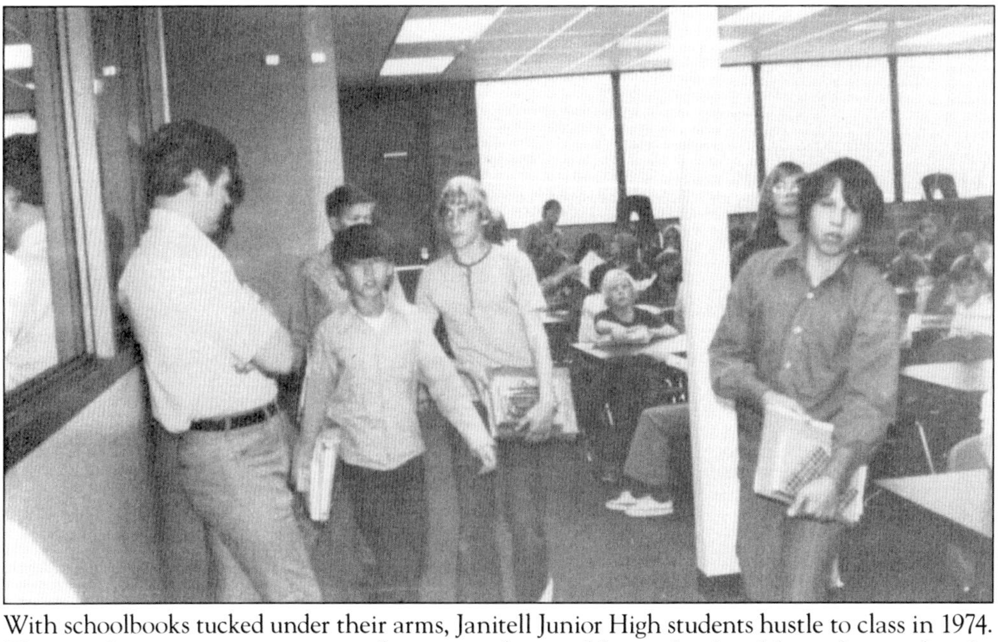

With schoolbooks tucked under their arms, Janitell Junior High students hustle to class in 1974. This was the common way to carry class materials to and from school and from class to class. In addition to the core curriculum, Janitell Junior High offered its first-year students Crochet Club, Ski Club, and Chess Club. (WSD.)

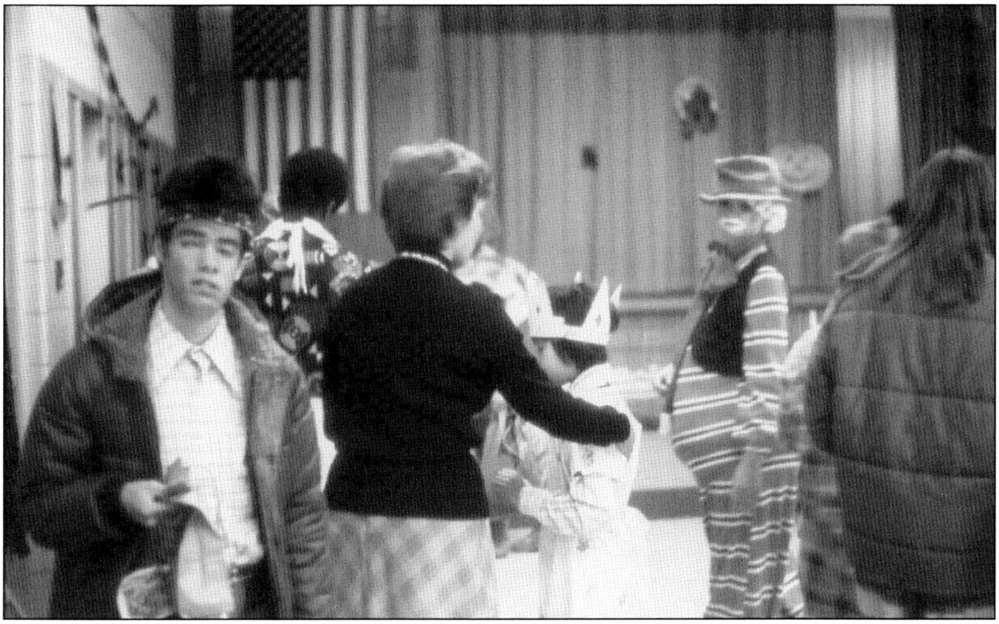

Special-needs student Leslie Thaden (left) is dressed up as an Indian for a Halloween party held in the cafeteria at S.A. Wilson School in 1977. In 1957, parents of children with disabilities approached the school board requesting a classroom and a teacher for their children. Widefield District met the needs of these children and eventually appropriated S.A. Wilson as a special education school. (NBT.)

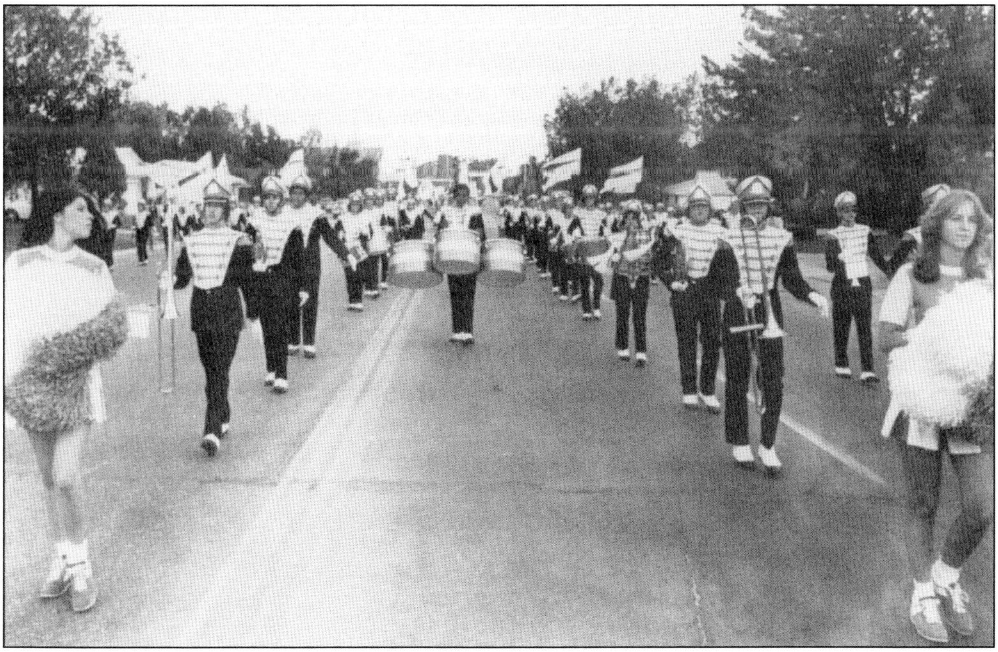

In 1977, the Widefield High School Band marches down Security Boulevard toward the high school in the annual homecoming parade. Many residents of the community turned out to watch the parade from the street curbs and later showed up at the stadium to watch their hometown football team play before an excited crowd. (WSD.)

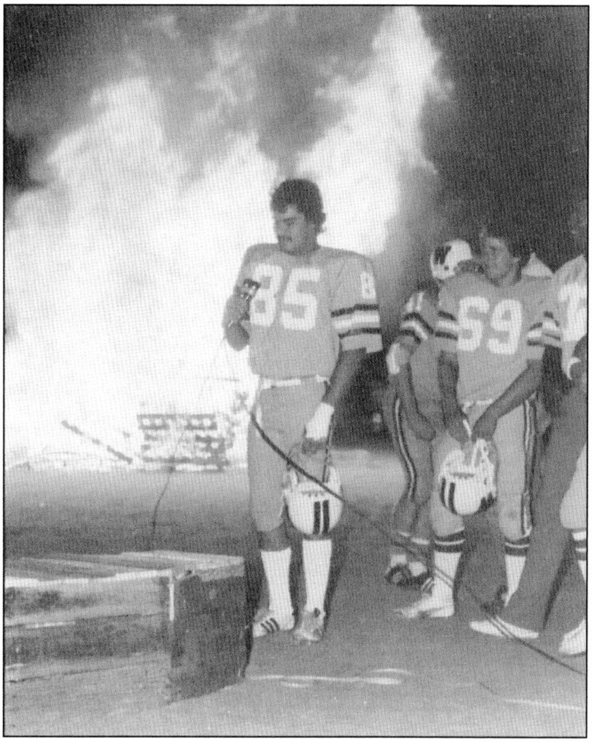

In his Columbia blue uniform, senior cocaptain Ralph Cintron addresses the stadium spectators at the homecoming bonfire in 1981. Bonfires generated enthusiasm for the homecoming football game. School alumni and former residents were welcomed back to the stadium. Homecoming events also included a dance and the coronation of the homecoming queen. (WSD.)

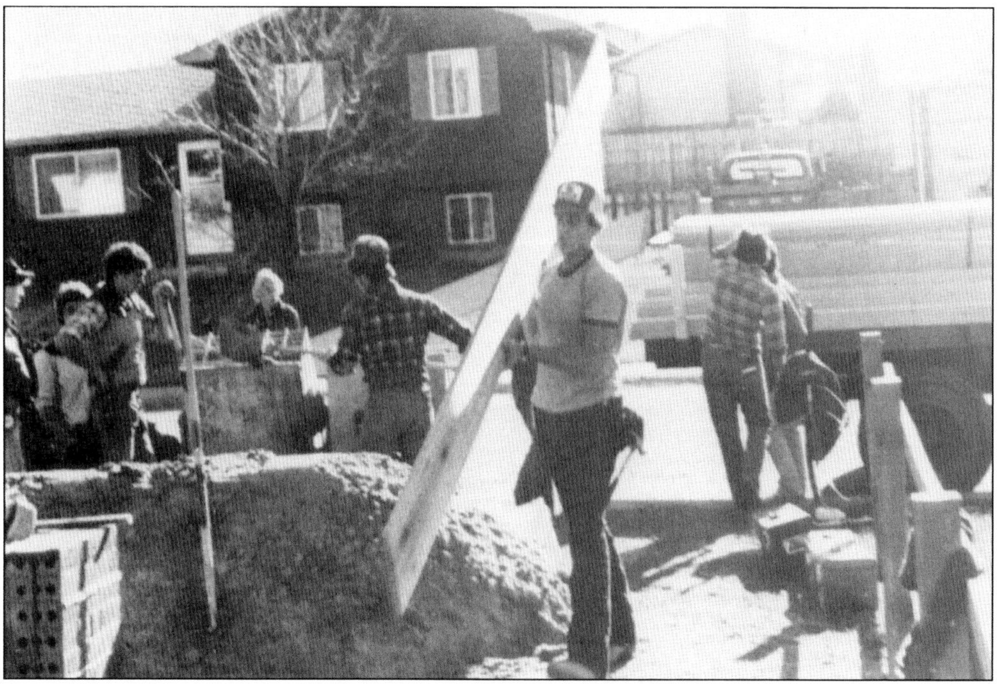

In the 1980–1981 school year, carpenter students in the VICA (Vocational Industrial Clubs of America) Club built a house on Drury Lane during their daily two-hour block. This unique class began in the late 1970s and was taught by Lynn Kopasz. Students gained valuable experience that proved useful when seeking employment upon graduation. (WSD.)

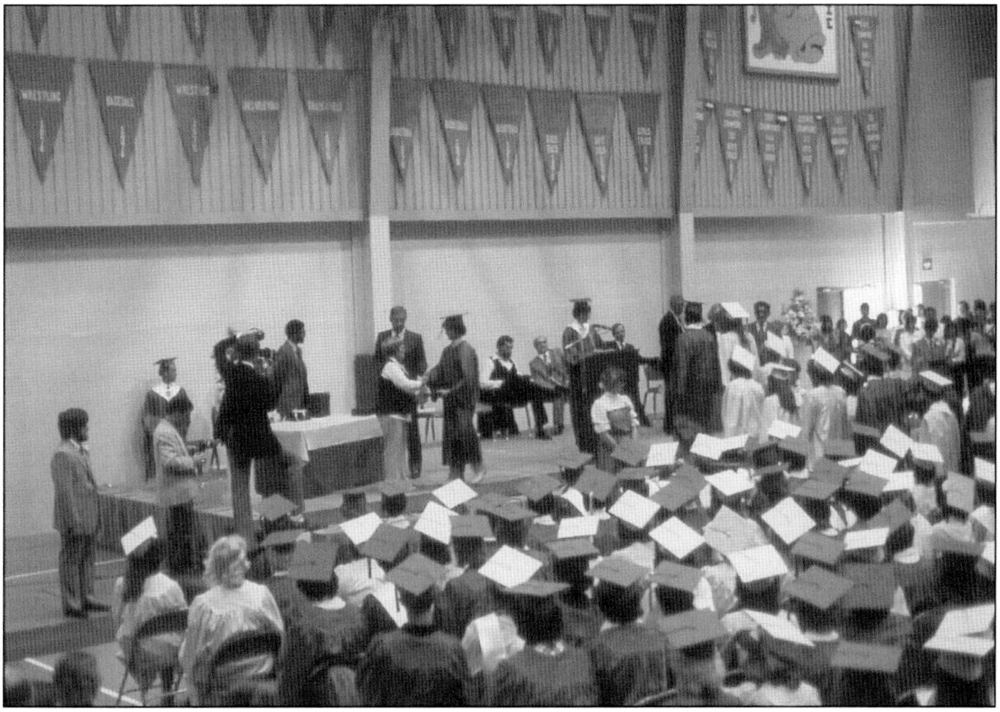

Fred Thaden, one of 511 graduates, receives his Widefield High School diploma from Candace French in 1983. The commencement exercises that year were held in the C.A. Foster Gymnasium on the high school campus. Prior to this time, they had been held outdoors next to the bleachers on the sunny football field. (NBT.)

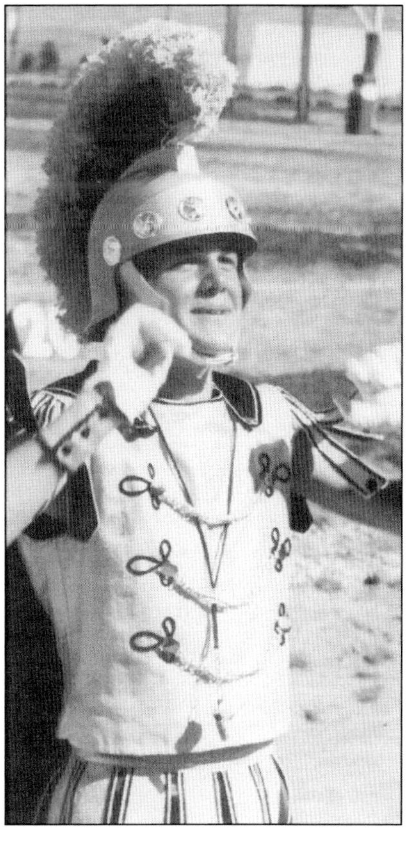

Thomas Wilson, drum major for the Widefield Gladiators high school band, leads the ensemble at a home football game in about 1985. Wilson's role as drum major required him to carry out the band director's instructions regarding practices and performances. His gladiator uniform was more elaborate than those worn by the musicians, and he was expected to add to the presentation of the band with his own performance. (WSD.)

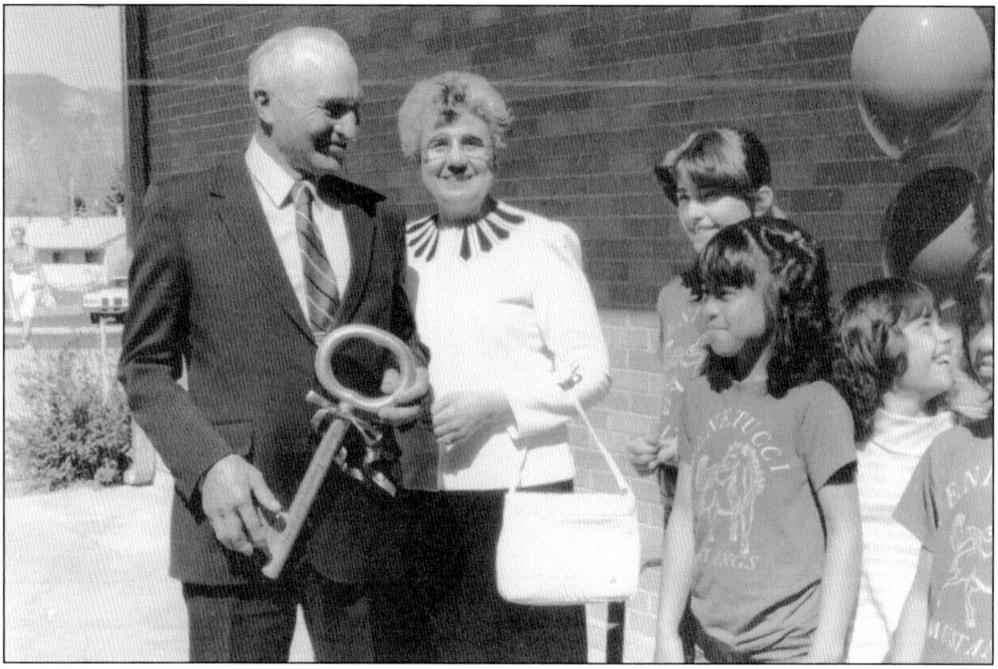

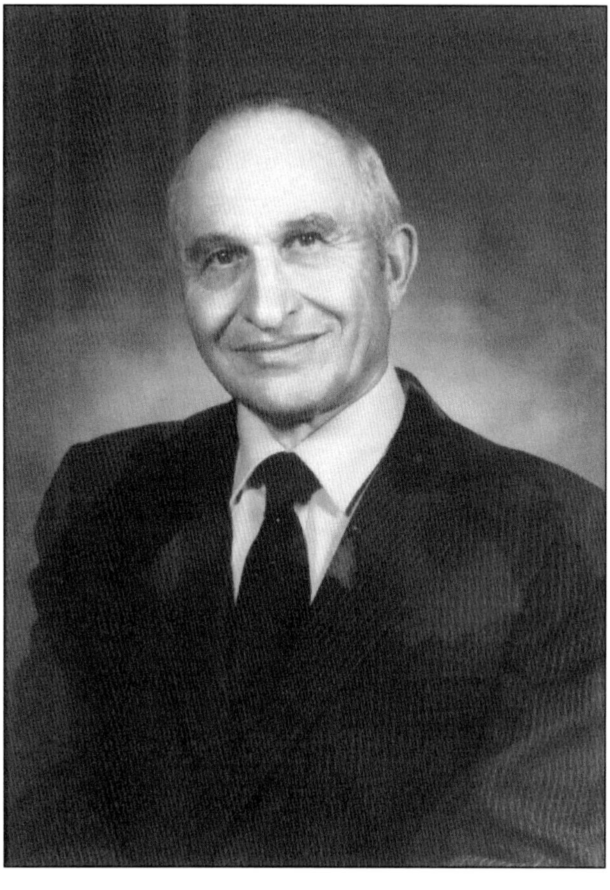

Nick Venetucci (left) and his wife, Bambi, attend a celebration in 1985 at South Security Elementary School. At this event, the name of the school officially changed to Venetucci Elementary in honor of Nick's many years of service to the schoolchildren in the Pikes Peak region. He expressed that his favorite memory was the smiling faces of children as they walked up and down his fields during his annual pumpkin giveaway. (WSD.)

Nick Venetucci spent many years caring for his elderly parents and ailing brother while keeping up the farmwork. Finally, in his 70s, he married his sweetheart of 27 years, Bambina Marcantonio, a former teacher of the deaf and blind. In spite of many opportunities to sell his farm, he chose to live a simple life. This allowed him to continue to bless the people of Security-Widefield with his endless generosity. (WSD.)

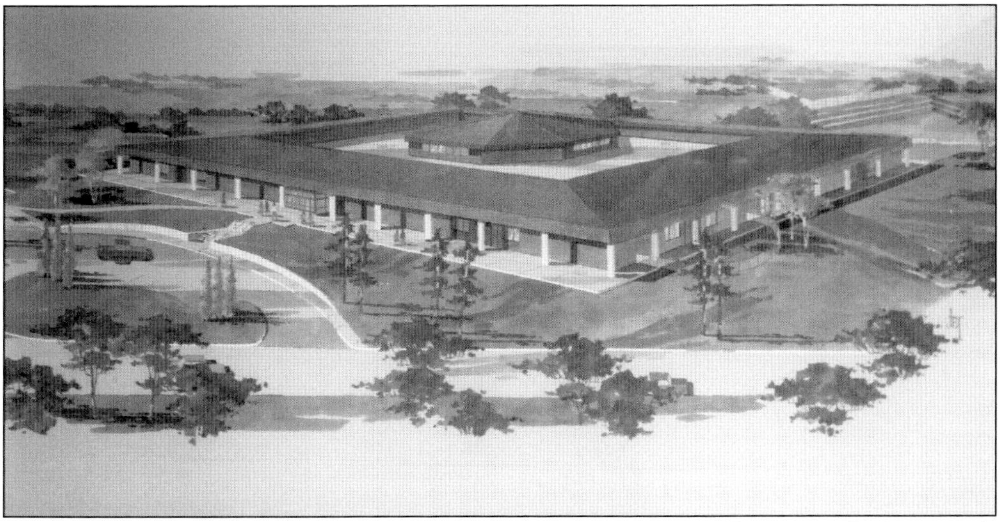

This architect's drawing shows Sunrise Elementary School on Grand Valley Drive, which was ready for the 1986–1987 school year. French Elementary School was built the next year using this same square design, which featured offices and classrooms surrounding the library and gym. (WSD.)

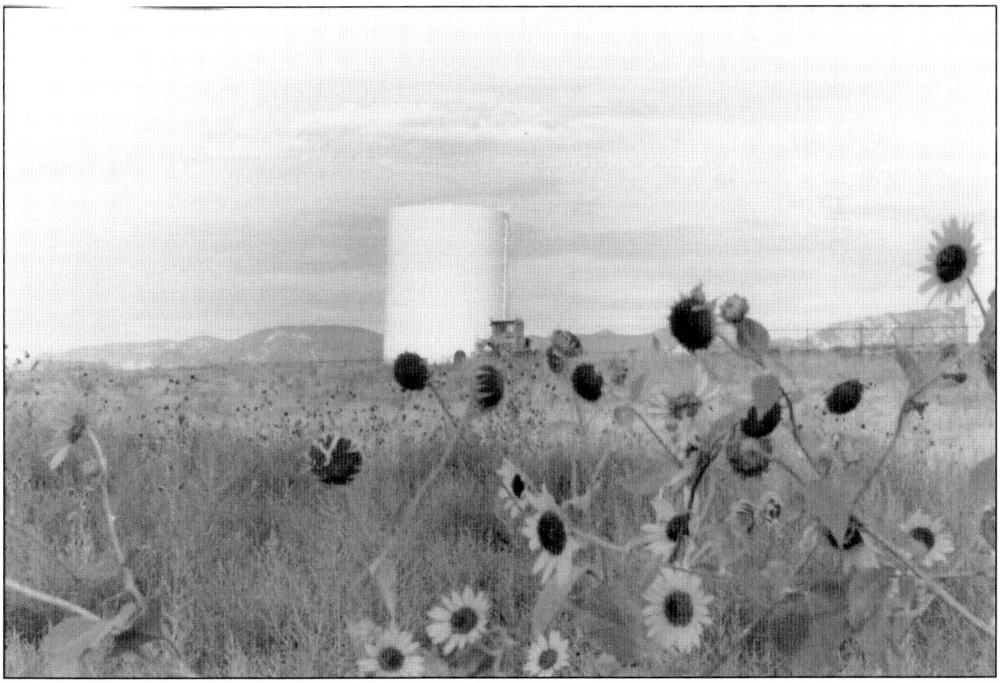

In August 1985, just before construction begins, a field of sunflowers near the large, white water tanks in the Sunrise Subdivision marks the location of the future Sunrise Elementary School. (WSD.)

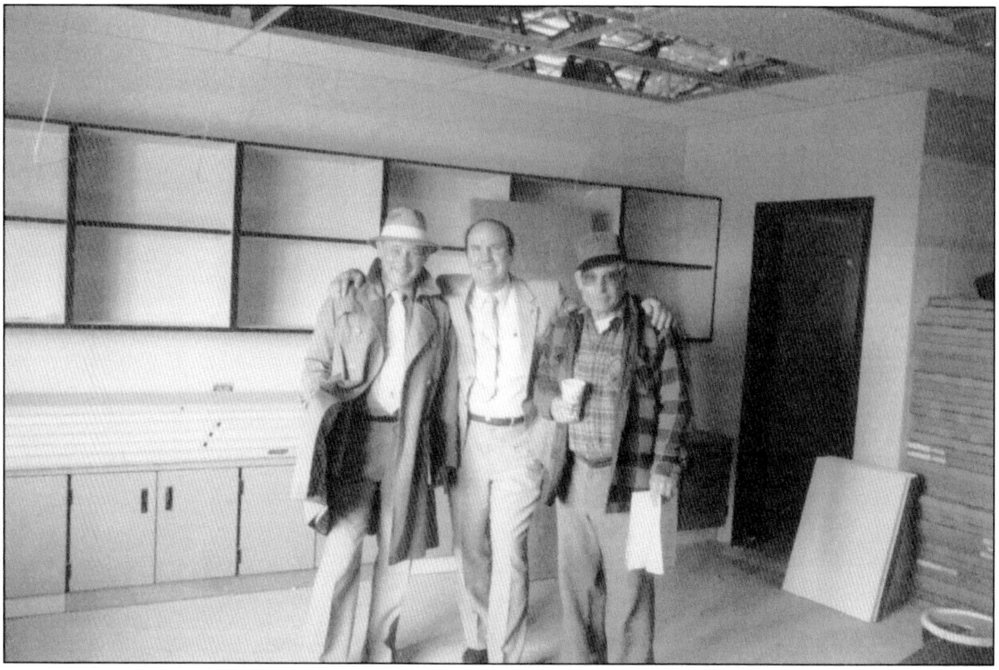

From left to right are architect John Guisti, school superintendent Phillip Cozzi, and job superintendent Jack Dubbs. They pause in April 1986 in one of the interior rooms of Sunrise Elementary School during one of their weekly construction inspections. (WSD.)

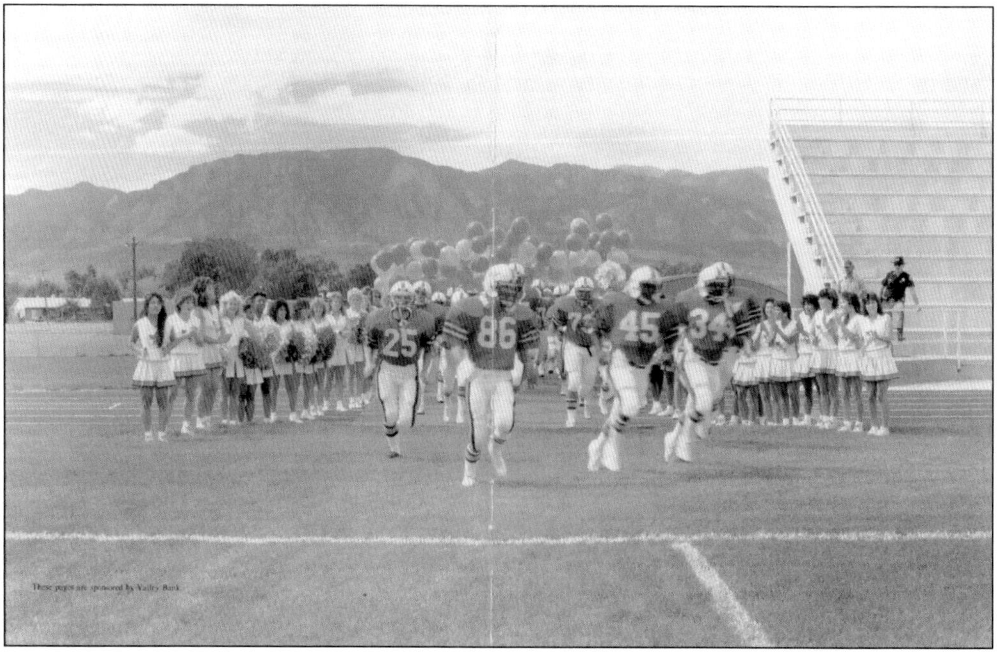

The Widefield High School Gladiators football team, flanked by the spirited school cheerleaders, enters the home field at the beginning of a game in 1986. (WSD.)

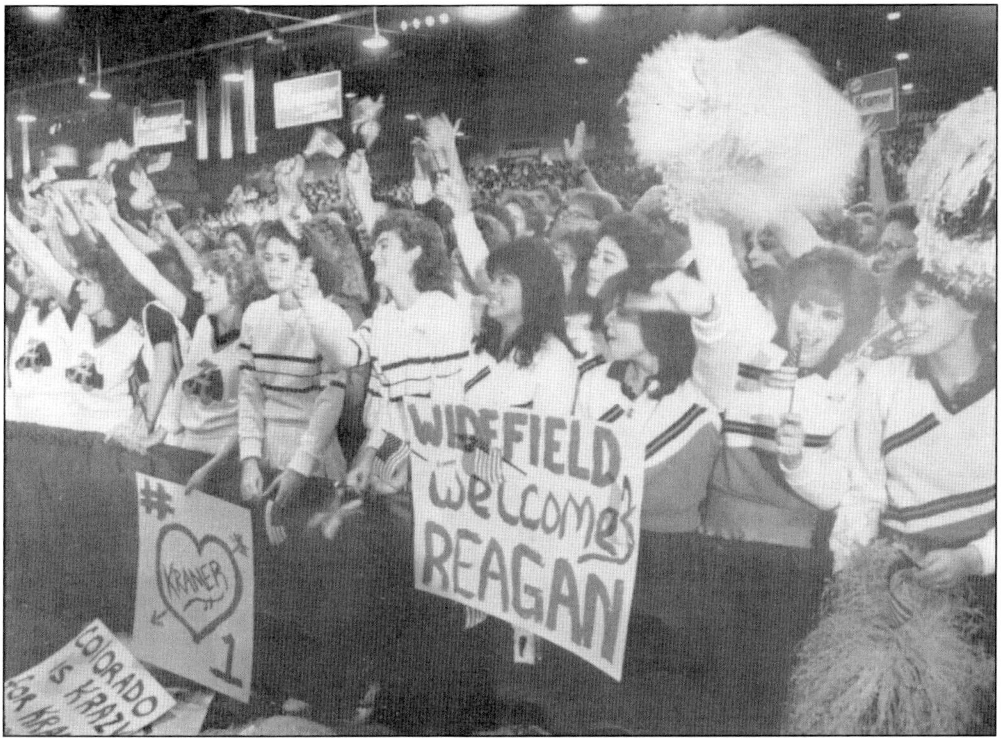

In October 1986, the Widefield High School cheerleaders represented the school while attending a speech by Pres. Ronald Reagan in Colorado Springs. At this rally, Reagan urged Colorado voters to elect Ken Kramer to the US Senate. (WSD.)

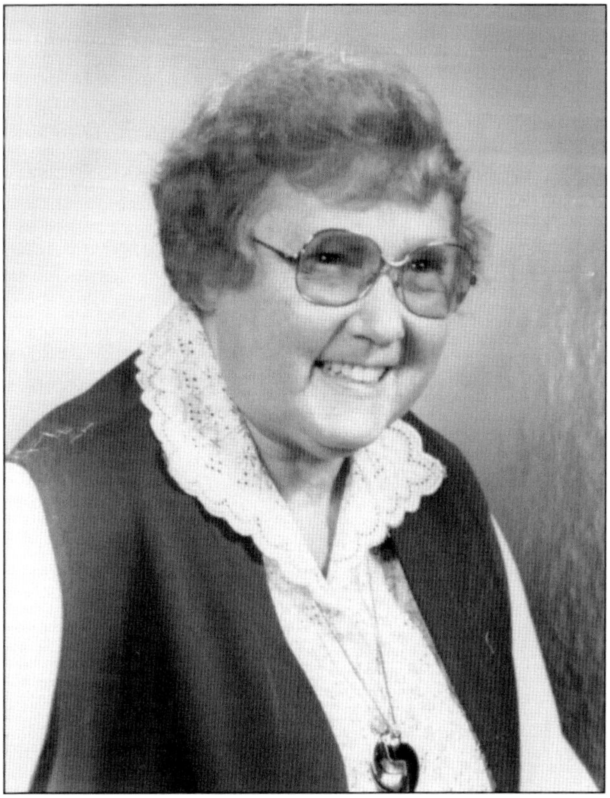

Candace A. French was a longtime employee of the school district; she worked as a teacher, administrator, and president of the school board. In 1987, Candace A. French Elementary School, located on Alturas Drive, was erected and named in her honor. (WSD.)

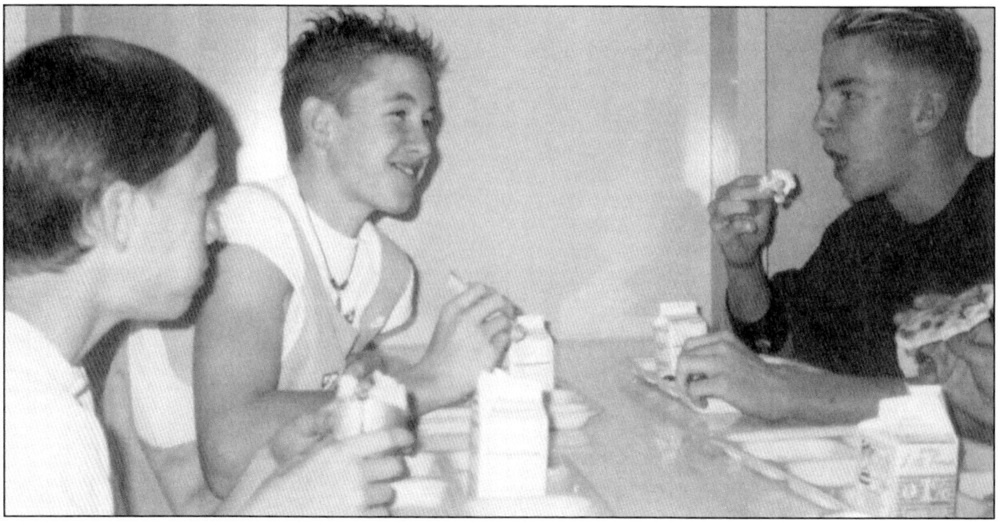

Eating their lunch in the 1990s are Sproul Junior High School students Shep Johnson, Cameron Mahnke, and Jonathon Rivera. In 1968, school lunch cost 30¢ for junior high students, and the meals were comprised largely of commodities provided through the federal government. School lunch evolved over the years until students could choose fast-food meals from the major chains in the 1990s. Recently, though, students have been limited to strictly healthy choices. (WSD.)

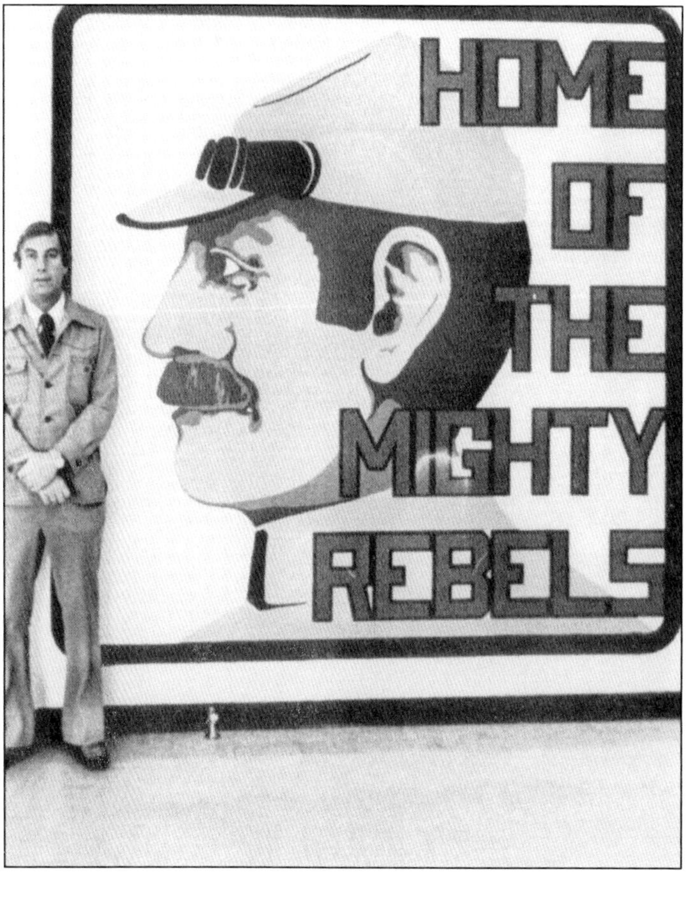

In 1977, Watson Junior High School vice principal Donald Hatchell stands next to a mural depicting the school's mascot. As Rebels, the band members' uniforms consisted of red sweaters and gray rebel caps. Many students went through their junior high years at Watson cheering for their Rebel sports teams. To the disappointment of many alumni, the school mascot was changed to the Wolverines in 1997 as a result of the nationwide mascot controversy. (WSD.)

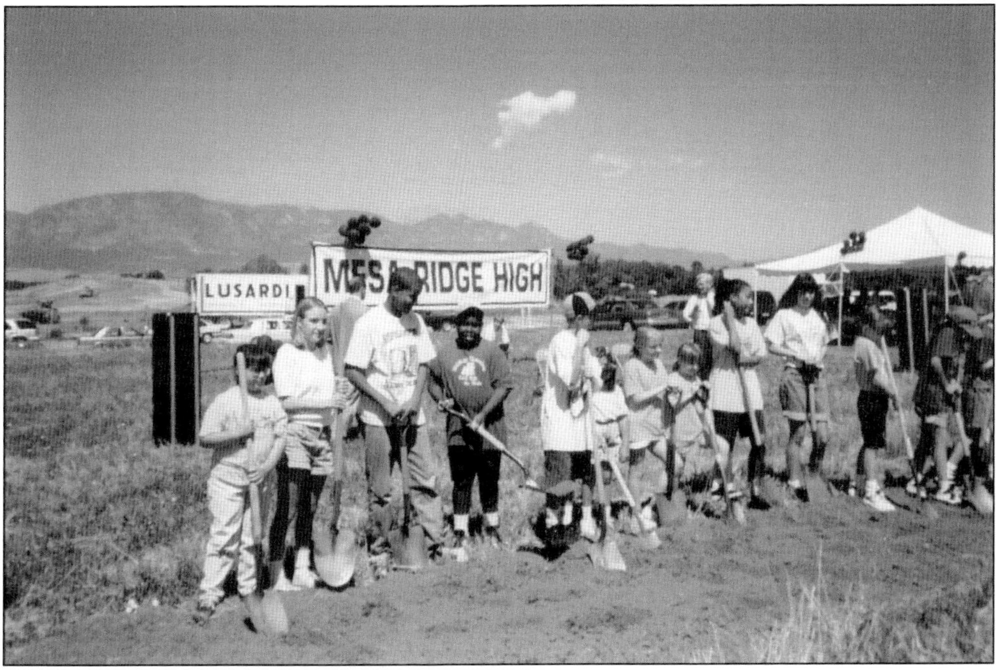

As part of the Widefield School District family, students from Widefield Elementary participate in the ground-breaking ceremony for the school district's newest high school, Mesa Ridge, in 1997. Students took an interest in this activity because they might later spend their high school years at this school. (WSD.)

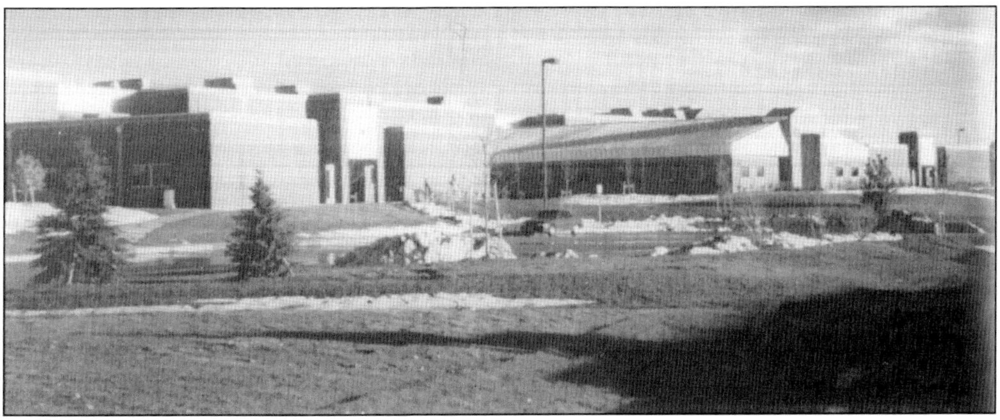

Mesa Ridge High School, home of the Grizzlies, is located on Mesa Ridge Parkway and was completed in 1998. It remains Widefield District's newest and most modern school. (WSD.)

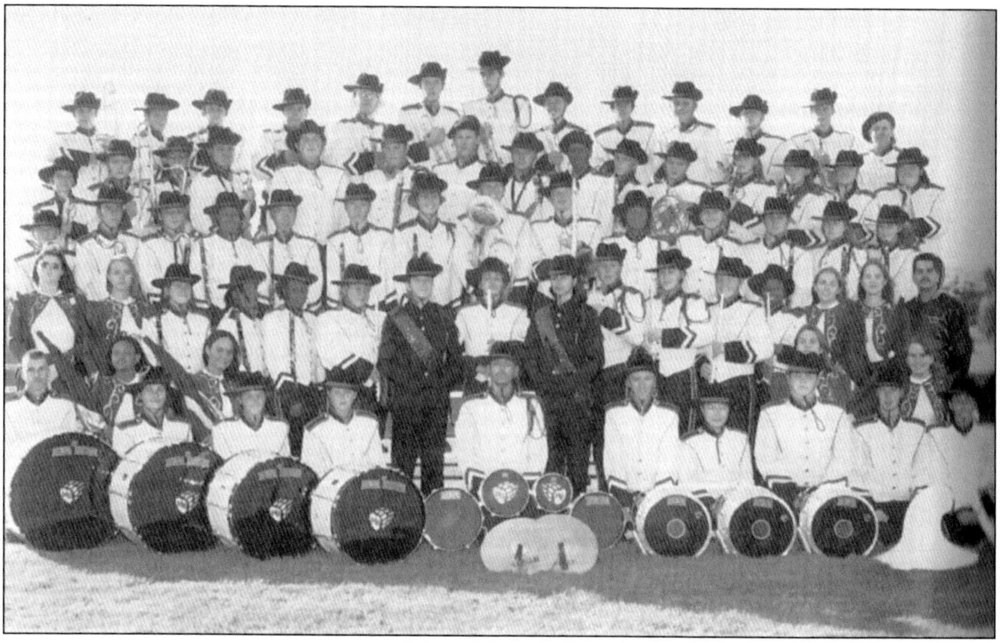

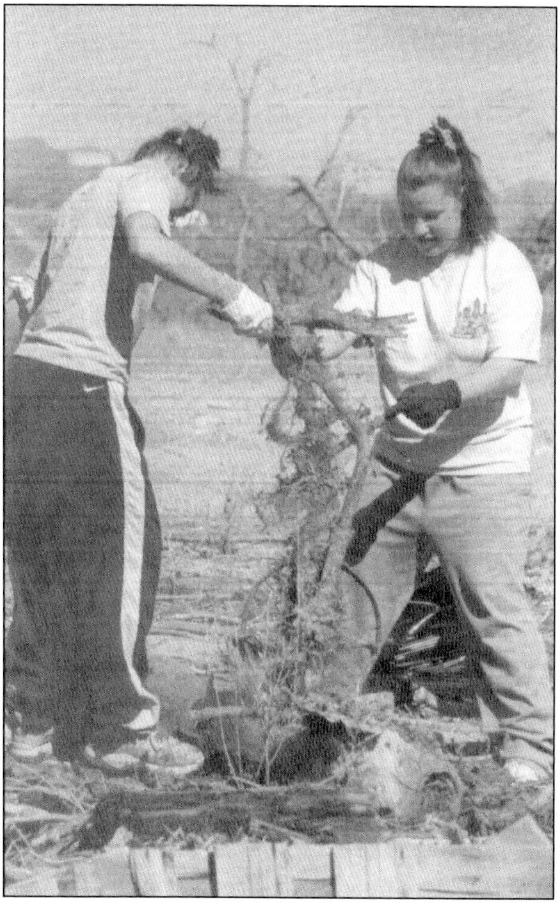

The Pride of Mesa Ridge High School Marching Band gathers in 2001 for this group photograph. The band truly has made Mesa Ridge proud with all the awards and honors it has earned. Indeed, the music program of the entire school district is superb, and many student musicians receive an excellent musical education. (WSD.)

As part of a Community of Caring organization, Mesa Ridge High School students participate in a cleanup activity in an effort to beautify their hometown. Yearly flooding leaves behind an array of interesting debris and plenty of work to do. (WSD.)

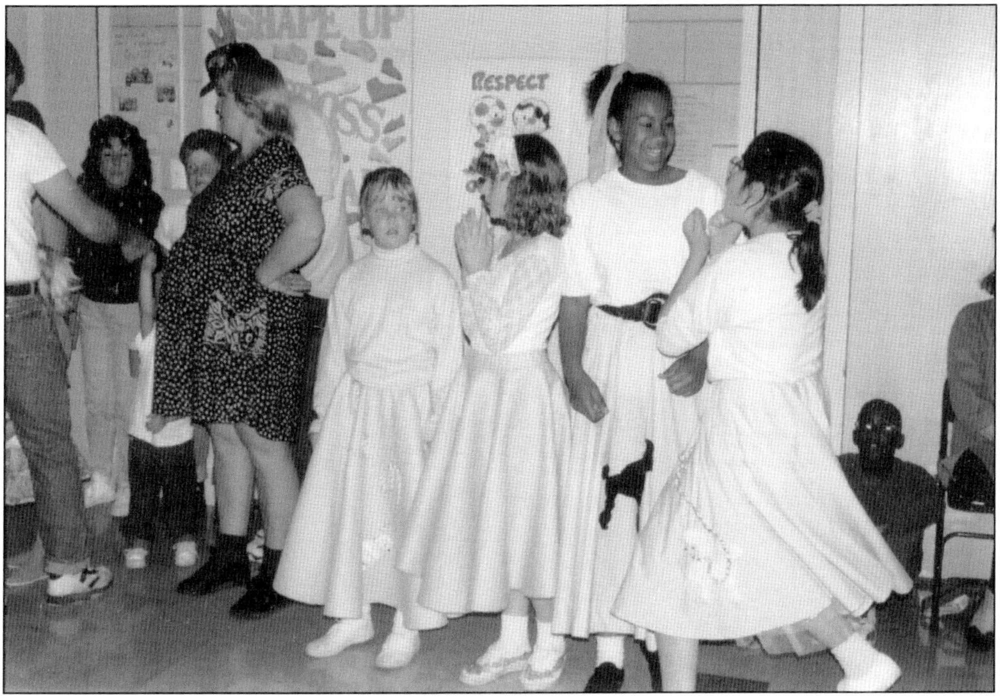

Pinello Elementary School held a 1950s-themed party sometime in the 2000s. Dressed in pink and blue poodle skirts are fifth graders Sally Paddak, Sadie Jones, Sarah Gonzales, and Britney Lacey. Such parties are popular among the district's elementary schools, and family members are invited to dress up, get out on the dance floor, and twist. (WSD.)

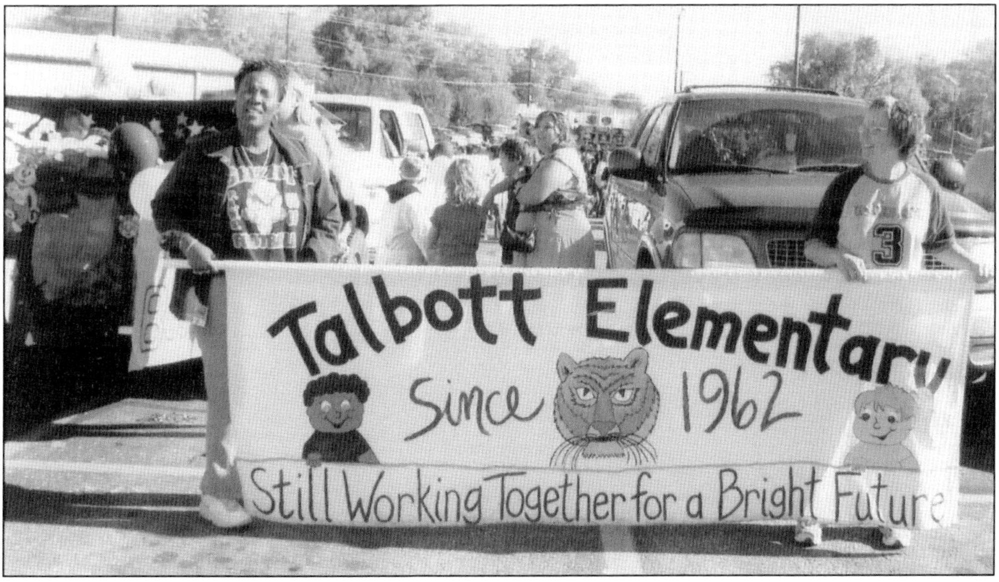

A group of students from Talbott Elementary School lines up in 2005 for the autumn Community Day parade. With the addition of another district high school in 1997, the annual homecoming events gave way to a combined effort. Locals and alumni from both high schools attend the parade and community barbecue, and the day ends with an exciting football game between the Gladiators and Grizzlies. (WSD.)

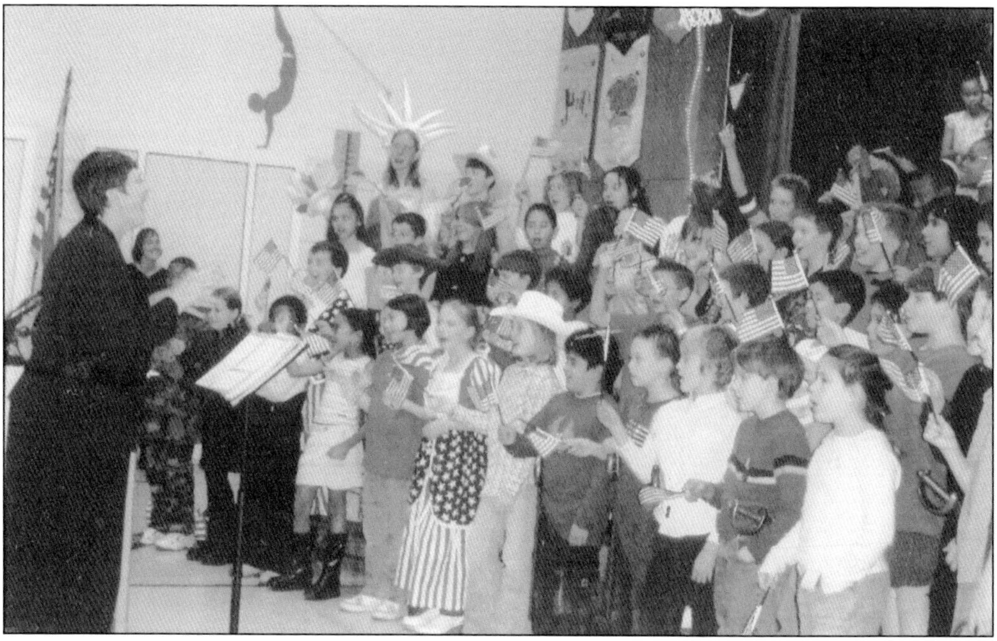

Talbott Elementary School students treat their audience to a Veterans Day concert in 2005. Widefield School District has always included a large percentage of military children whose parents serve the country and work at nearby military installations. Therefore, patriotism runs high in Security-Widefield, and appreciation abounds for the community's large number of active-duty and retired personnel. (WSD.)

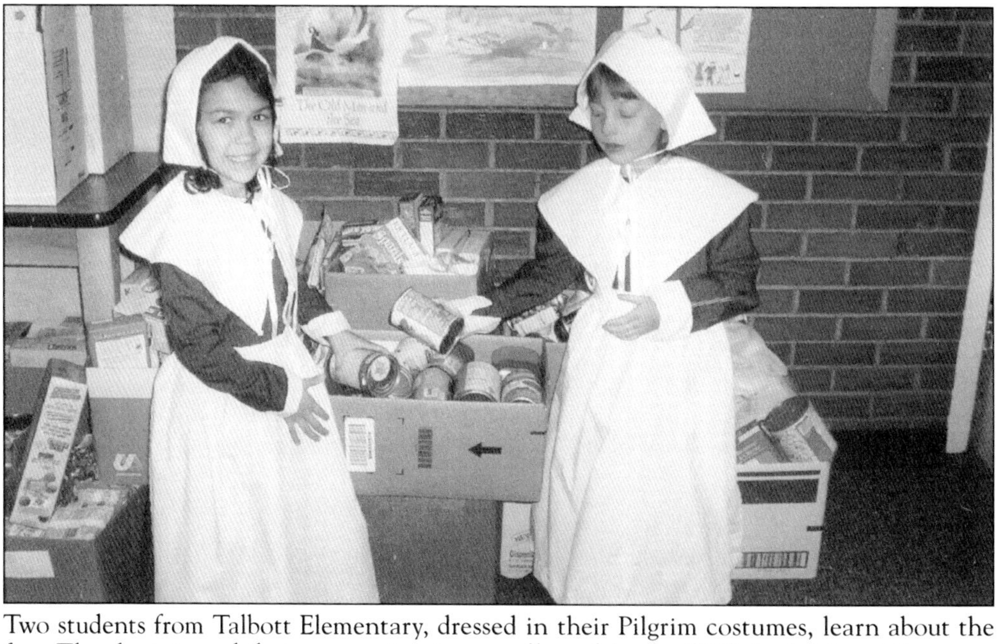

Two students from Talbott Elementary, dressed in their Pilgrim costumes, learn about the first Thanksgiving while inventorying items collected in the 2010 food drive. Like many organizations across the country, Widefield District schoolchildren collect canned goods from home in the spirit of thanksgiving and sharing. The food is later donated to shelters in the Pikes Peak region. (WSD.)

Five

Handshakes, Promises, and Prayers

The 7-Eleven convenience store at the Security intersection opened in 1956 as one the first businesses in the area. Another opened at the Widefield intersection in the early 1960s. Both served the many construction workers building new homes, and they continue to offer convenience to the residents of Security-Widefield as they hustle back and forth to school and work today.

The Safeway supermarket opened in the Fountain Valley Shopping Center in 1960 and later moved to the Widefield Mall. The local Dairy Queen has been serving up ice cream since the 1970s. The *Security Advertiser and Fountain Valley News*, founded by H. Kay Larson and Carl Weiss, began its publication in 1958 from an office near the Security intersection. Residents continue to receive this weekly newspaper delivered directly to their porches.

Ted Foltz operated the first business in Widefield, known as the Conoco Service Station, in 1962. In his spare time, he raced stock cars and participated in the annual Pikes Peak Hill Climb with fellow Security resident Grier Manning. Later businesses on Widefield Boulevard included the Widefield Homes office, a liquor store, and McDonald's.

Almost everything one needed could be purchased from the businesses in the Security Shopping Center, the Fountain Valley Shopping Center, the Widefield Mall, and various stand-alone shops. Even the German population could pick up rye bread, kaiser rolls, wursts, and sausages at the Zugspitze delicatessen in the Widefield Mall. Likewise, anyone who desired could find a local church or charitable organization to join. Eventually, Security-Widefield became known as a very caring community, one of the jewels of El Paso County.

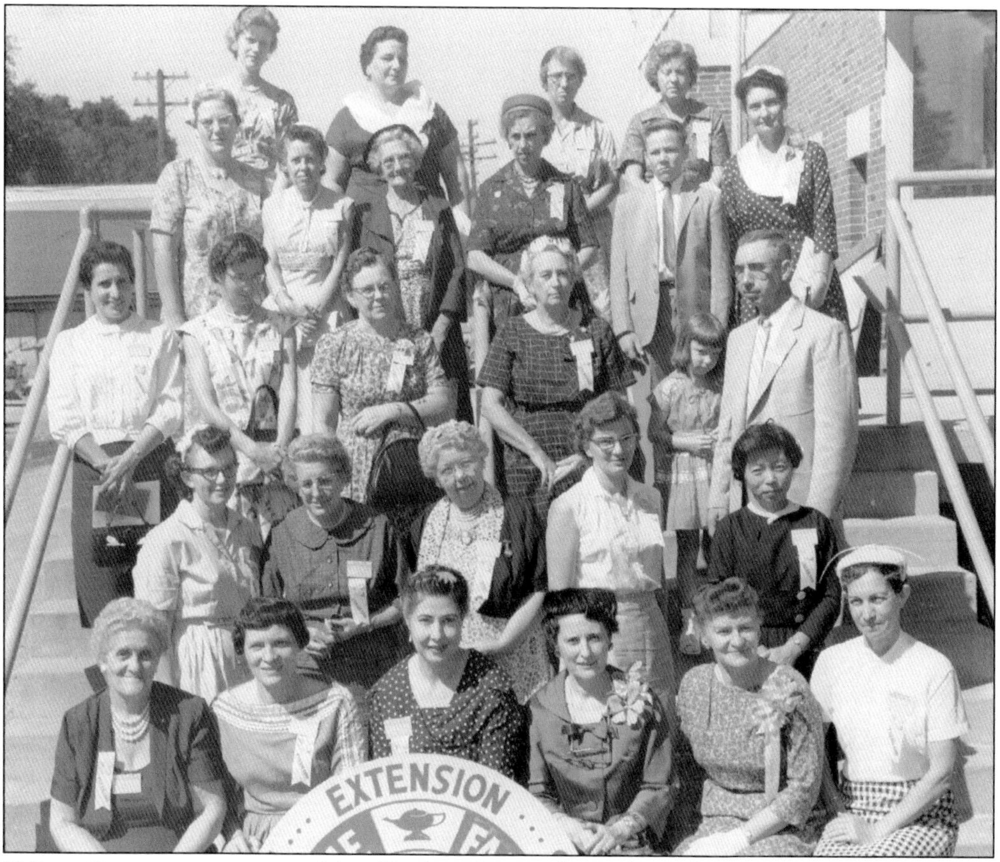

El Paso County representative Mae (Cuchares) Janitell stands on the far left in the third row of this group of delegates from the Colorado State Extension Service. Members of this organization provided agricultural and home-economics information to Colorado's rural communities. Home economists taught homemakers how to preserve produce through storing, drying, and canning, and how to make do with what was on hand. (MAS.)

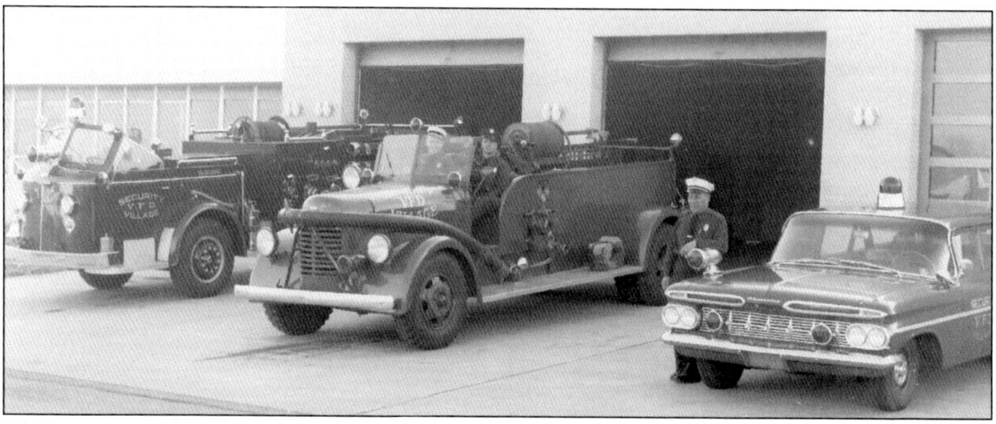

The Security Volunteer Fire Department was organized in 1956. After spending a few years in a tin Quonset hut, the fire department moved to this new brick home constructed in 1959. Parked in front of the fire station are, from left to right, a 1927 American LaFrance Pumper, a 1941 Peter Pirsch donated by the Security developers, and the chief's car. (SFD.)

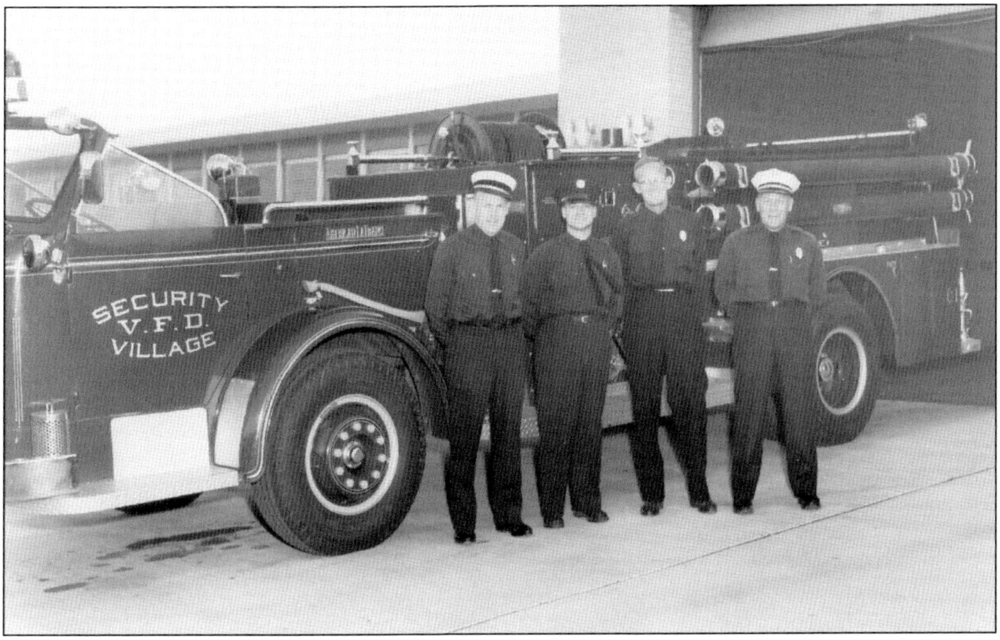

From left to right are Roger Fay, Lou Harding, Tom Salmon, and Chief Rusty Hart. In addition to serving as the fire department's first chief, Fay also served as county commissioner over roads and as a member of the Security Library Board in the 1960s. The fire department recognizes charter members Roger Fay, Louis Harding, John Sinnes, Donald Wiltgen, Allen Murray, and Wilbur Douglas, with their names engraved on the sign in front of the station. (SFD.)

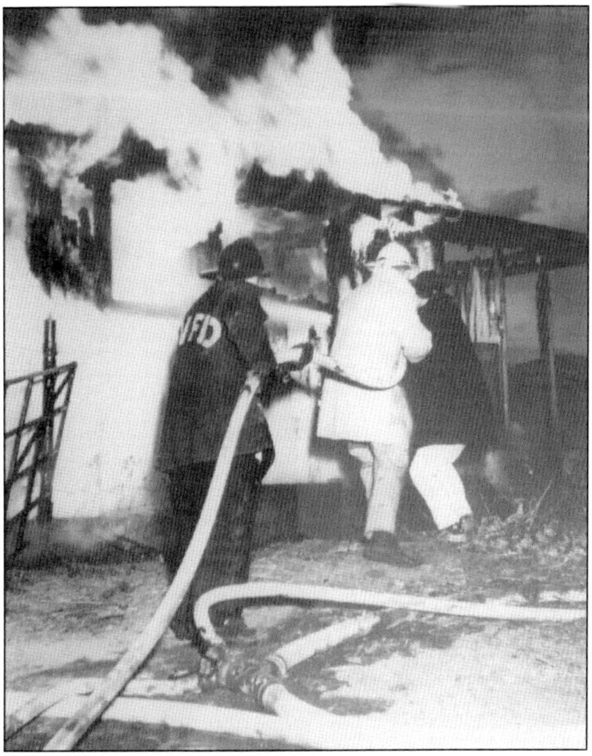

Members of the Security Volunteer Fire Department respond to a structure fire. Security's firefighters answer the typical range of emergency calls, including medical situations. Many motorists were stranded during the 1965 flood and rescued by the fire department, which took them to the firehouse to wait for the waters to recede. The department also assists the Colorado Springs fire crews on occasion when emergency situations in their area spread their resources thin. (SFD.)

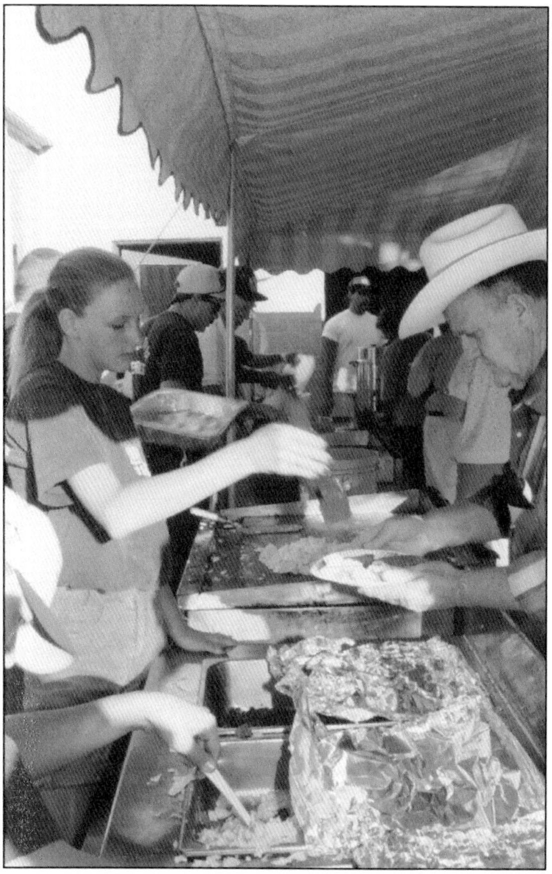

Jim Johns (right) fills his plate at the annual Fourth of July pancake breakfast sometime in the 1990s. The fire department has been hosting this community event for many years. Security-Widefield residents look forward to starting the holiday's activities at the fire station. Funds raised at this event are used for charitable projects. (SFD.)

About 2001, little Jessica Stambaugh gives thought to what she would like to ask from Santa Claus. He visits the fire department every year to greet the children of Security-Widefield. For many years, the fire department worked with the businessmen's association and, later, the local school district in setting up and presenting an annual Fourth of July fireworks display at the high school football field. (SFD.)

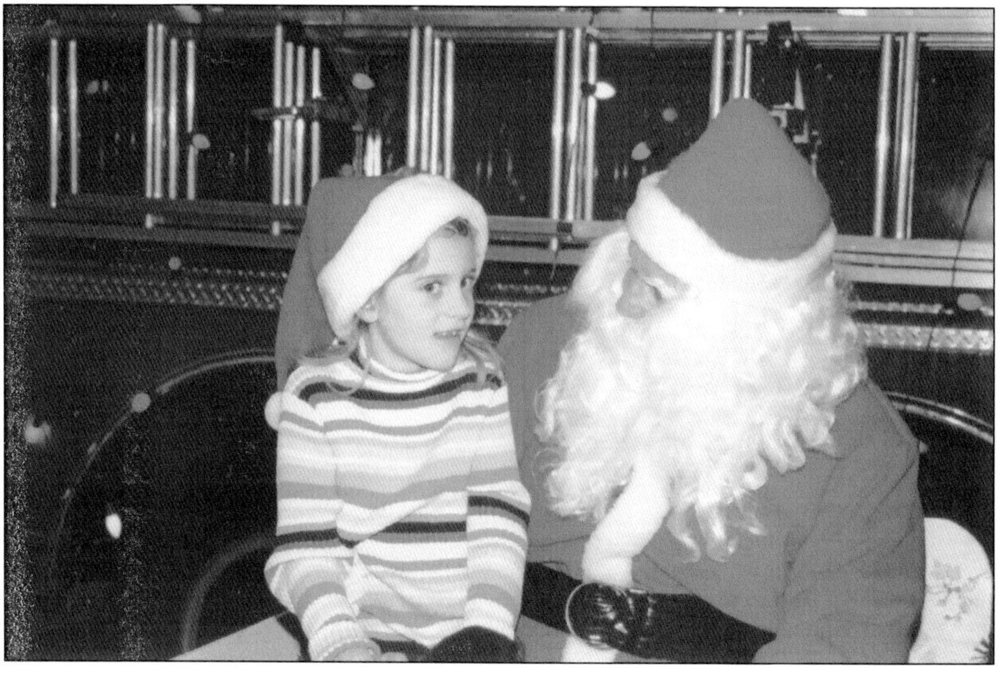

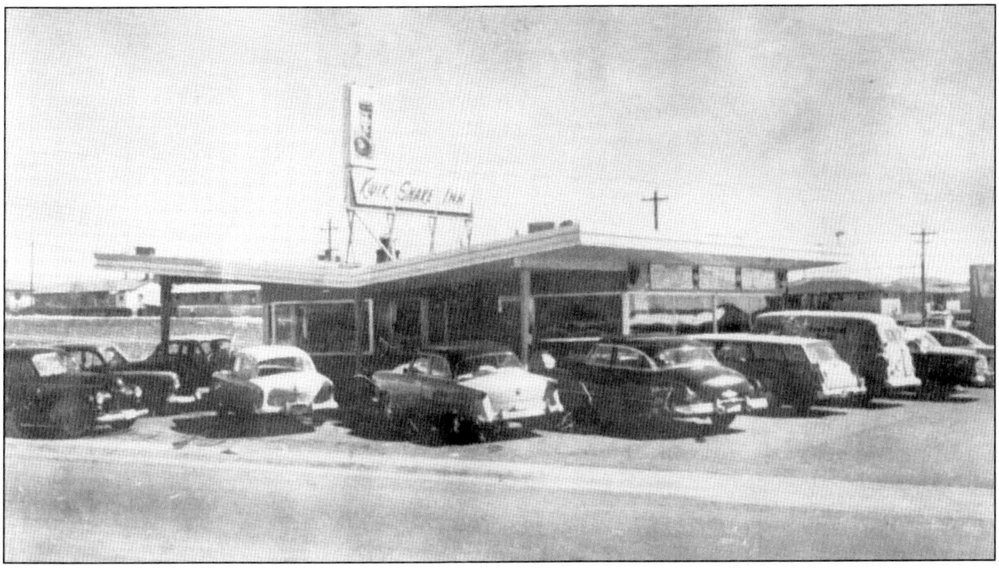

Tom Kennedy opened the Kwik Shake Inn in 1956 as the first business in Security. Three years later, the restaurant moved to this location at the corner of Marquette Drive and Main Street. Over four decades, Kennedy made many renovations and additions to the building to keep up with modern changes in the fast-food business. (TK.)

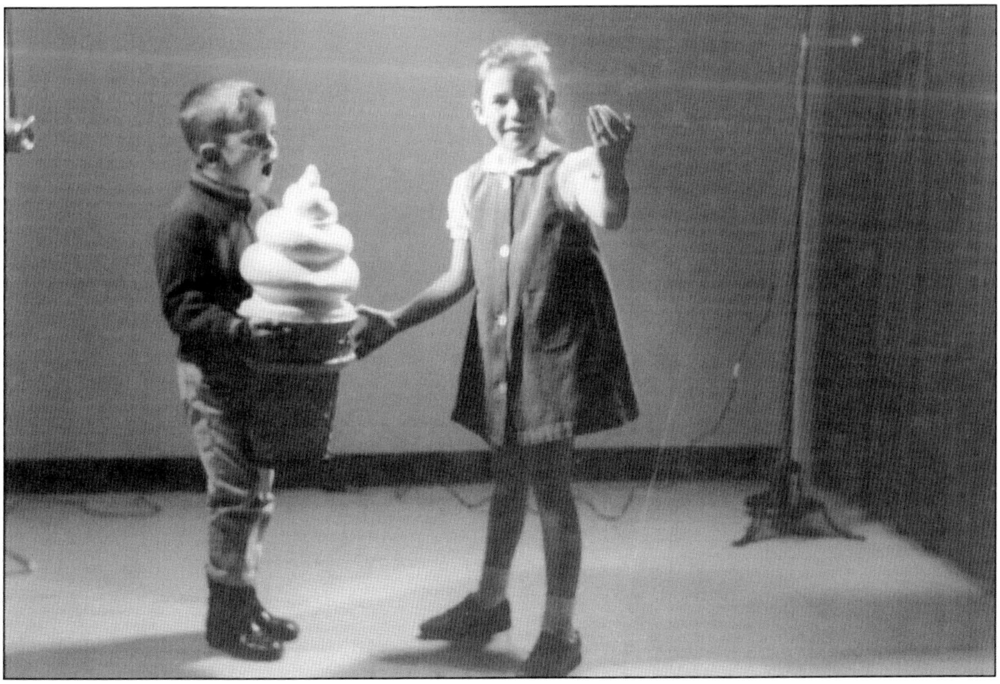

Scott and Lori Kennedy help in the family business when they pose for this photograph in the early 1960s. The image appeared in a local newspaper advertisement for Kwik Shake Inn. (TK.)

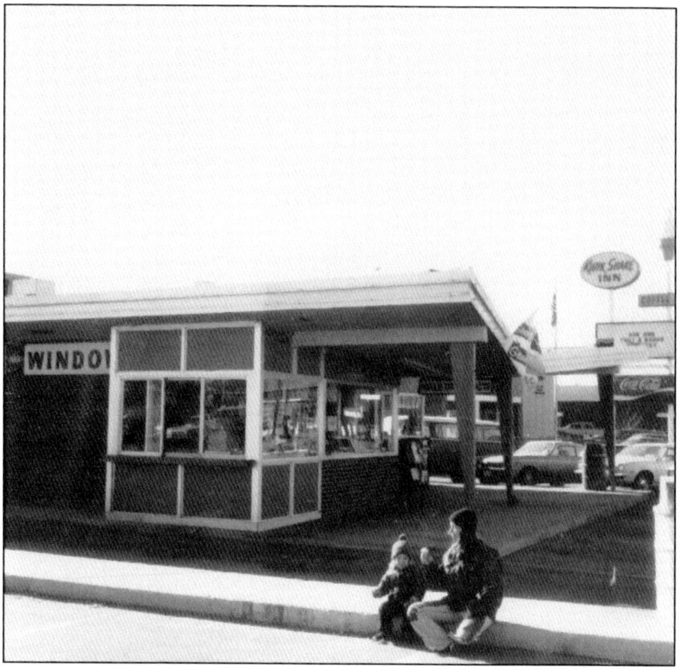

On a chilly December day in the 1970s, a young woman and a small child enjoy an ice cream cone from the Kwik Shake. Retired men met here for morning coffee, and high school kids congregated here after school for a Vanilla Coke. (TK.)

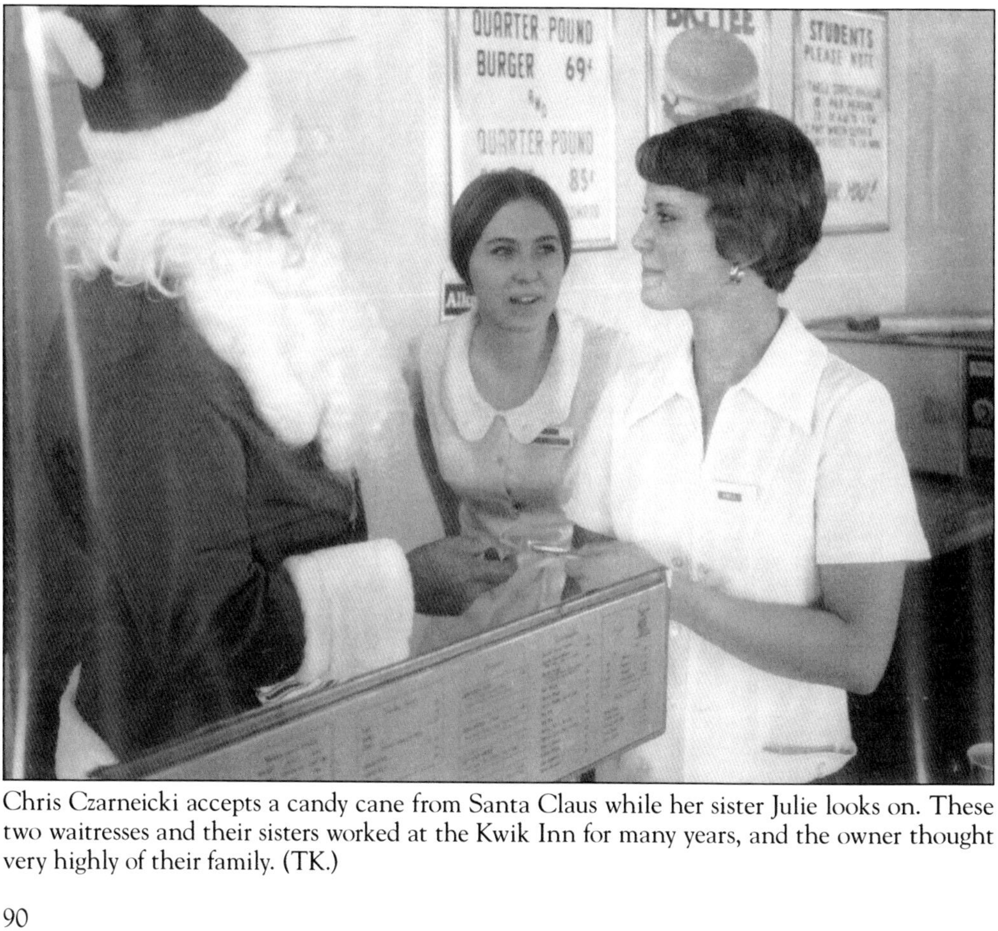

Chris Czarneicki accepts a candy cane from Santa Claus while her sister Julie looks on. These two waitresses and their sisters worked at the Kwik Inn for many years, and the owner thought very highly of their family. (TK.)

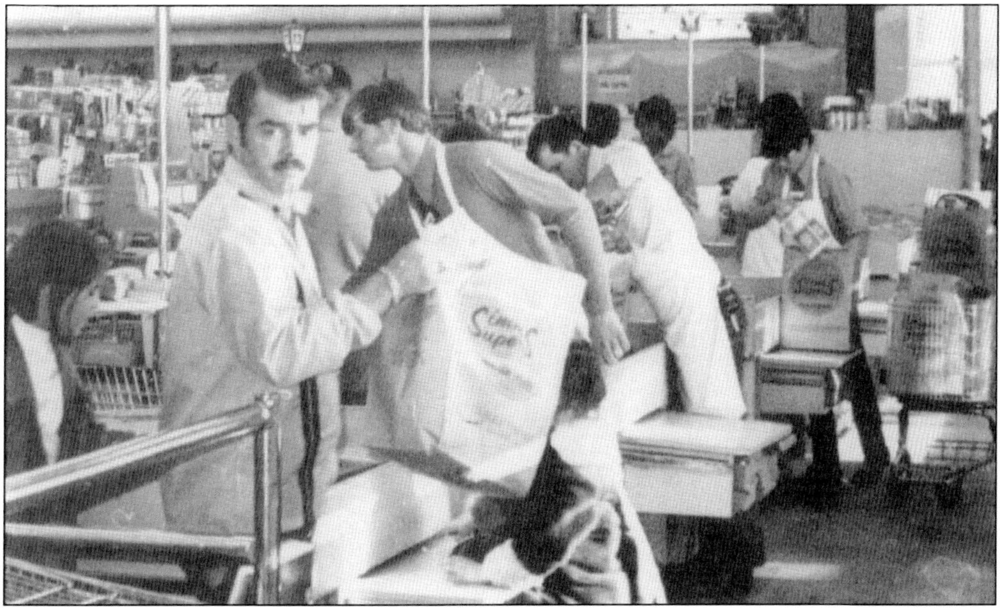

Security Shopping Center's first tenant in 1956 was Simm's Super Market, pictured here in 1973. The store quickly became a favorite place to shop for food. It was a nice convenience for the residents of Security, who no longer had to drive to Fountain or Colorado Springs for groceries. It has been said that owner Earl Simms often gave groceries away to folks who needed a little help. (WSD.)

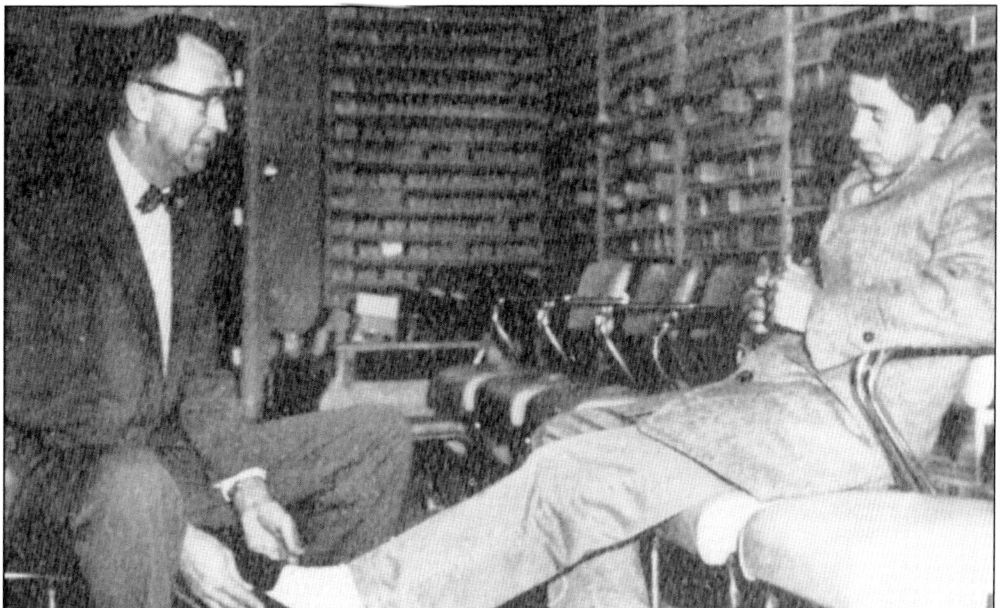

A customer tries on a pair of penny loafers at Ralph's shoe store in the Security Shopping Center in 1960. These loafers had a convenient slot on the front of the shoe for inserting shiny copper pennies. Many students outfitted themselves with their one pair of school shoes here at the local shoe store. Store clerks used a shoe sizer to measure the customer's right foot and then retrieved several styles and colors of shoes from the back room for trying on. (WSD.)

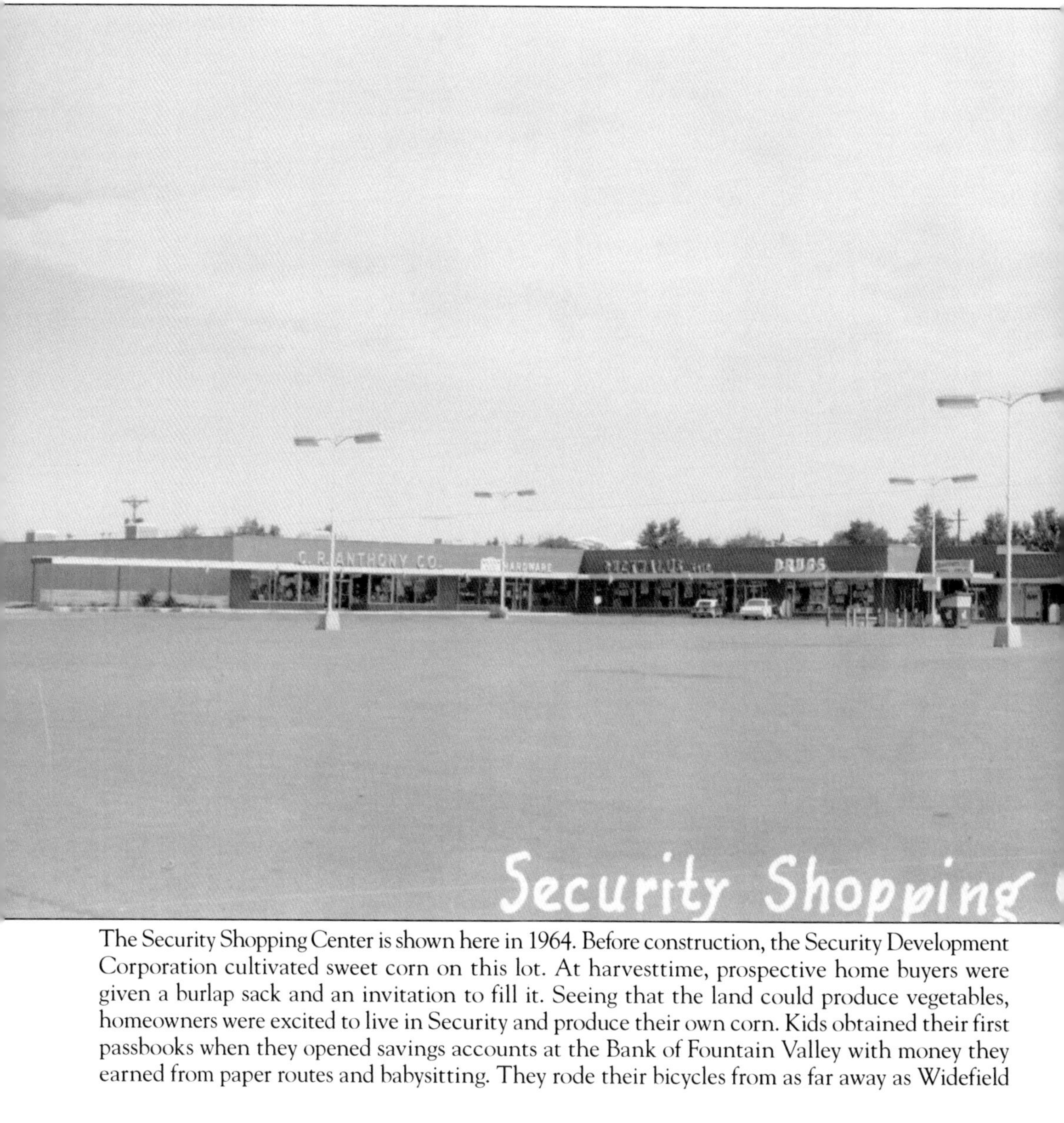

The Security Shopping Center is shown here in 1964. Before construction, the Security Development Corporation cultivated sweet corn on this lot. At harvesttime, prospective home buyers were given a burlap sack and an invitation to fill it. Seeing that the land could produce vegetables, homeowners were excited to live in Security and produce their own corn. Kids obtained their first passbooks when they opened savings accounts at the Bank of Fountain Valley with money they earned from paper routes and babysitting. They rode their bicycles from as far away as Widefield

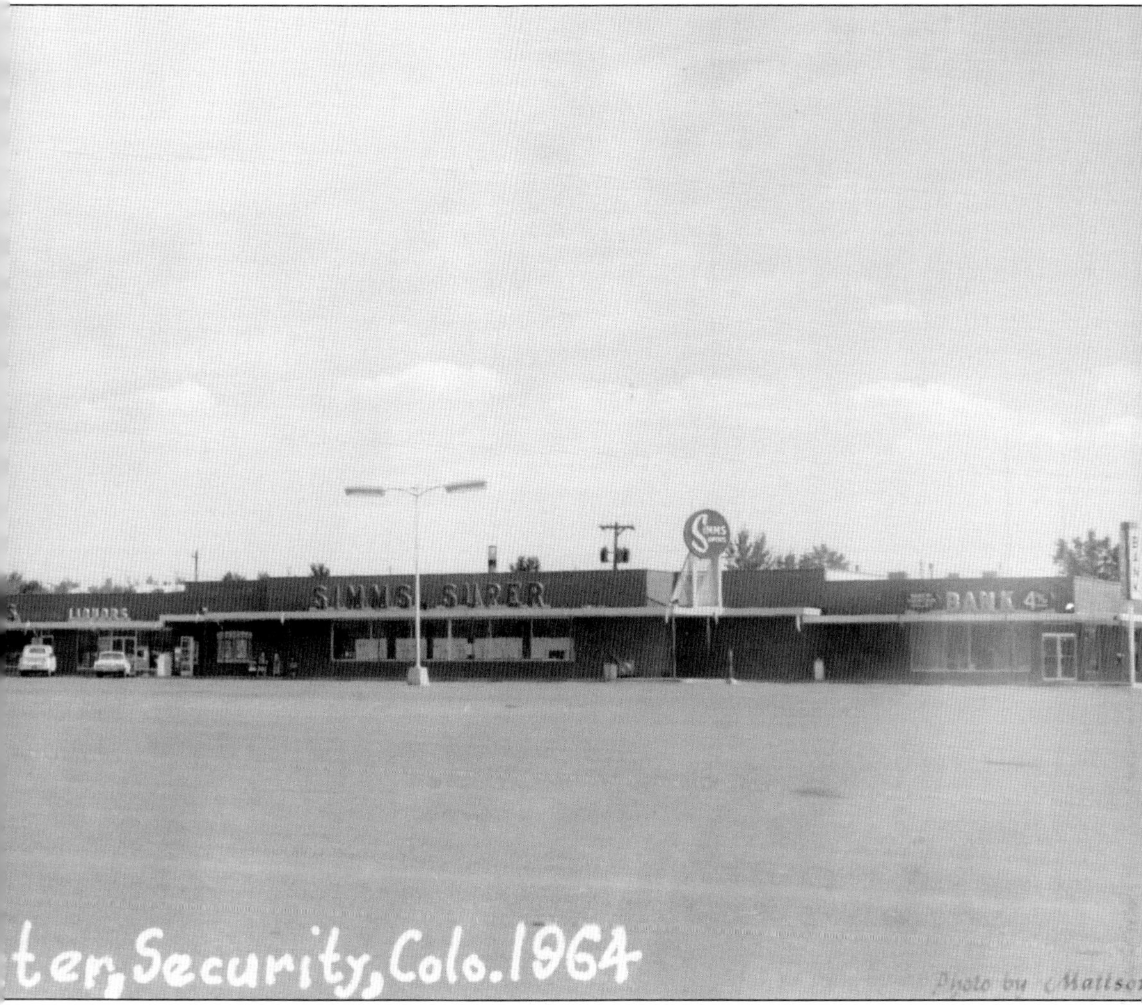

to this shopping center to buy paper dolls and candy from Duckwall's. A visit to Western Auto took care of bicycle repairs. For back-to-school shopping, a pair of shoes was purchased at Ralph Rieves's shoe store, and a visit to C.R. Anthony's clothing store produced a new pair of jeans. The west side of the Anthony's store was painted white to function as a screen for outdoor summertime movies. Families brought blankets, lawn chairs, and shopping bags full of popcorn. (CJ.)

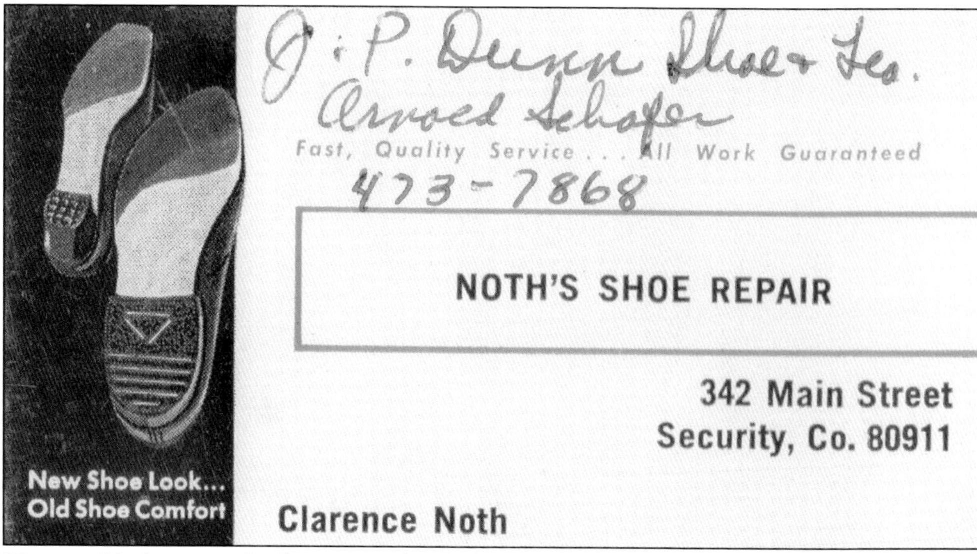

Clarence Noth operated a shoe-repair shop behind Ralph's shoe store. His business card includes a handwritten reference to a shoe repairman in downtown Colorado Springs. Noth tended his baby grandson in the shop and, as the boy grew, taught him the art and the business of shoe repair. Noth's grandson now runs the repair shop. (JN.)

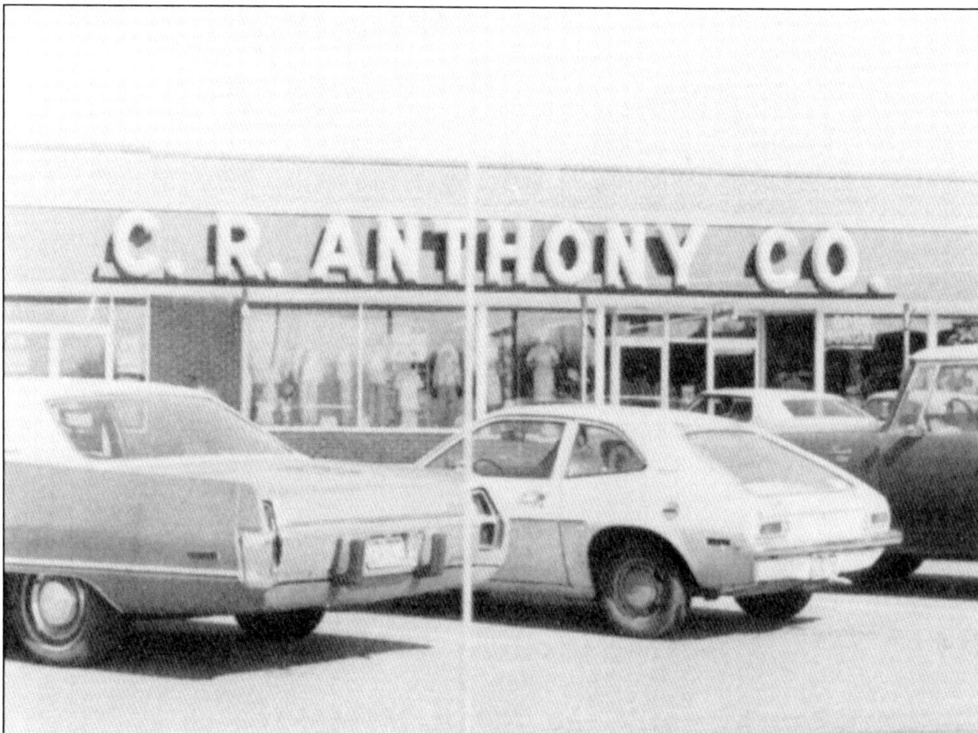

C.R. Anthony's Department Store is pictured here in 1977. Located in the Security Shopping Center, it offered high-quality clothing to the residents of Security-Widefield. In support of the high school, the owners of the store willingly displayed flyers announcing school events in the store's front windows. (WSD.)

A hesitant toddler receives his first haircut from Manny Sigala, who opened Manny's Main Barbershop in 1962 in the Security Shopping Center. For over 50 years, the establishment has operated in the Security-Widefield community. Sigala's fellow Security residents and Korean War veterans were especially fond of him. Remarkably, all seven of his children completed barber school and came back to work in the family's neighborhood barbershop. (RS.)

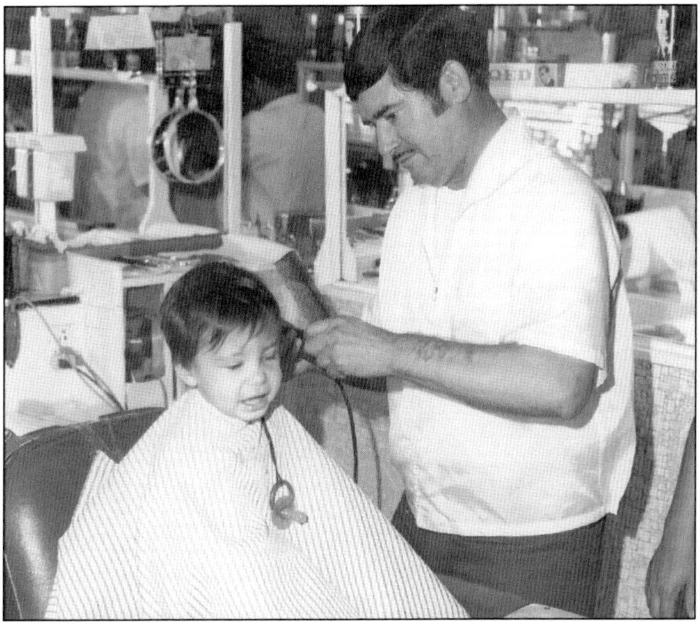

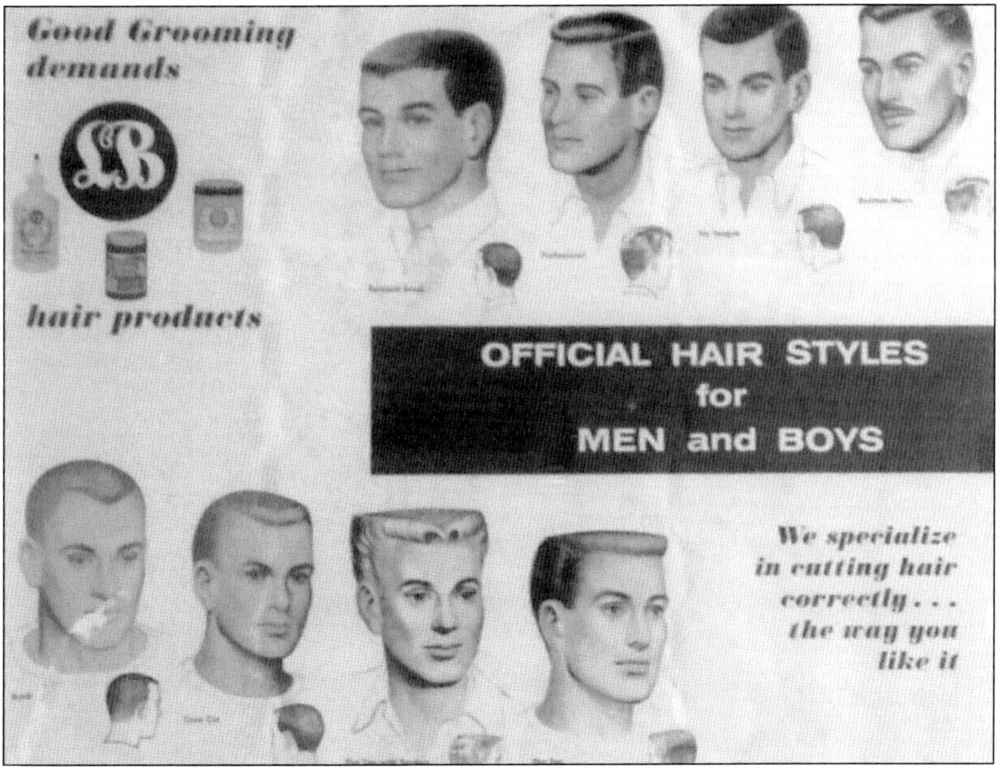

This poster of various men's hairstyles has been hanging in Manny's Main Barbershop since 1962. Members of the Sigala family pride themselves on their ability to cut anyone's hair in any style with only barber clippers, which is a dying art. They have had the pleasure of cutting the hair of famous athletes, state politicians, and foreign dignitaries, and they are pleased to now be serving the great-grandchildren of their very first customers. (RS.)

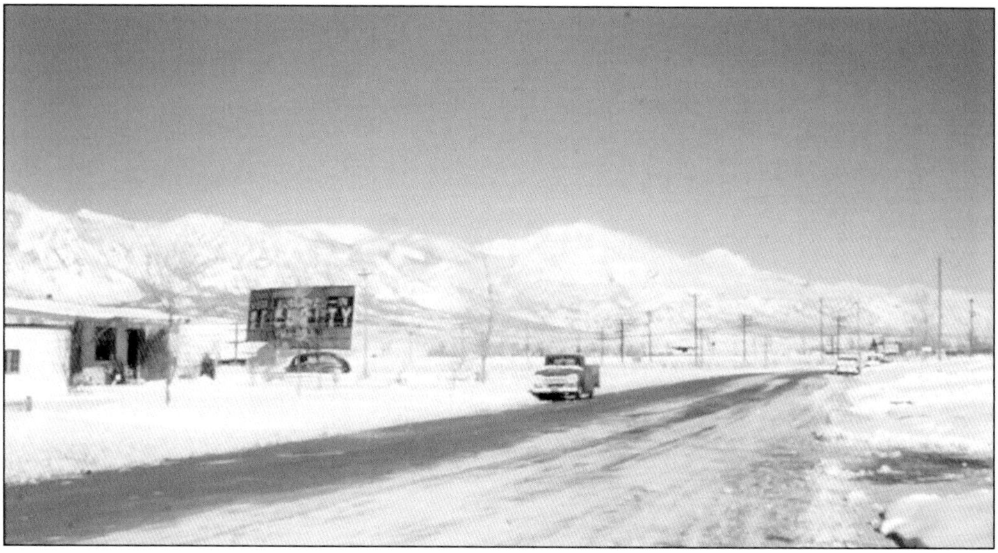

Snow blows off the top of Pikes Peak on this cold day in the late 1950s. From Security Boulevard, the Vista-Vue Drive-in screen is visible in the background. Until the 1980s, the drive-in entertained dating couples, families, and carloads of teenagers. The driver paid an admission fee and parked in front of the screen next to a speaker box. The driver positioned the speaker on the car window and adjusted the transistor radio–like sound. (MS.)

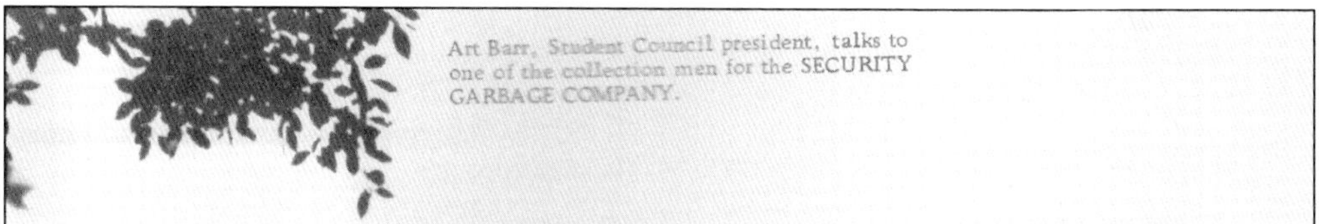

In this image from 1959, Widefield High School Student Council president Art Barr talks to one of the collection men for the Security Garbage Company. Tom Salmon started the business in 1956, and it grew to be the second-largest trash-collection business in Colorado Springs. Now known as Waste Systems, the company functions in the Fountain Valley under the ownership of Salmon's son-in-law and grandson. (WSD.)

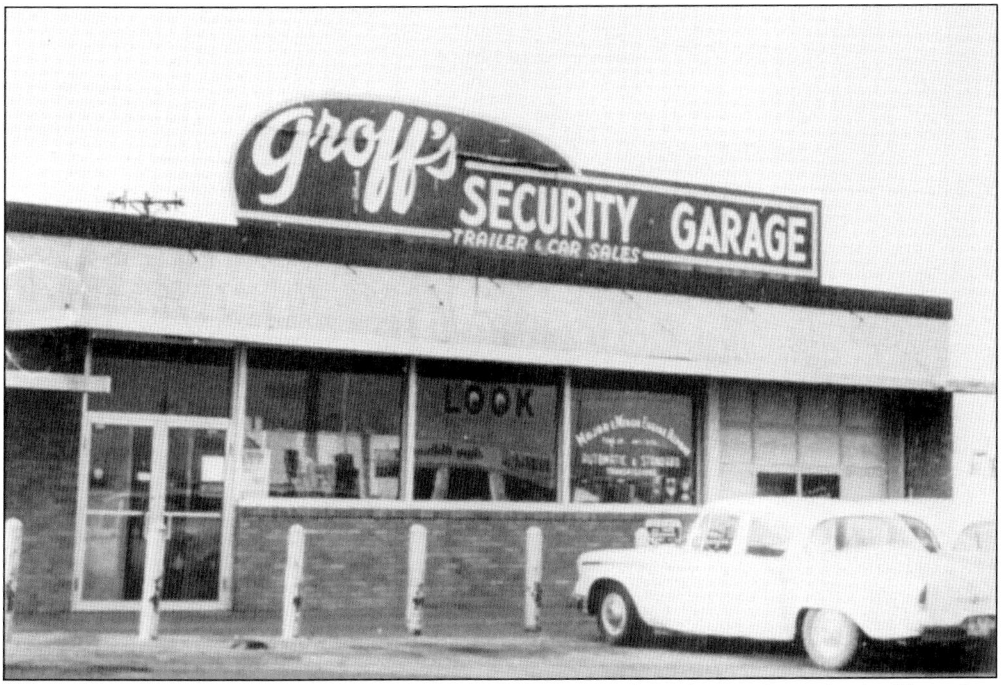

The Groff family opened Security Garage on Security Boulevard in 1958 in the building that had previously housed Simm's Super Market. The garage received a great amount of business from the many residents of Security who had recently moved into the new housing development. Three generations later, and under a slightly different name, Groff's Automotive still satisfies the residents of Security-Widefield and surrounding areas. (WSD.)

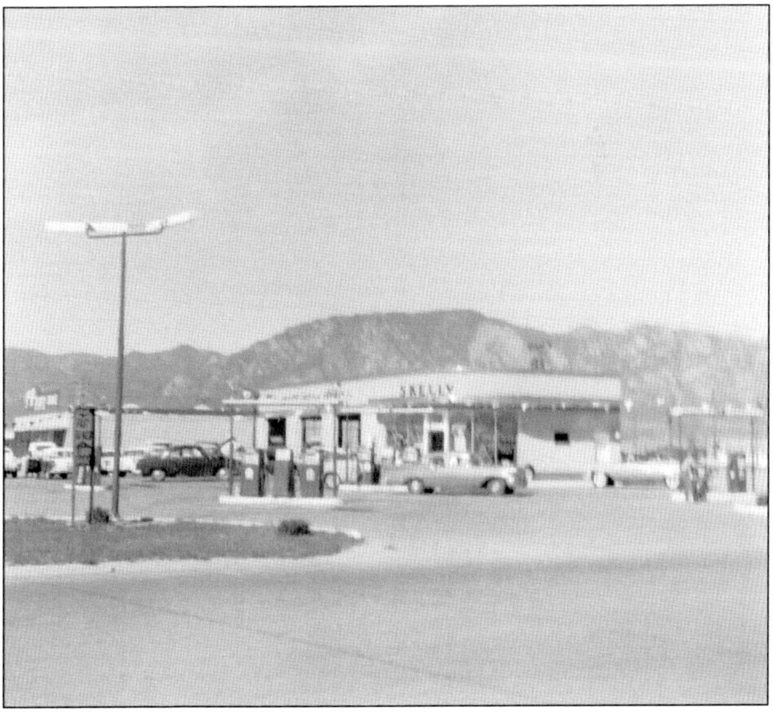

Next door to Groff's Security Garage, P.L. Groff maintained the Skelly Service Station, which opened in 1956. At one time, Groff's was one of 12 service stations operating simultaneously in Security-Widefield. Workers at a full-service station filled the gas tank, washed the windshield, and checked the automobile's fluids while the customer waited in his car. (DG.)

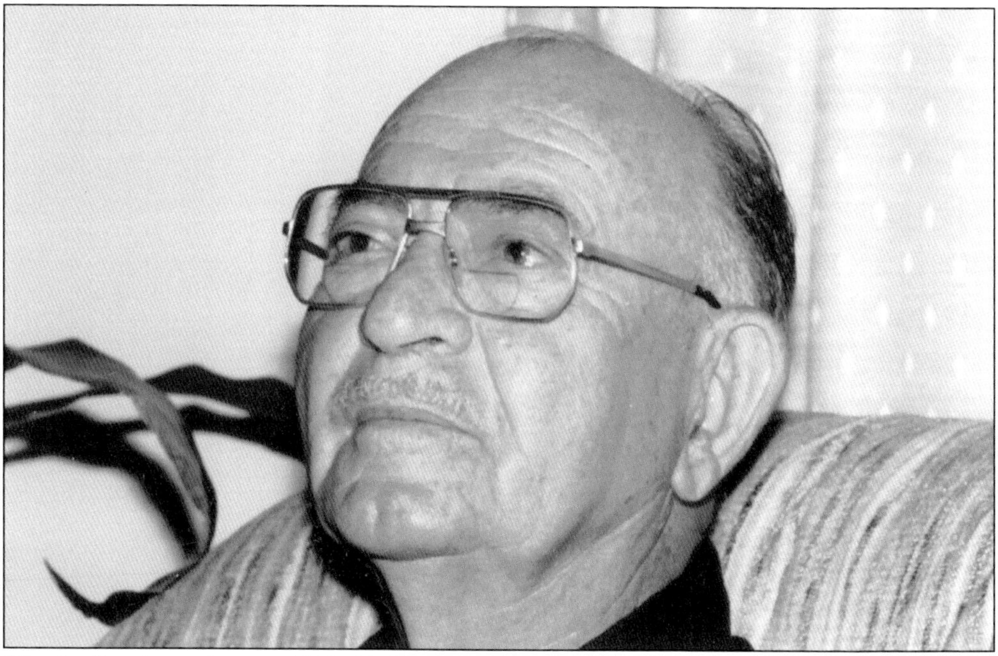

P.L. Groff is shown here in 1988. Children in the community knew him as "Pappy." He greeted his customers at the Skelly service station with a wave and a smile and kept a pocketful of suckers to hand out to the children who came by with their parents. Even the neighborhood teenagers knew about Pappy's suckers and would stop in to receive one. Groff is remembered as a very kind man. (DG.)

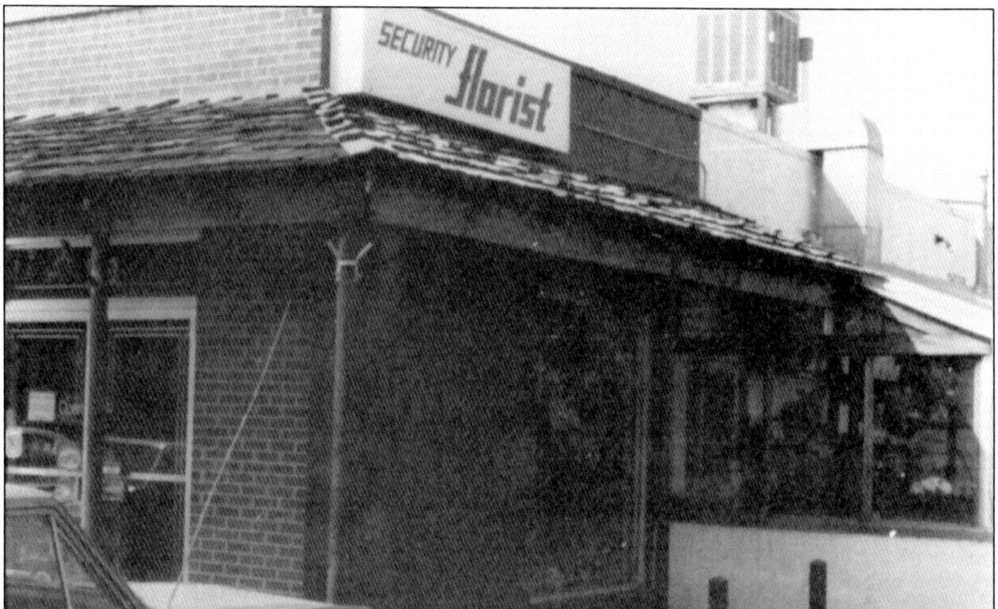

The Security Florist opened for business in 1967. It began under the ownership of Dorothy Sproul and was later operated by her daughters. Sproul's granddaughter now runs the business, which provides its clientele with floral arrangements for local weddings and funerals. Boutonnieres and corsages for high school proms are also handled by the florist shop. (WSD.)

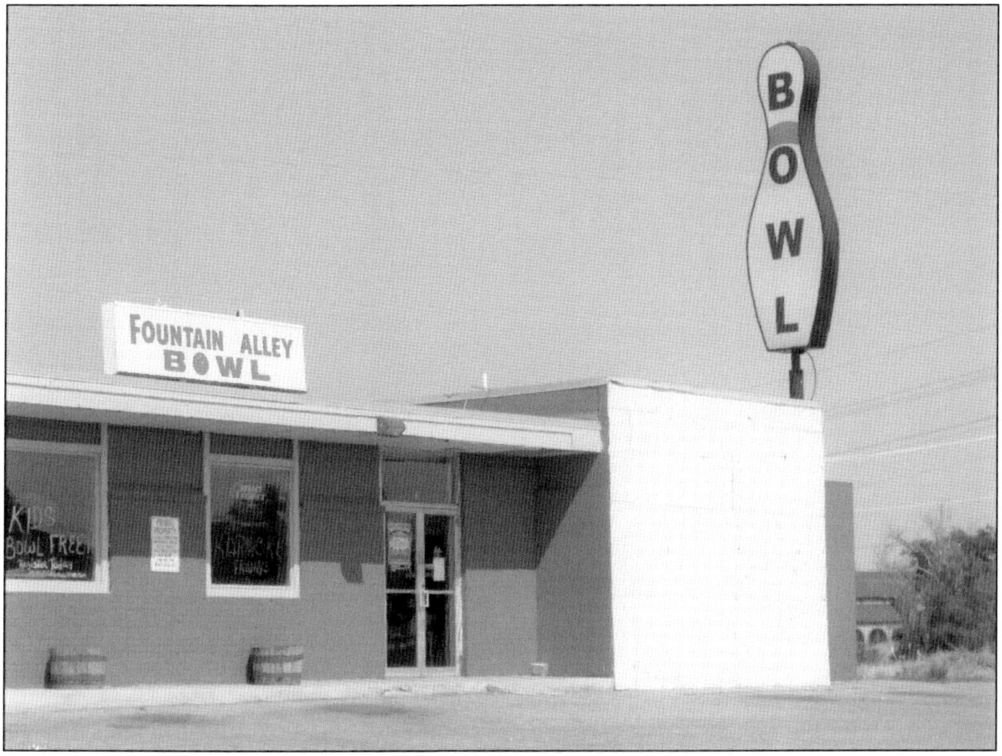

At one time, the brightly lit bowling pin above the bowling alley, located near the Security Shopping Center, slowly pivoted around during the nighttime hours. Fountain Valley Bowl has been serving the bowlers of Security-Widefield for 60 years by providing a place for friends and families to meet and compete. (ATH.)

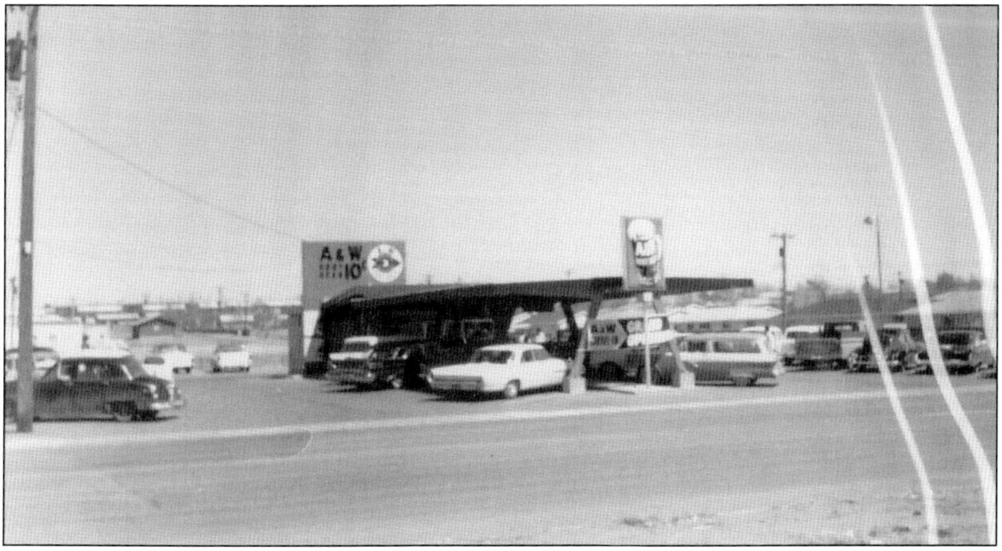

Tom Kennedy's A&W Drive-in was located at 507 Security Boulevard and opened in 1962. At this type of restaurant, a carful of friends or family drove into a parking stall and chose their orders from a menu posted there. The driver pushed a button and placed the order through a speaker, and a carhop showed up shortly with the food. (TK.)

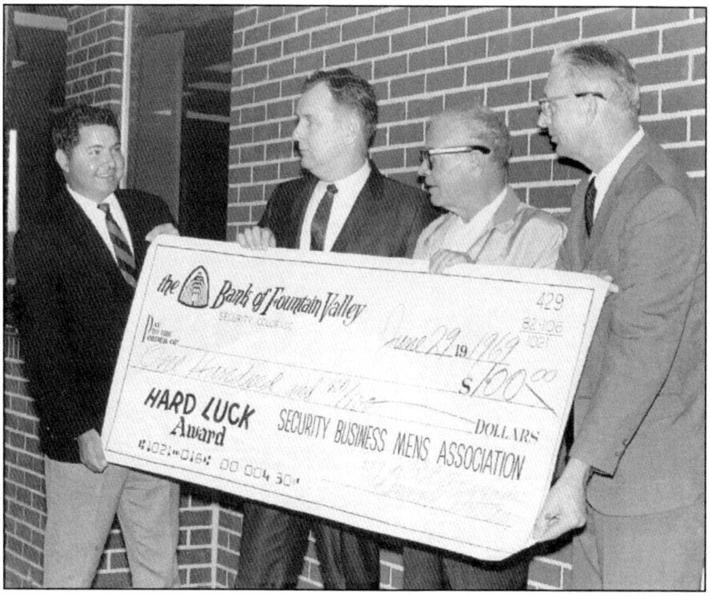

Members of the Security Businessmen's Association appear here in 1969. Everett "Dutch" Sproul, owner of Dutch's Liquors in the Security Shopping Center, stands second from right. The organization, created in 1959 with Earl Simms as president, promoted local business and hosted several events, including window-decorating contests and visits from Santa Claus. (Photograph by Carl H. Brattin, courtesy of CJ.)

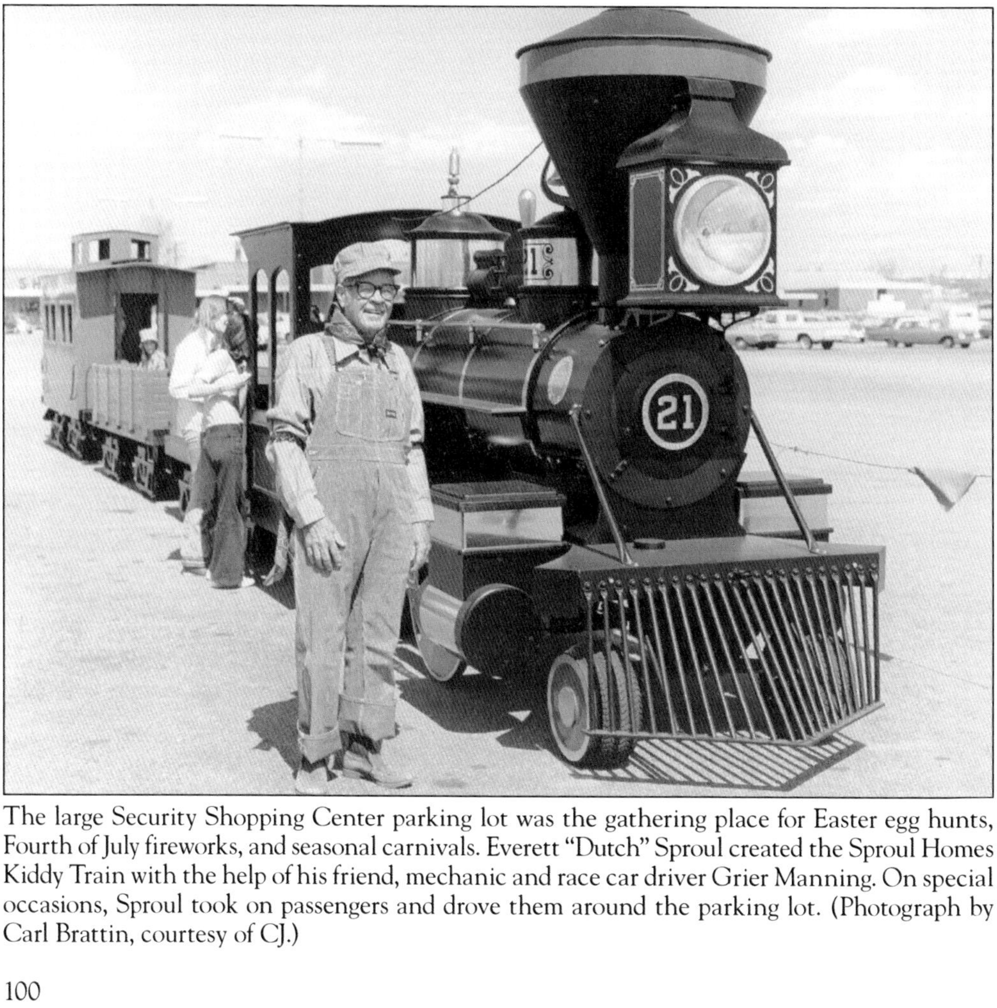

The large Security Shopping Center parking lot was the gathering place for Easter egg hunts, Fourth of July fireworks, and seasonal carnivals. Everett "Dutch" Sproul created the Sproul Homes Kiddy Train with the help of his friend, mechanic and race car driver Grier Manning. On special occasions, Sproul took on passengers and drove them around the parking lot. (Photograph by Carl Brattin, courtesy of CJ.)

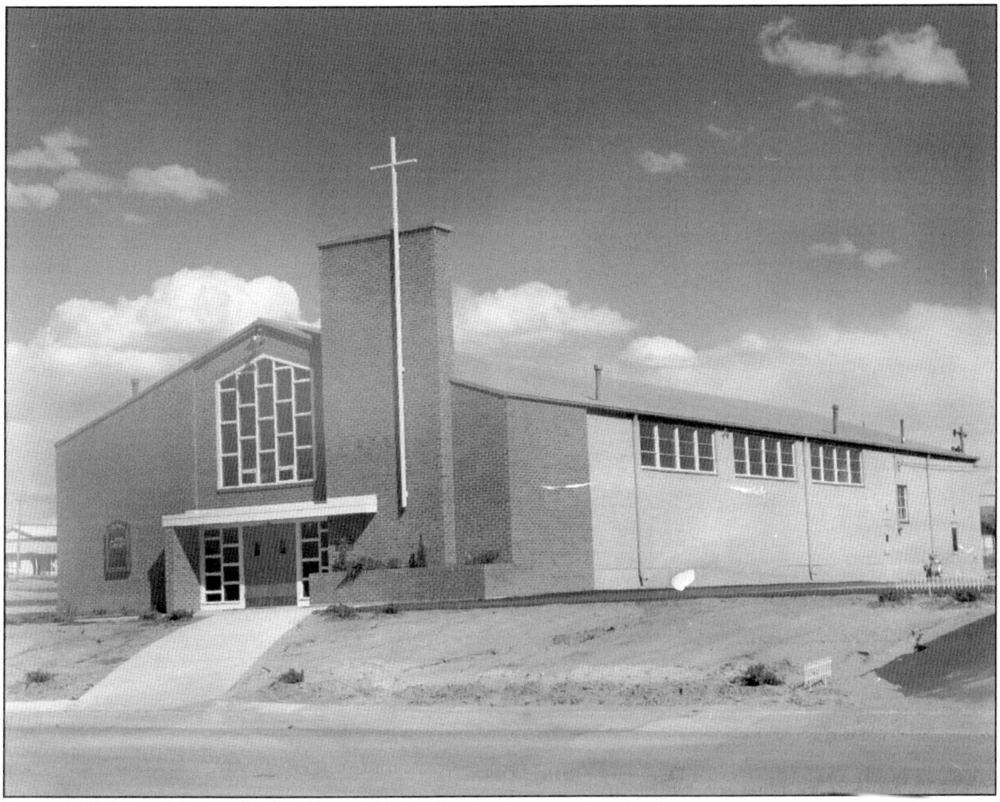

Holy Family Parish was founded in 1957, and the church building on Main Street was constructed a year later. Two important additions were completed in the 1960s, and Holy Family administered to the Catholic population of Security-Widefield for the next 40 years. (SDP.)

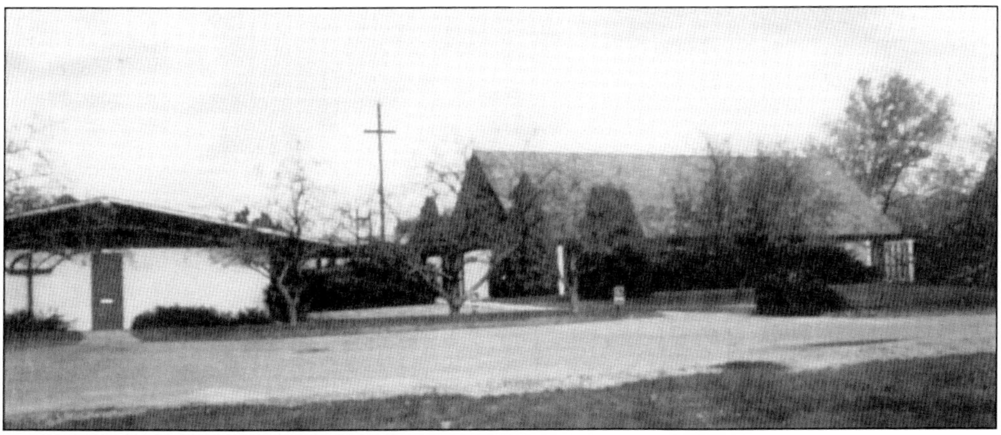

St. Raphael's was organized as a mission at the end of 1959. The congregation met in the home of Harry Anderson until the church on the left was erected on land donated by Fred Sproul on Leta Drive. Security's Episcopalian congregation moved next door into the current sanctuary in 1967. (SEC.)

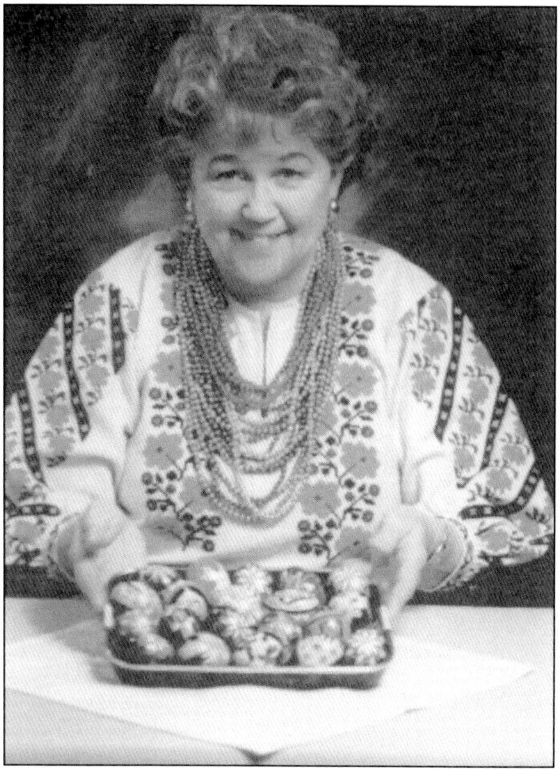

Helen Tostanoski displays *pysanky* (Ukrainian Easter eggs), which she makes during Lent and brings as an offering to the altar of St. Raphael's Episcopal Church. This is an old Orthodox tradition that is kept alive throughout generations. Pysanky are exchanged as greetings and given as gifts of love and friendship. (SEC.)

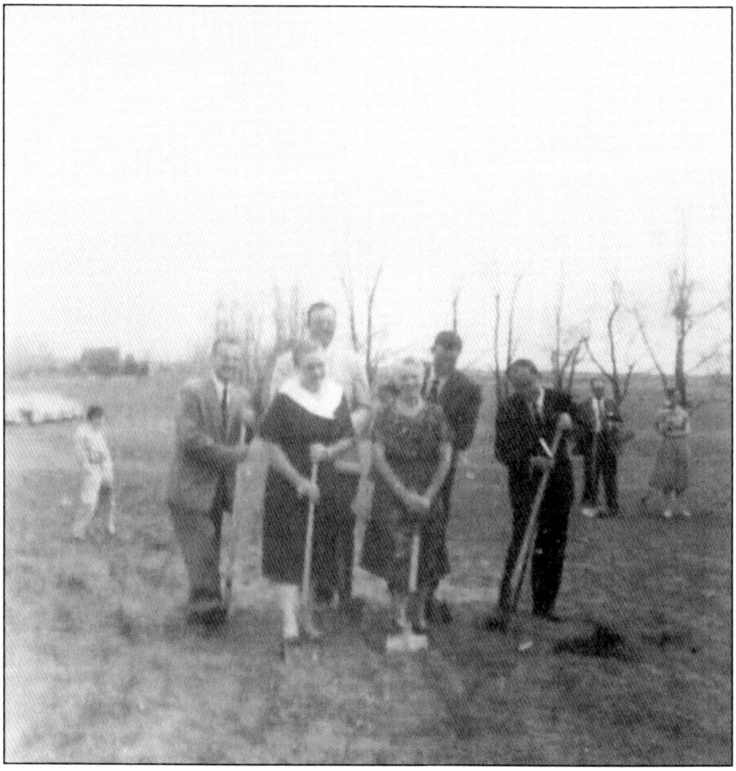

In May 1960, members of the Evangelical United Brethren Mission ceremoniously break ground for their new church building on farmland that was donated by Alta Cunningham. The small membership temporarily met in the parsonage until construction on the new Good Shepherd meetinghouse on Leta Drive was finished. In 1969, the Evangelical United Brethren merged with the Methodist Church to form the United Methodist Church. (BW.)

In March 1956, a small house on Hackberry Drive was the site of the first gathering of 60 Lutherans in Security. Within three months, the congregation started meeting in a large tent on the lot on Security Boulevard acquired for the church. Before the year was over, Security's Faith Lutheran Church building, pictured here, was opened to the congregation. Furniture was built by members of the congregation, and the ladies made the pastor's stole and altar paraments. (MS.)

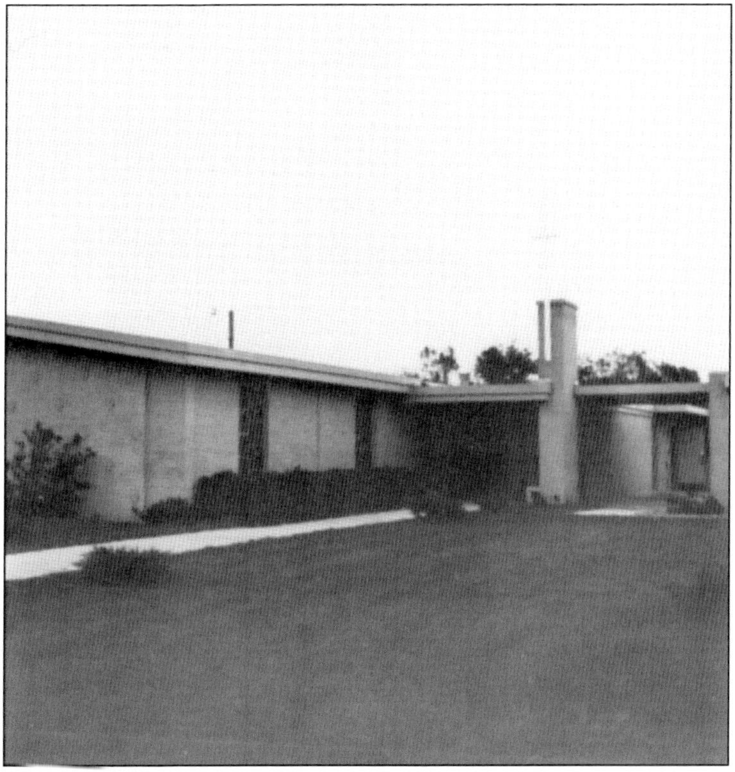

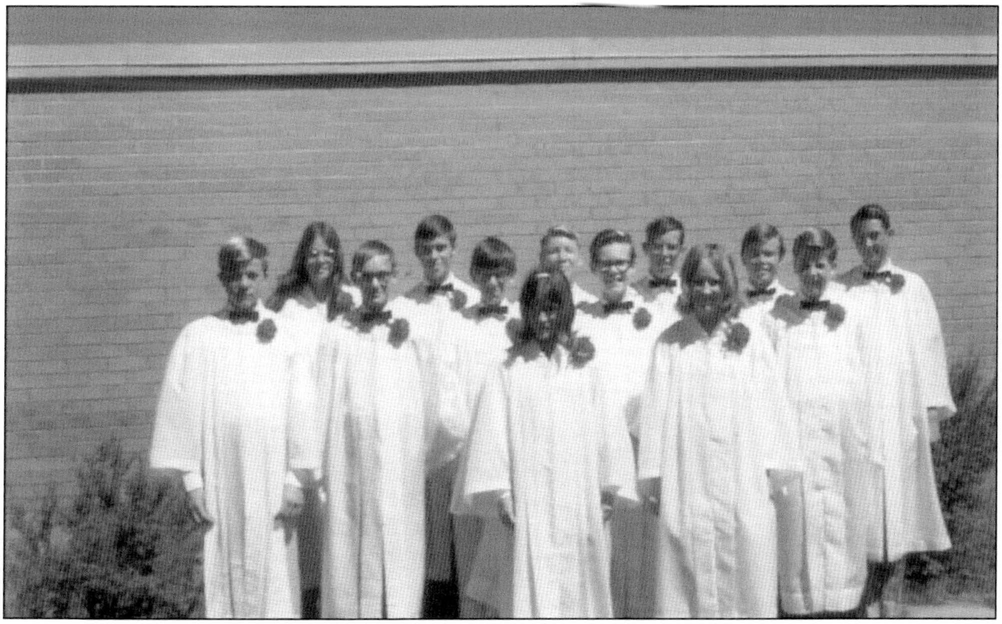

Karl Simon (second row, far right) stands with his confirmation class next to Faith Lutheran Church in the early 1970s. They are dressed in white robes and red corsages. Lutheran children begin catechism classes at an early age. When the children reach the approximate age of 14, they participate in the rite of confirmation, in which they publicly profess their faith and pledge devotion to Christ. (MS.)

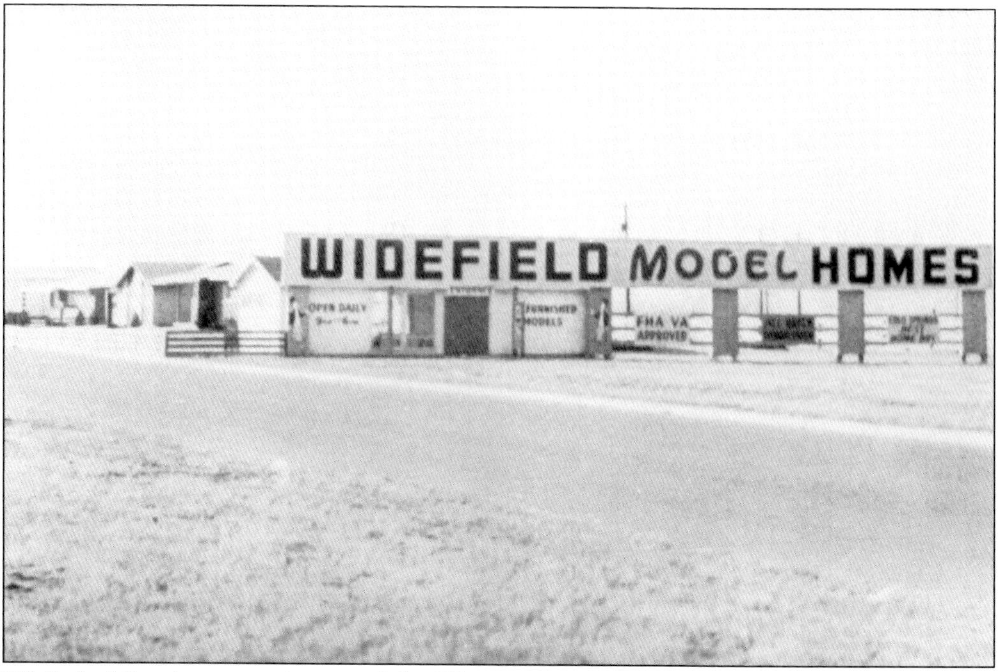

While building homes in Arizona, Jules Watson saw an opportunity in the Fountain Valley. Fort Carson was scheduled to expand and bring more soldiers to the area, and Watson created Widefield Homes in 1958. The business became a family affair when Watson's three children began working for the company. Watson's grandson has joined the team, now known as New Generation Homes. (WSD.)

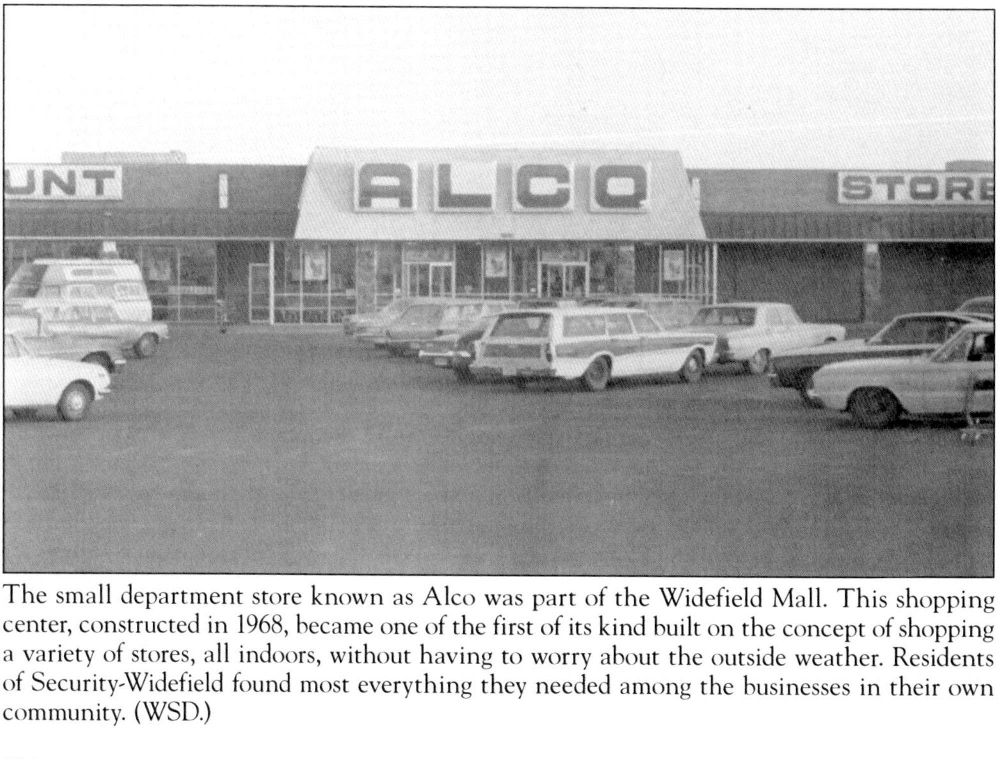

The small department store known as Alco was part of the Widefield Mall. This shopping center, constructed in 1968, became one of the first of its kind built on the concept of shopping a variety of stores, all indoors, without having to worry about the outside weather. Residents of Security-Widefield found most everything they needed among the businesses in their own community. (WSD.)

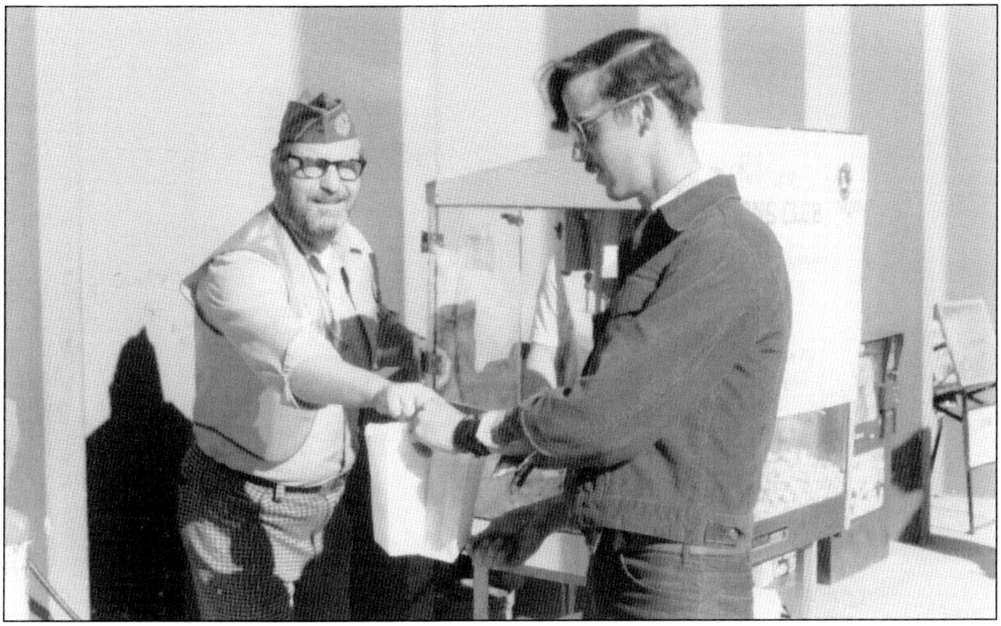

In 1977, a member of the Security Lions Club sells popcorn outside the Albertsons grocery store in the Security Shopping Center. The sign on the popcorn machine reads, "Help Your Lions Club Purchase Eye Glasses for Needy People!! Your Contribution may help a child to Read!!" During this time, the Lions also collected old newspapers and magazines for recycling. The money earned from this project was donated for improvements to Pi-Ute Park. (DB.)

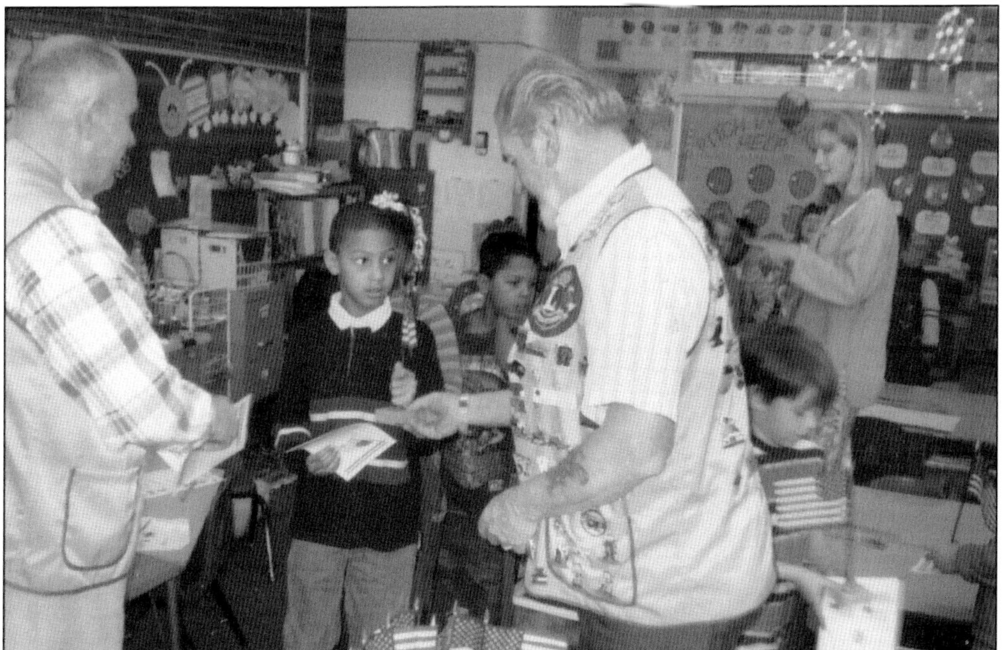

In the 1990s, the Security Lions Club began handing out flags to first graders in the Pikes Peak region. In this activity, the Lions help young students learn about the American flag. In the summer, the club also sponsors shopping trips for children to receive school clothes. (DB.)

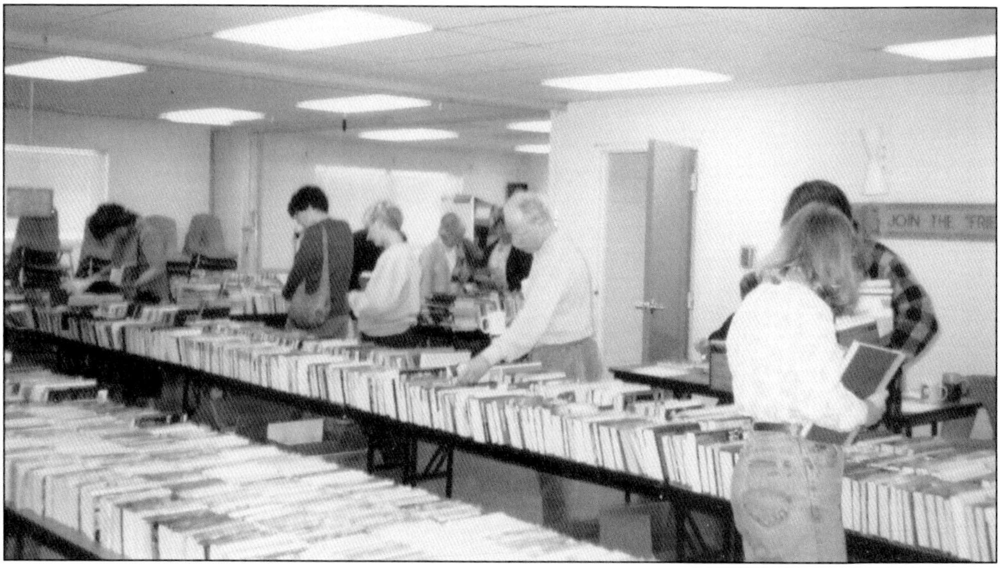

In 1998, booklovers browse through many selections in the community center meeting room. This book sale is hosted every spring and fall by the Friends of the Security Public Library, a group of volunteers that recognizes that a good library is an asset to the community and endeavors to enhance the library's community programs. (SPL.)

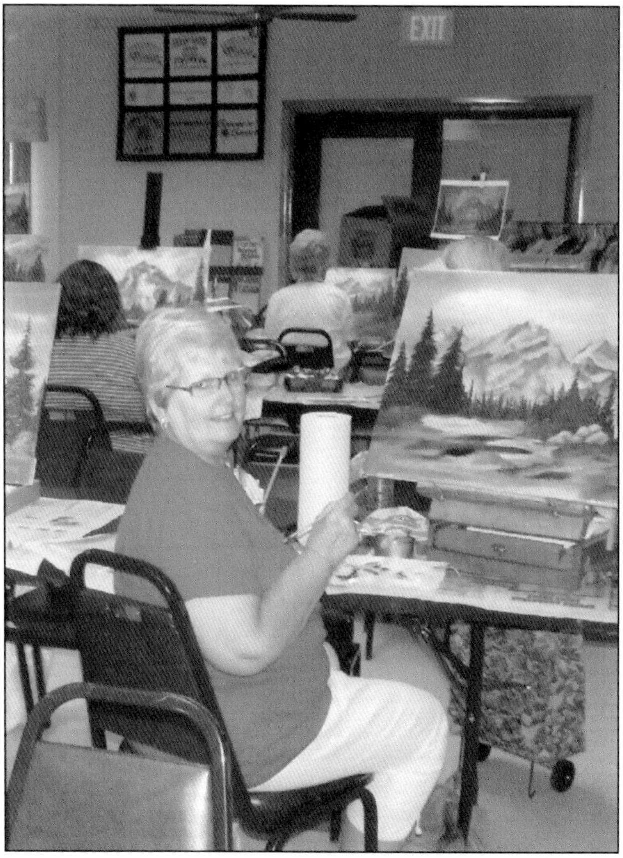

Art students attend an oil-painting class at the Fountain Valley Senior Center in 2006 under the instruction of Frances Duran. The Fountain Valley Senior Center was organized in 1975 in the Kittie Paster School, formerly known as the Widefield School, and provides services and activities to the area's older adults, encouraging them to stay involved in the community. (FVSC.)

Six

The Best-Kept Secret

Security-Widefield's best-kept secrets are those delightful, sometimes unknown or forgotten, and unusual tidbits that culminate in the community's identity. For instance, only the earliest pioneers of Security remember the ice rinks at Pi-Ute Park and the park district's sledding hill in the vicinity of Leta Drive, which opened daily in the winter afternoons and evenings as long as a sufficient amount of snow covered the ground.

The large military population resulted in a transient community. However, many of the personnel came back to retire in this hamlet. The valley's pleasant climate and the suburb's proximity to the post appealed to active-duty military personnel as well as retirees. Since most of these families had traveled the world, the result was a very diverse community. At one time, a Little Germany existed within the neighborhoods. This group consisted of young German women who had married American servicemen and made the United States their new home. The kaffeeklatsch tradition helped them to stay connected with each other in their new burg, and they succeeded in making many unique contributions to the area.

Longtime residents lament what they identify as deterioration in the little village they pioneered. Growth and progress have depleted its small-town quality. However, the attributes and desirability of this peaceful bedroom community are not lost on newcomers and visitors, especially those from larger metropolitan areas, who value this location as a desirable place to live and raise a family.

The people of Security-Widefield continue to enjoy the small-town atmosphere and sense of security in this quiet community. Most everyone is friendly, and a helping hand can always be found if needed. The school district has a statewide reputation of providing a safe and caring learning environment. It is no wonder that many district graduates return here to live and teach in the same schools they attended as children. A school administrator explained that Security-Widefield is indeed a place where people come home to make a difference in their community.

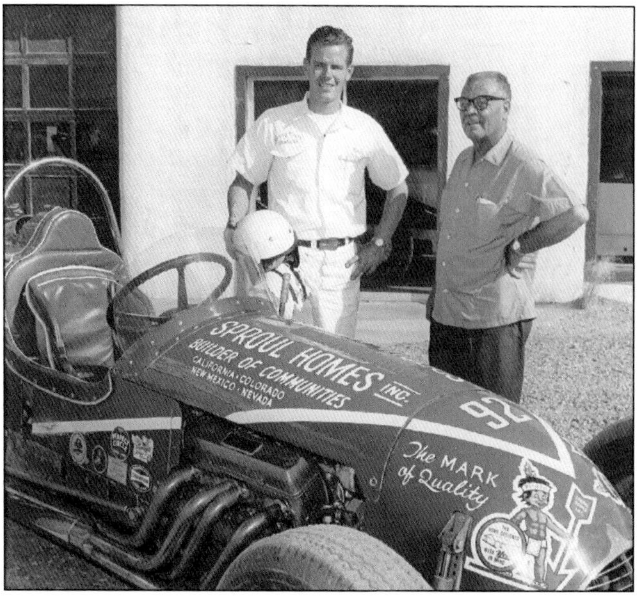

Bobby Unser (left), winner of the Pikes Peak Hill Climb in 1963, stands next to Everett "Dutch" Sproul and the No. 92 car sponsored by Sproul Homes. Unser finished the 12.42-mile race in 12.5 minutes. Sproul likely painted the advertising on the car, which features the Sproul Homes logo: a Piute Indian with a red arrow. Sproul headed up the sign department for his nephews Fred and Elmer at Sproul Homes. (Photograph by J. Frederick Laval, courtesy of CJ.)

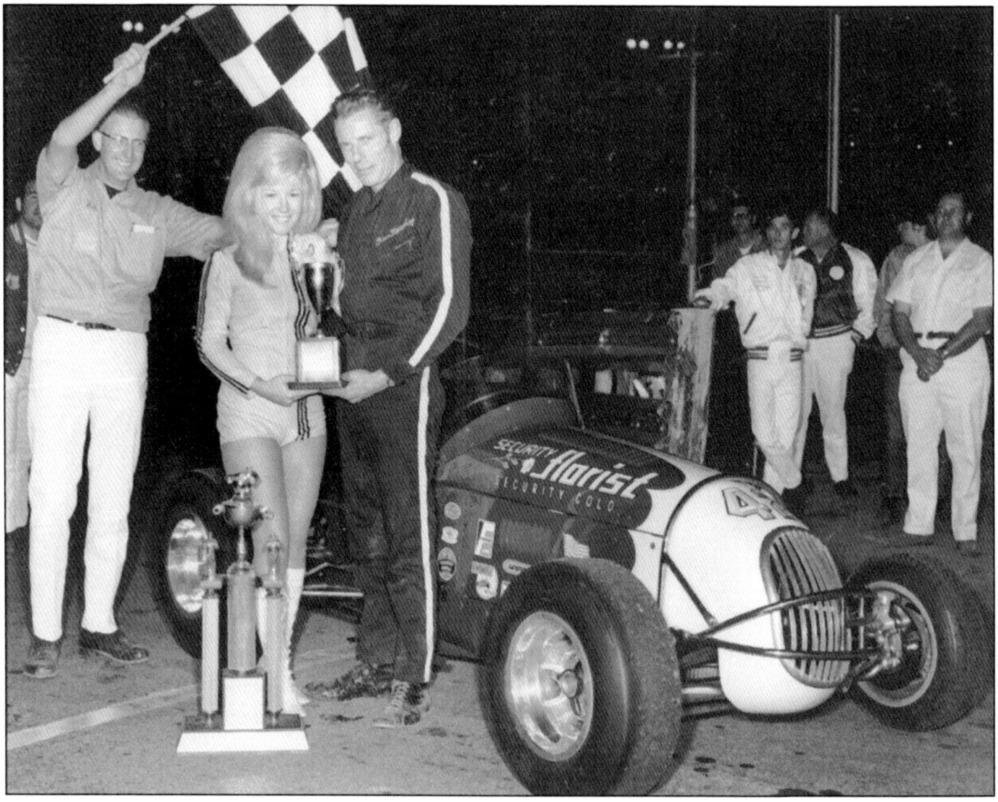

In 1969, Security's own Grier Manning, pictured here with his trophies, became the Rocky Mountain Midget Racing Association champion. The candy-apple-red No. 42 car was sponsored by Security Florist. As a mechanic, Manning built most of the cars he drove in the races in the region, including the Pikes Peak Hill Climb. Artist Everett "Dutch" Sproul painted the advertising on the car. (Photograph by Leroy Byers, courtesy of CJ.)

Janet Wallis appears here with Blinky the Clown in about 1963 during her birthday party in the television studio of *Blinky's Fun Club*. Blinky the Clown lived in Security. Also known as Russell Scott, he came to Security with American Builders and set up a miniature circus at the sales office on Security Boulevard. He and his troupe entertained the children while their parents wandered through the model homes. Later, he hosted young guests on his television show at KKTV in Colorado Springs. (JWA.)

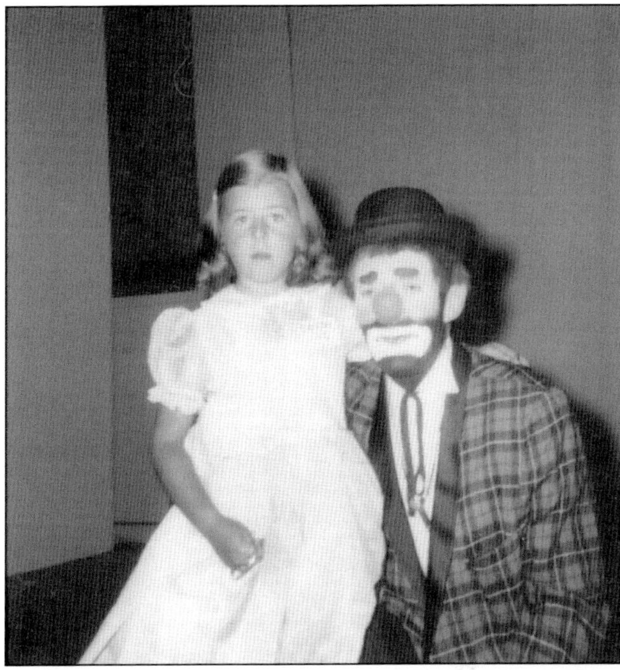

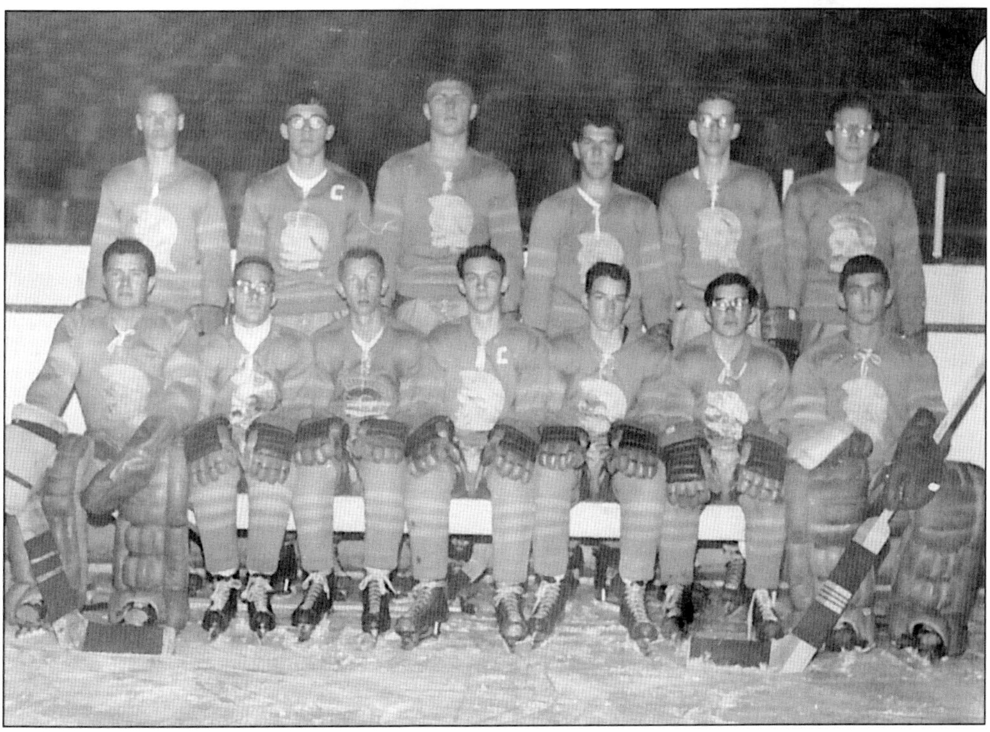

The Widefield High School Gladiators hockey team poses here for a team photograph in 1965. The Gladiators played their games at the Broadmoor World Arena. The players are, from left to right, (first row) Mike Herman, Bob Rhinehart, Peter Townsend, Bruce Brian, Roger LaTour, Jerry Frazee, and Larry Hazelett; (second row) Lonis Brown, Tom Fay, Dennis Morgan, Pete Spiers, Tom Shouse, and Alan Bohner. Brown played the game so hard he lost a tooth. (LB.)

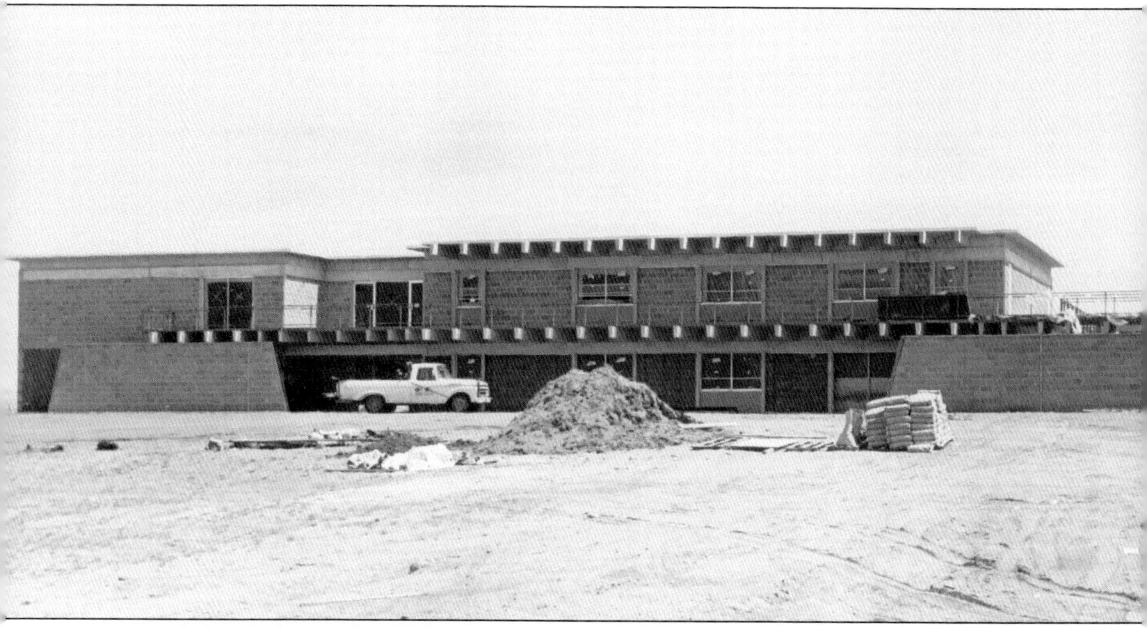

In 1965, the residents of Security came together with a common goal when they voted to create a community center complex within the Security Metropolitan Park & Recreation District. The unusually large percentage of young people living in Security and the fact that the nearest recreational facilities were several miles away in Colorado Springs emphasized the need for a community center. The architect modeled the Park & Community Center Complex in a Southwestern style, and the exterior was finished in earth-tone stucco. The Security 4-H Club executed some of the first landscaping, planting trees around the new building. School district

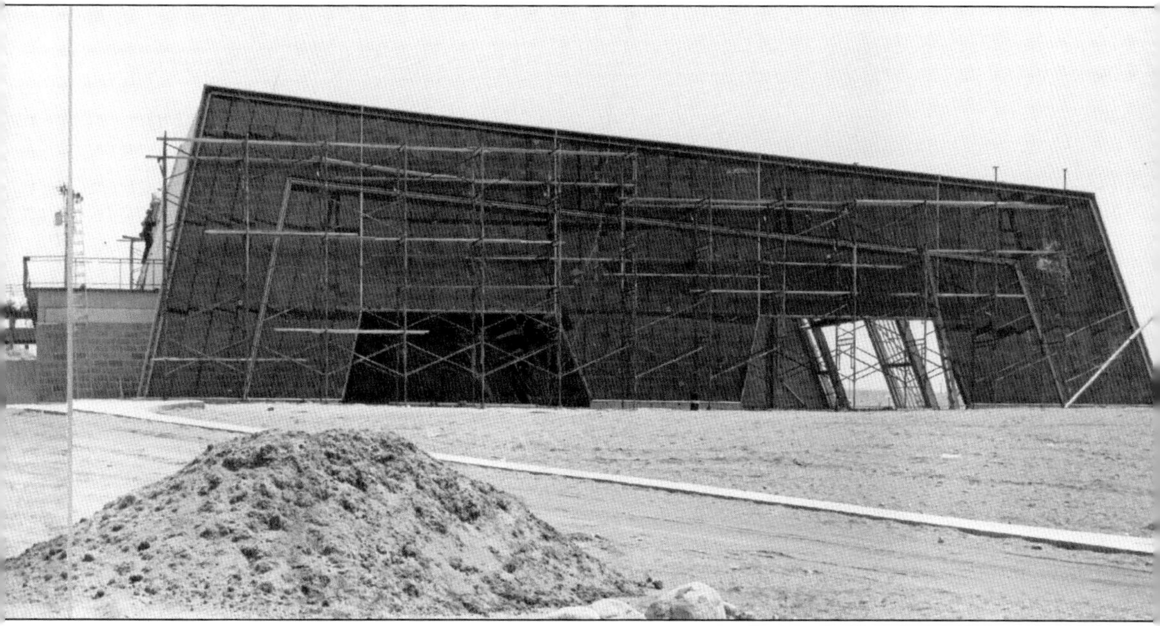

facilities continued to be used for athletic programs so that the new community center could be utilized for a wider range of activities. Plans for the community center included playgrounds, picnic areas, ball fields, and parking, as well as a garden outdoor theater, indoor ice rink, library, kitchen, meeting room, teen center, swimming pool, and craft room with a kiln. After experiencing financial difficulty, Security Metropolitan Park & Recreation District requested the county assume the parks and programs. When the county declined, the school district absorbed the community's parks and community center complex. (WCC.)

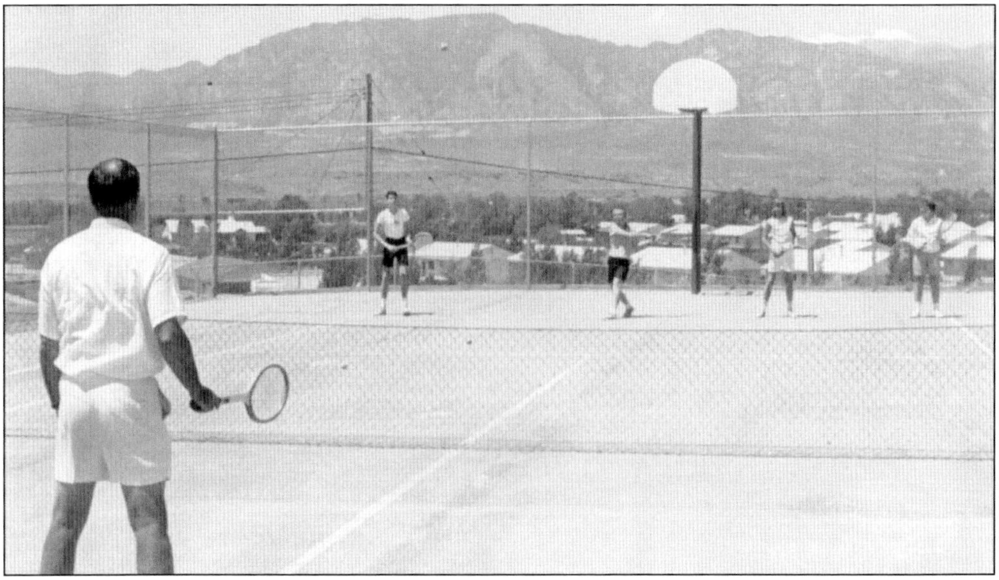

The Security Metropolitan Park & Recreation District was organized in 1960 at Pi-Ute Park, and school district facilities were utilized for the many programs offered. In this photograph, summer tennis instructor Charles Emery (left) watches students loft a ball above the court at Sproul Junior High School in about 1964. Approximately 40 youngsters were active in the tennis program. (WCC.)

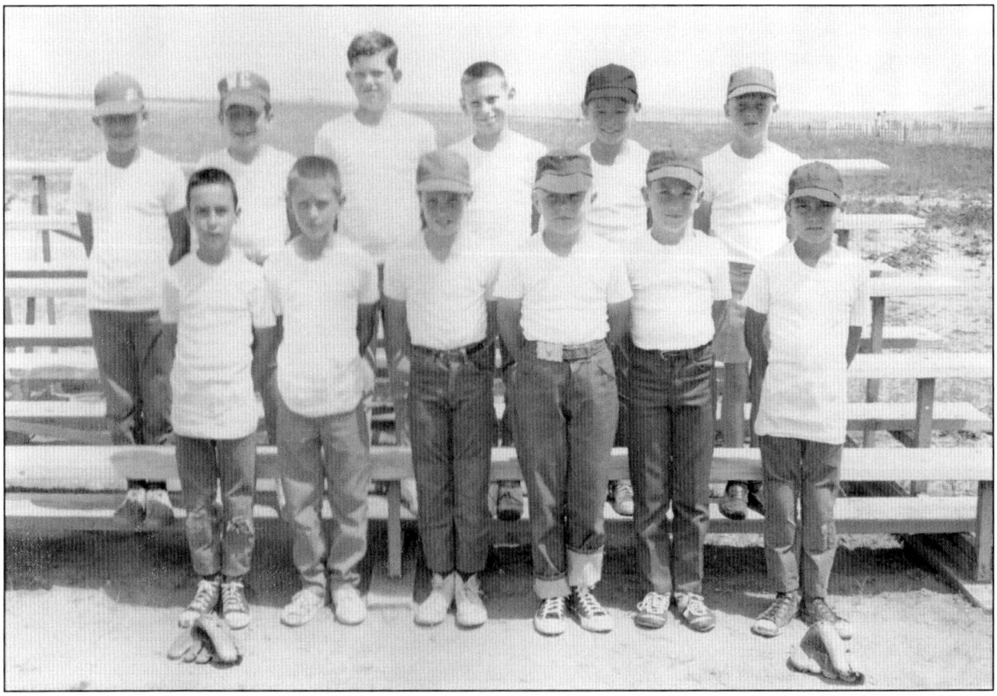

A Little League baseball team gathers for a group photograph in 1967. By this time, the park and recreation program had been expanded to include Widefield and all other residents within the school district. The program director this year was Phillip Cozzi, who eventually became a devoted and well-respected employee of Widefield School District. (WCC.)

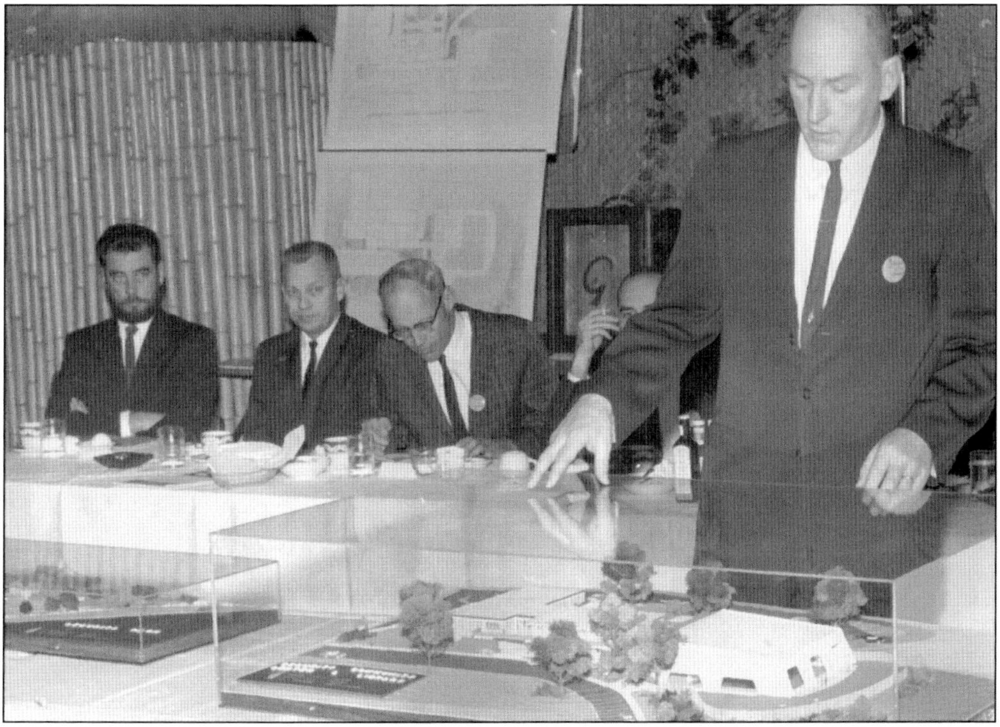

Glenn Driscoll (right), vice president of the Security Park & Recreation District, unveils a model of the proposed new community center in 1965. Land for the building was purchased from the Fountain Valley Boys School. Looking on are, from left to right, architect Walter Weber, School District 3 superintendent Richard Taylor, Colorado Springs National Bank vice president John Armstrong, and park board president J. Gentile. (WCC.)

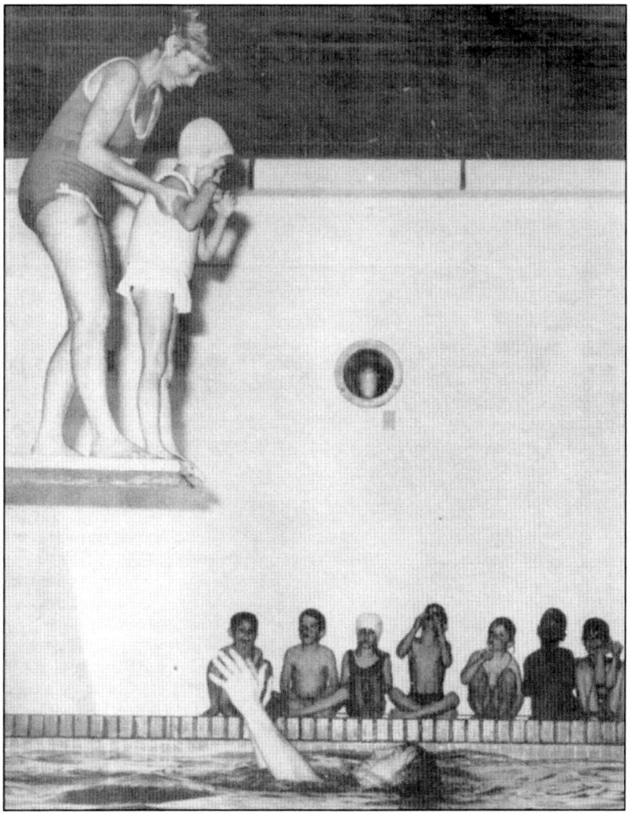

Published in the local newspaper in about 1968, this photograph advertised swimming lessons for all ages at the Security Parks & Recreation pool. In addition to lessons, the pool has offered numerous water activities, including exercise, lap swims, and open swim sessions. The high school swim teams practice here and host swim meets. (WCC.)

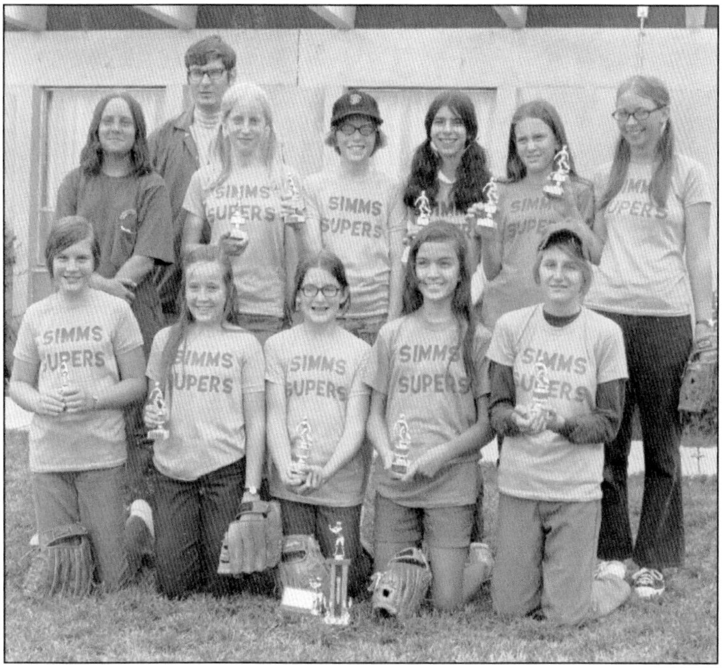

Members of the Simms Supers girls' softball team show their trophies after winning the league championship in 1972. Providing Security-Widefield youth with sports opportunities and other activities was truly a community effort. Parents paid minimal fees, while the community center organized the sports activities. Uniforms were simple T-shirts purchased by the sponsor, who received advertising in return. (WCC.)

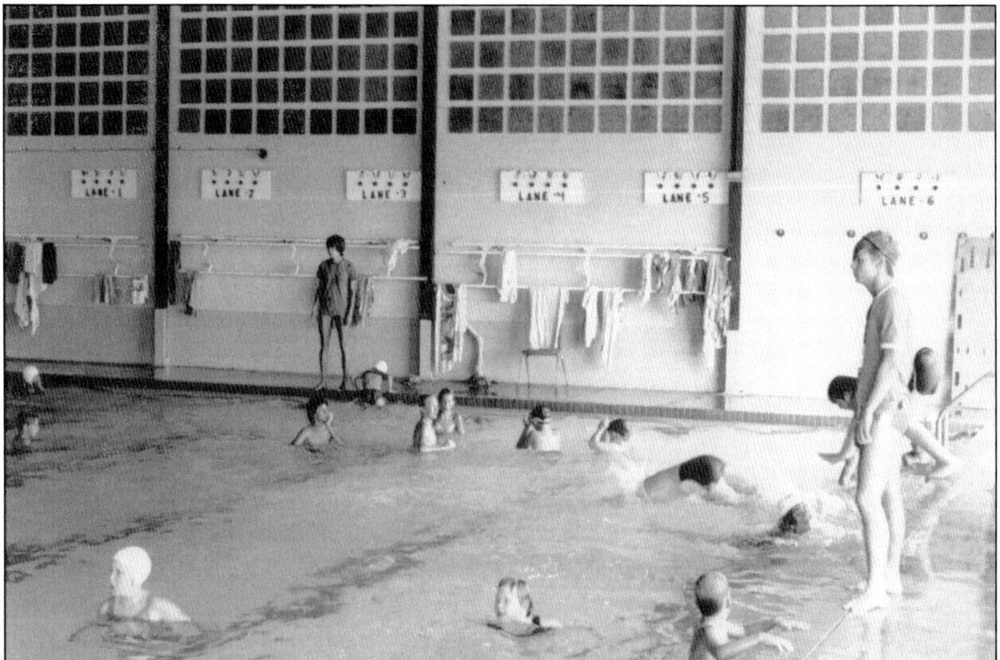

The new community center complex building included indoor and outdoor swimming pools. Swimmers are seen here at the pool in about 1976. The pool has continued to be a popular summertime spot for residents of Security-Widefield to have fun and cool off from the heat. (WCC.)

Youngsters practice here with their bows and arrows in about 1976. Archery was just one of the many activities offered by the Security Park and Recreation District. At this time, the department had been serving the people of Security-Widefield for about 15 years, offering playground programs, family nights, exercise, arts and crafts, drawing, and golf. (WCC.)

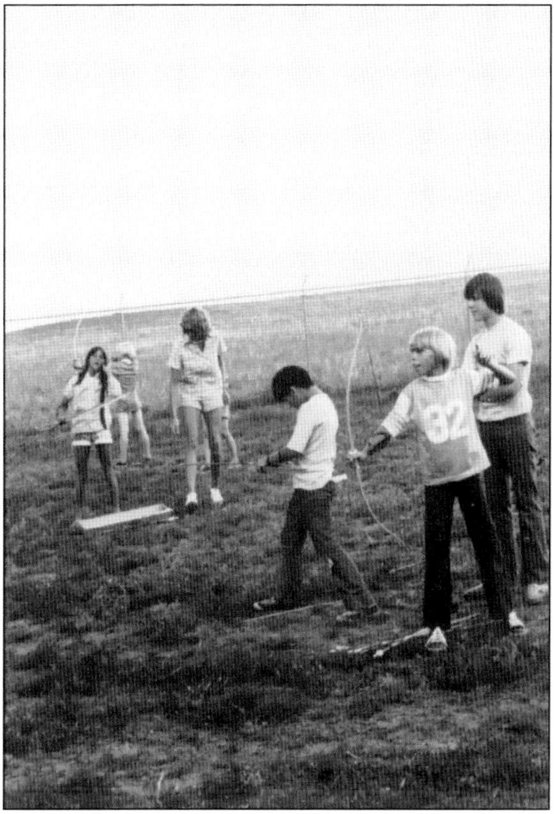

The Security Public Library, shown here in the 1980s, opened to patrons in 1965. For seven years, volunteers worked to create a public library for the growing community. After 1,200 book donations were collected from residents of Security and Colorado Springs, circulation commenced in 1961 in the basement of Sproul School. A year later, the library collection was moved into the administration building next door to Widefield High School. (SPL.)

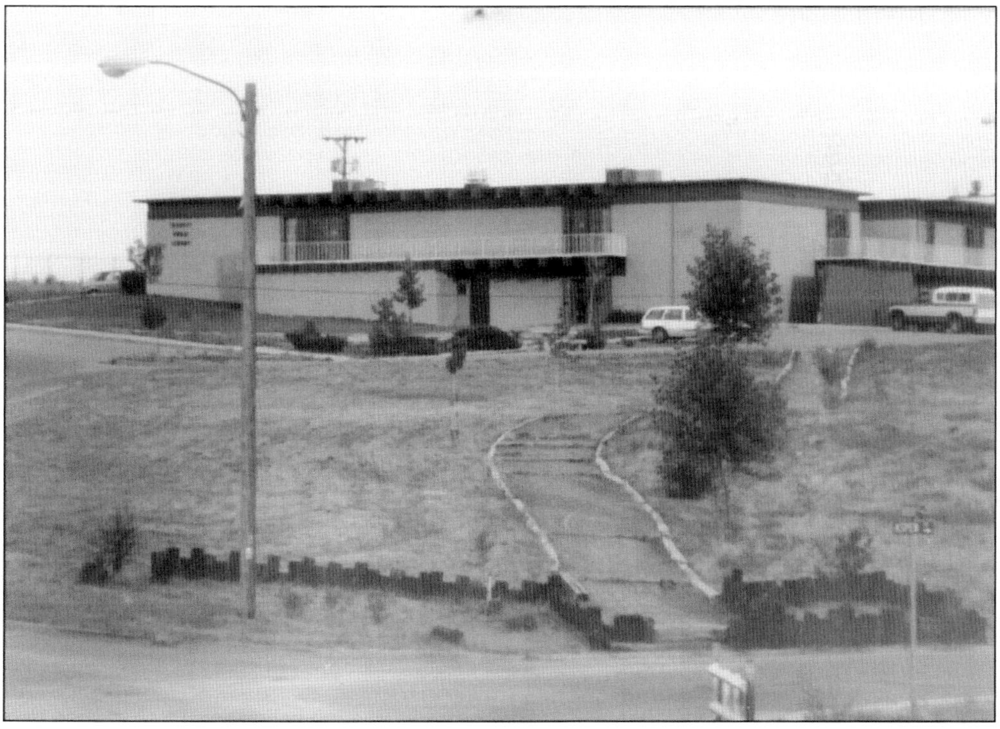

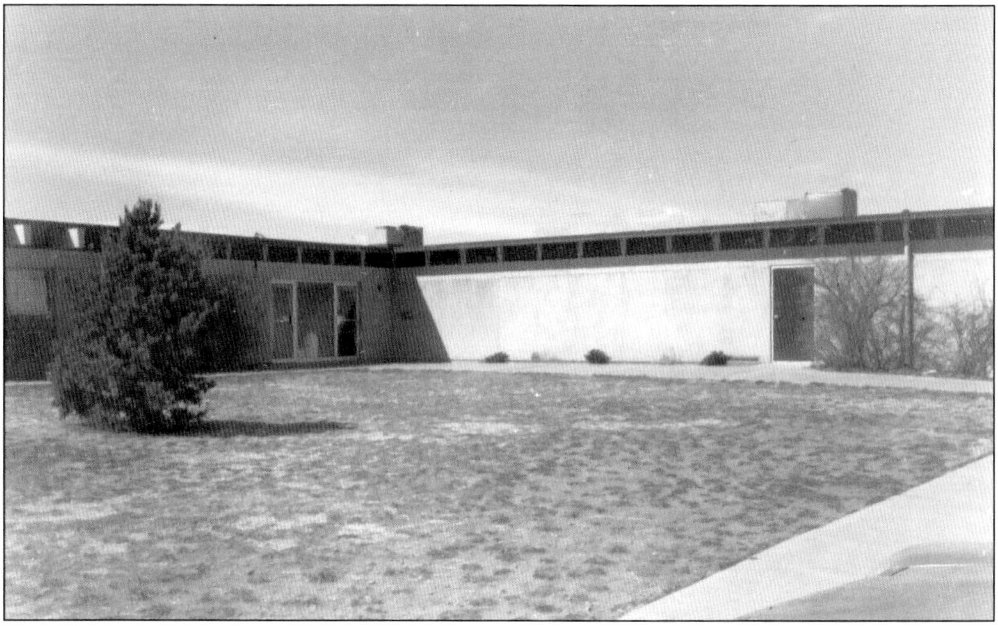

The library committee sought funding from several government entities, but it was to no avail because Security was an unincorporated community. Finally, the library was able to receive an operating budget from the Widefield School District, and with these funds it became available to all of the residents within the school district. The Colorado State Library lent great support and assistance to Security's library, pictured here in 1976. (SPL.)

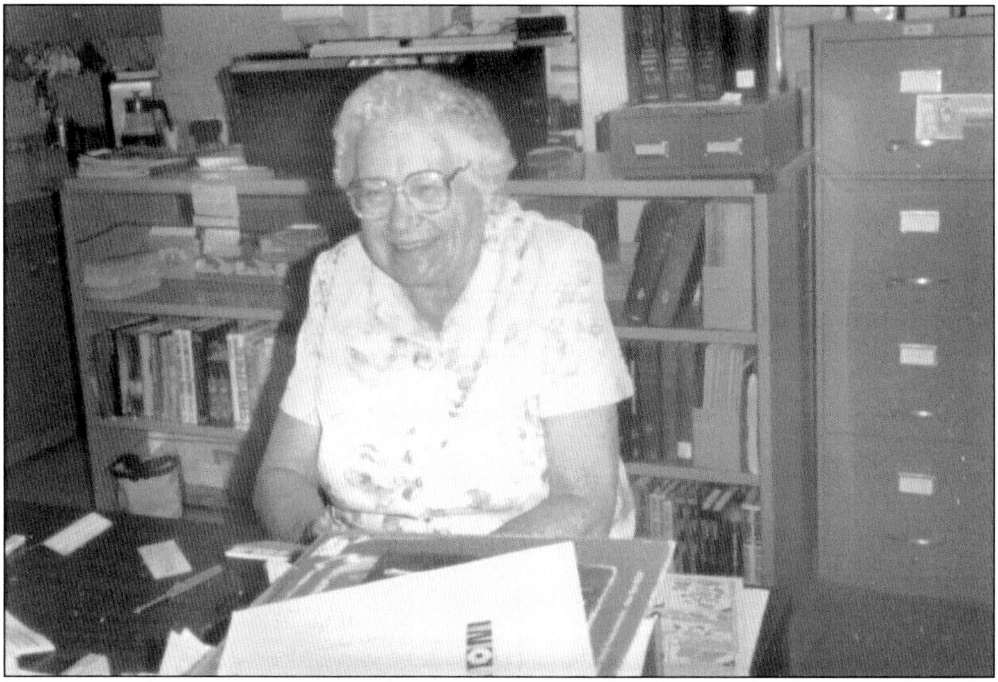

Professional librarian Barbara Hamilton was hired in 1964, and the library grew at a rapid rate under her supervision. She is remembered for her modest and pleasant personality and quiet efficiency. (SPL.)

When the Security Public Library opened in the Park & Community Center Complex, the adult reading section accommodated dozens of patrons, and an interlibrary loan service was implemented to help people borrow books from other libraries in the state. The library also offered summer reading programs; story contests; and talented magicians, storytellers, and musicians from the Pikes Peak region. The glass display case featured reading prizes and personal collections. (SPL.)

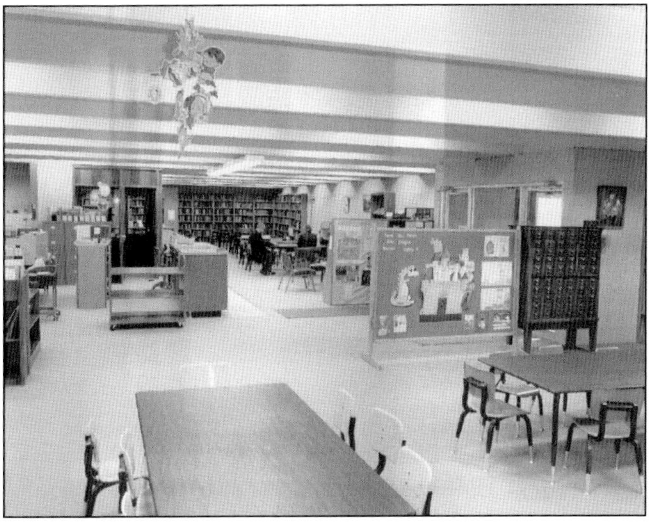

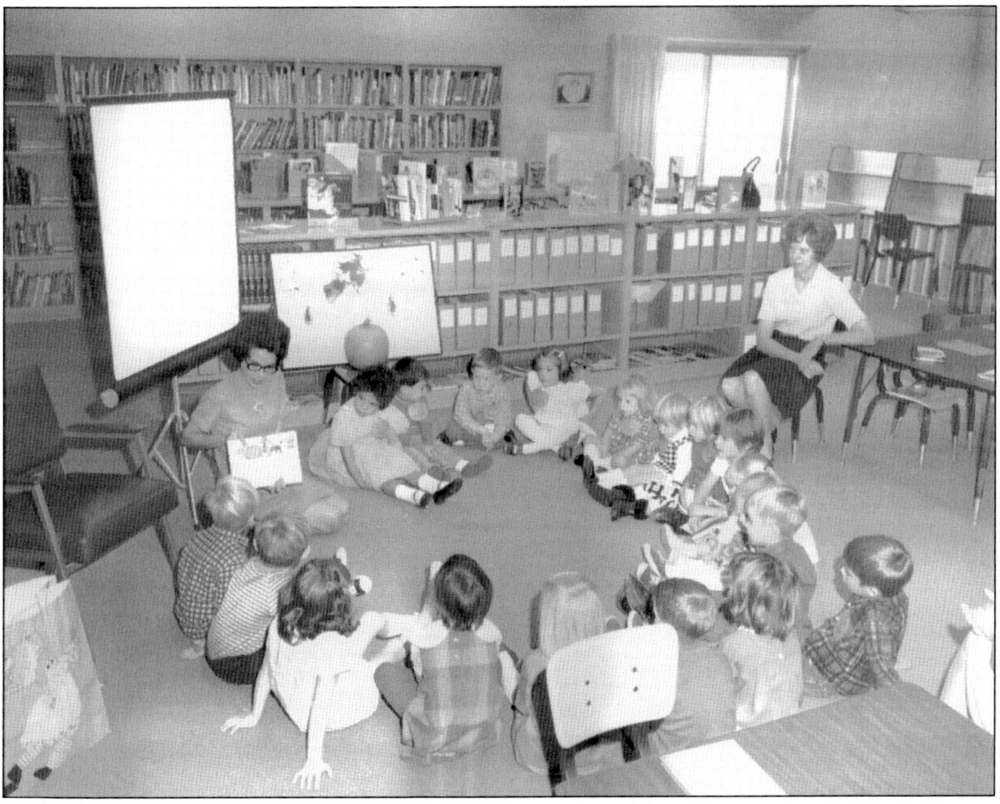

In the 1960s, Amabel Sanchez (left) tells stories during Story Hour Time in the children's library. She is assisted by Thelma Wiebke. After the stories, children watched films borrowed from the state library. The children's section of the library was located on the west side of the main floor but was moved downstairs in 1971 to where the community center's athletic equipment was once stored. (SPL.)

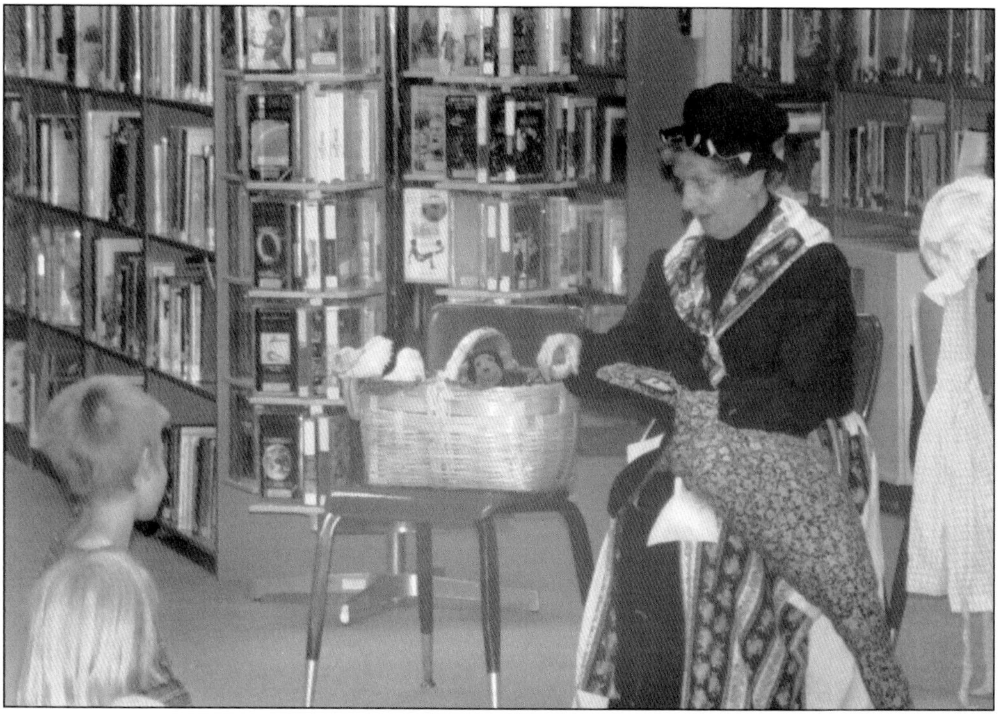

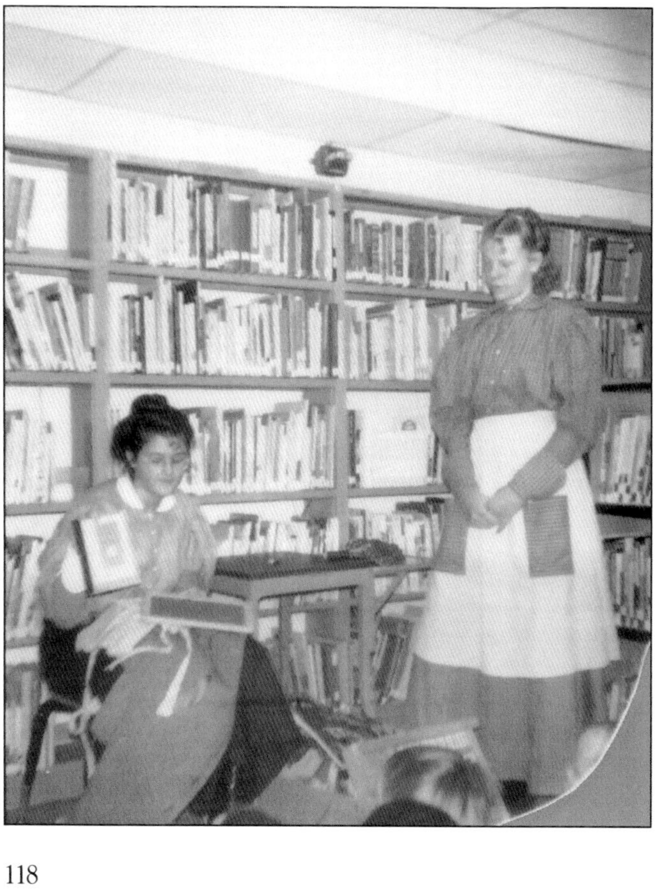

Former school librarian and local storyteller Mollie Harris entertains children at the Security Public Library in 1996 as she presents "The Hungry, Hungry Python." Dressed in a ruffled Mother Goose cap, she invites children to pick a story from one of the many pockets in her skirt. Harris encouraged the children to read as she told stories in her delightful British accent and animated presentation. (SPL.)

Historical interpreters Maria Hahn (left) and her friend Desirae Pollard visit the children at the Security Public Library in 1996 for a presentation on how children lived in the olden days. Among the items they brought in to show are a washboard, a slate, a sunbonnet, and a McGuffey Reader. (SPL.)

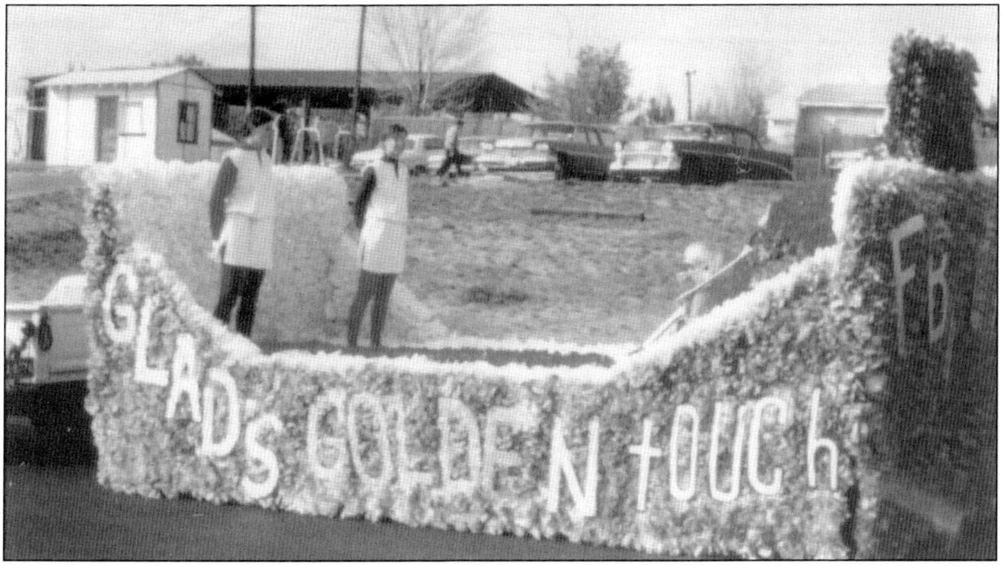

The theme of this float in the 1970 Widefield High School Homecoming parade was "the Golden Touch," and it portrayed a queen touching a golden football player with her sword. The float was created by the FBLA (Future Business Leaders of America) and won the first-place award. The parade started on an October afternoon at 4:00 p.m. at Pi-Ute Park and made its way to Security Boulevard through the neighborhood before returning to the park. (WSD.)

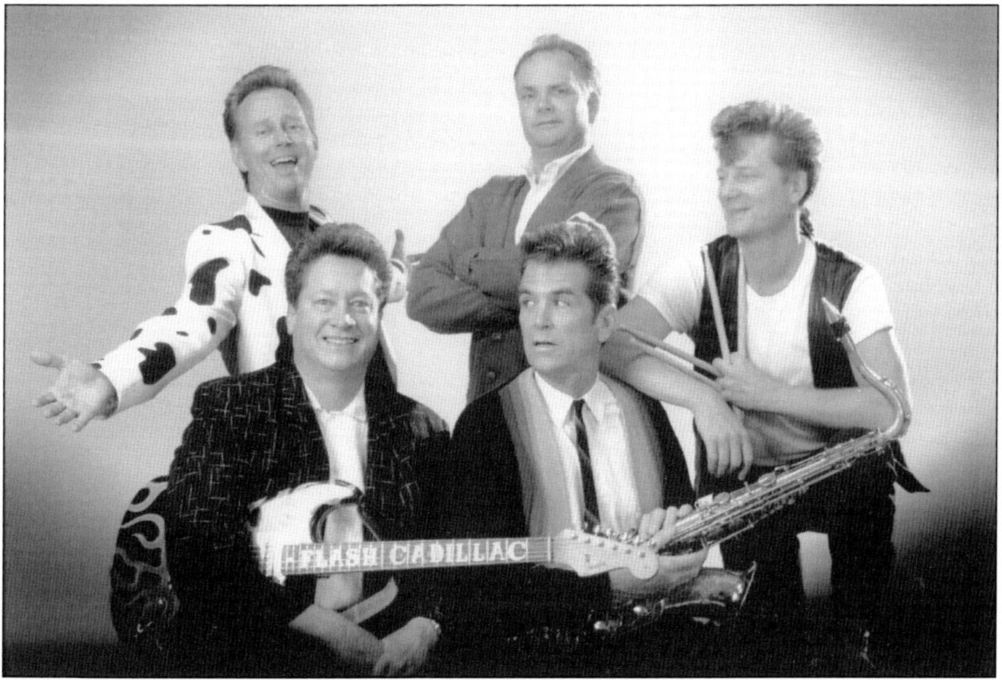

Flash Cadillac and the Continental Kids are pictured in the 1980s. The band members are, from left to right, (first row) lead guitarist Sam "Flash" McFadin, Dwight Bement, and Dave "Thumper" Henry; (second row) Kris Moe, and Warren Knight. McFadin served as senior-class president at Widefield High School in 1970. The band gained quick fame in the early 1970s with its musical presentations of popular songs from the 1950s. (SOA.)

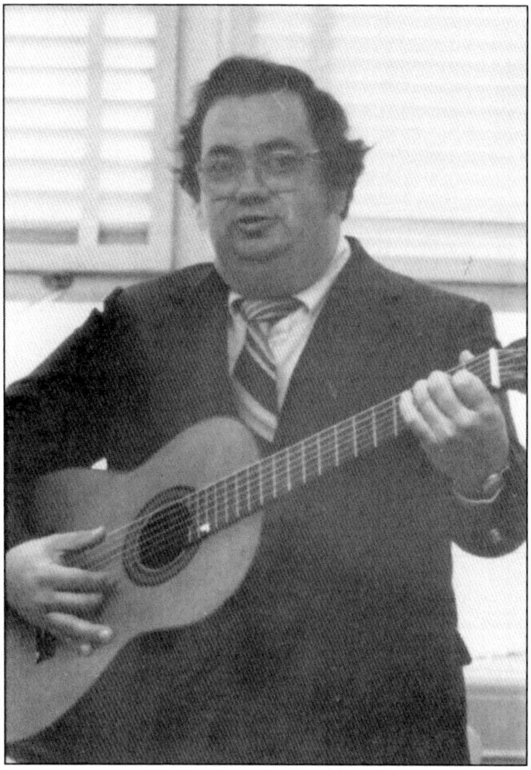

Herr Robert Sennert taught German for many years in Widefield schools. In the early 1970s, four-fifths of his students were children of military fathers and German mothers. He is pictured here in the 1970s teaching German folk songs to the German Club. Sennert included German history in his instruction. The club learned German Christmas carols and went to Memorial Park to sing German folk songs as members skated on the ice. (WSD.)

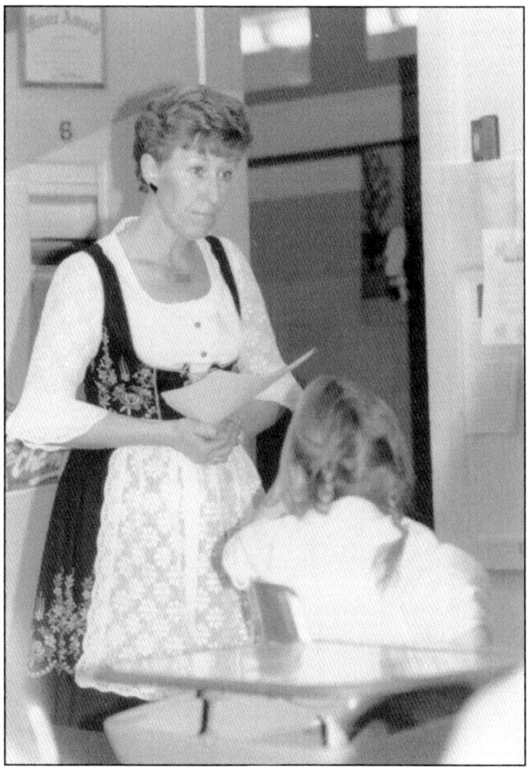

In the 1970s, Ursula Zimkas speaks to area schoolchildren about her life as a young girl in Germany. Zimkas was one of hundreds of young, post–World War II German women who found a new home in Widefield after realizing a better opportunity awaited them in America. Their presence added to the diversity of the community, and their characteristically well-manicured yards enhanced the beauty of the neighborhoods. (UZ.)

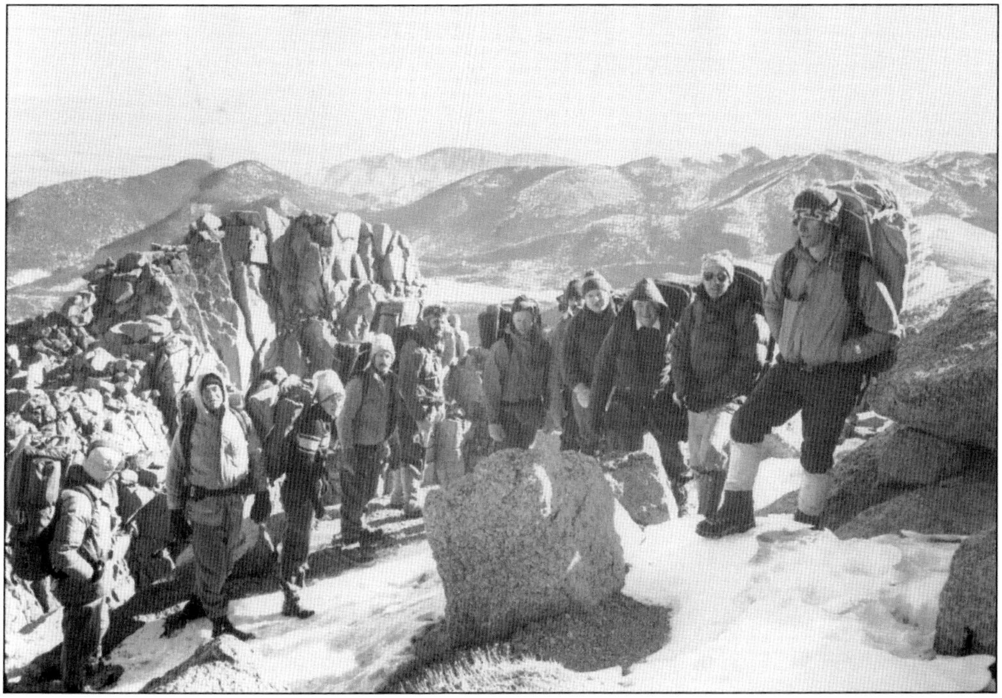

Security business owner Tom Kennedy (second from left) takes a break with the AdAmAn Club as members make their way to the summit of Pikes Peak. Kennedy joined the AdAmAn Club in 1979. Each year, the club hikes for two days up Barr Trail until climbers reach the top of the mountain on New Year's Eve. At midnight, they ring in the New Year with fireworks, which can be seen from down below in Colorado Springs and outlying areas. (TK.)

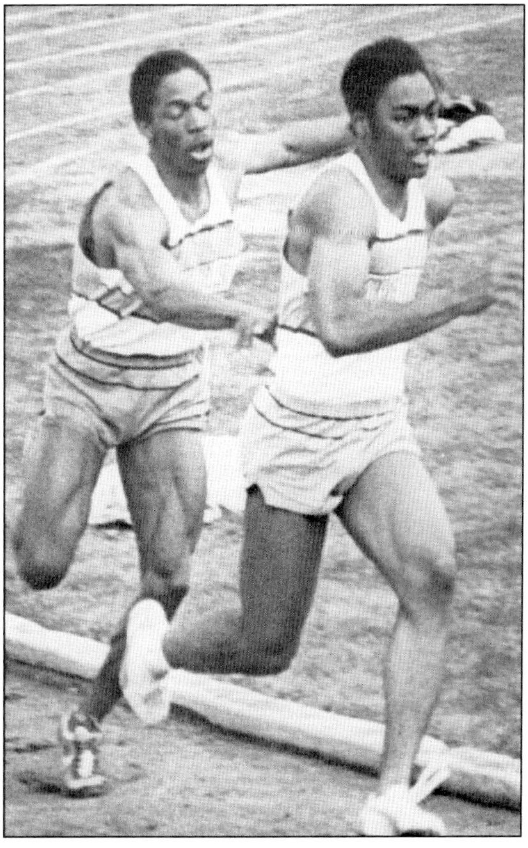

In 1980, Ron Pollard (left) passes the baton to Darryl Clack in the 440-yard relay. Clack later graduated from Widefield High School. In his college days, metal noisemakers, called "Darryl Clackers," were sold to fans at sports events. He later spent three years playing professional football for the Dallas Cowboys, and he was inducted into the Colorado Springs Sports Hall of Fame in 2006. (WSD.)

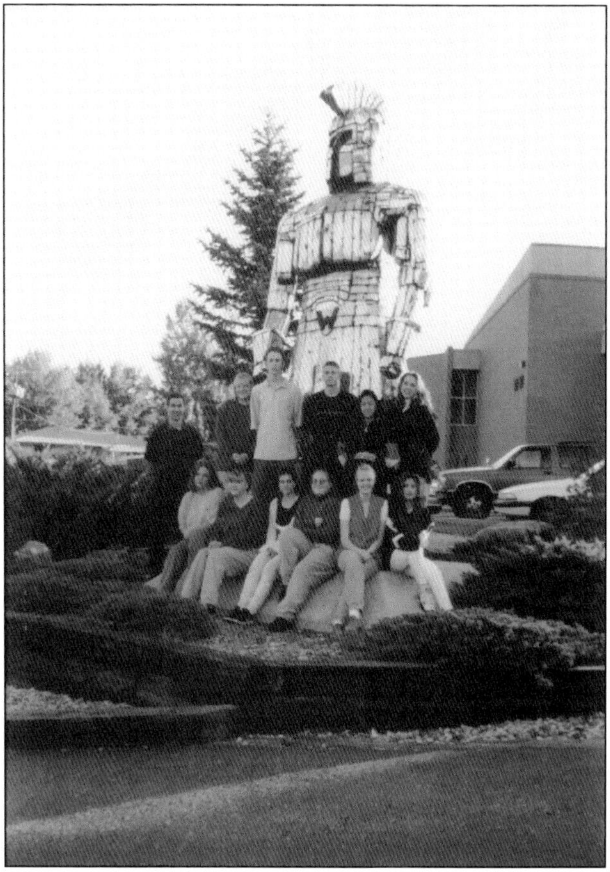

Students gather around Charlie the Gladiator in 1988. The gleaming statue stands watch over Widefield High School. The class of 1987 took two years to complete the statue, which is built entirely of chrome car bumpers donated by local auto-parts dealers. Widefield alumni of all ages are very pleased with the sculpture. (WSD.)

Participants in the 1989 Security Sprint start the 5K run on Morningside Drive in Security. This event was held on the morning of the Fourth of July. Runners paid a $6 entry fee, and the proceeds benefitted the Security Public Library's Interior Beautification Project. The run was one of many fundraisers organized by the community's schools, businesses, organizations, and citizens for the library in an effort to accumulate $30,000 for doors, carpets, and windows. (NBT.)

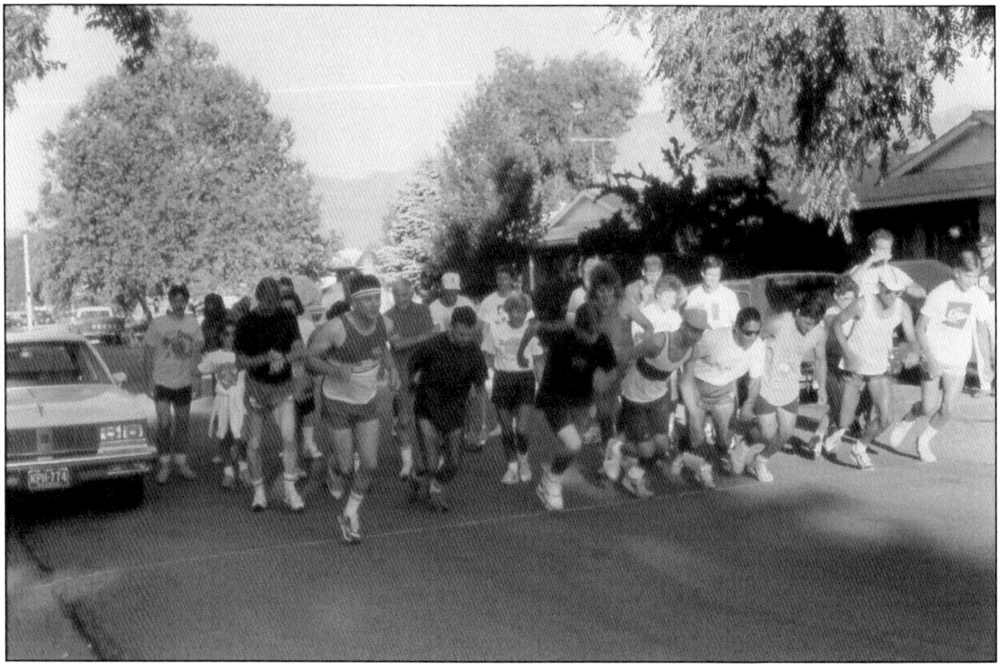

Candace French started working in Widefield School District 3 in the late 1950s, and her career lasted about 30 years. During this time, she filled many rolls: teacher, senior-class sponsor, dean of students, and school board member. She became a legend among Widefield alumni for her strict discipline. It was rumored she was a Marine veteran, but many remember her kind counsel and amazing ability to remember names. (WSD.)

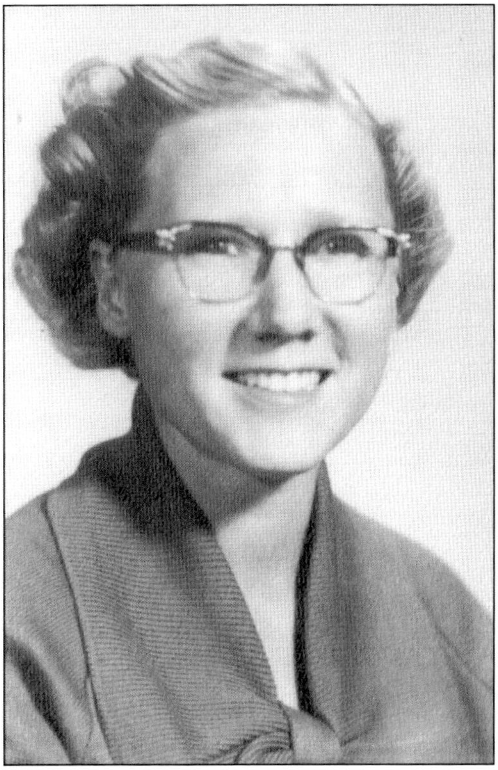

Search-and-rescue personnel look for signs of life among the wreckage of a United Airlines aircraft that crashed into Widefield Park on a peaceful Sunday morning in March 1991. Tragically, they found no survivors among the 25 passengers and crew on board. The crash stunned the Widefield neighborhood. (KD.)

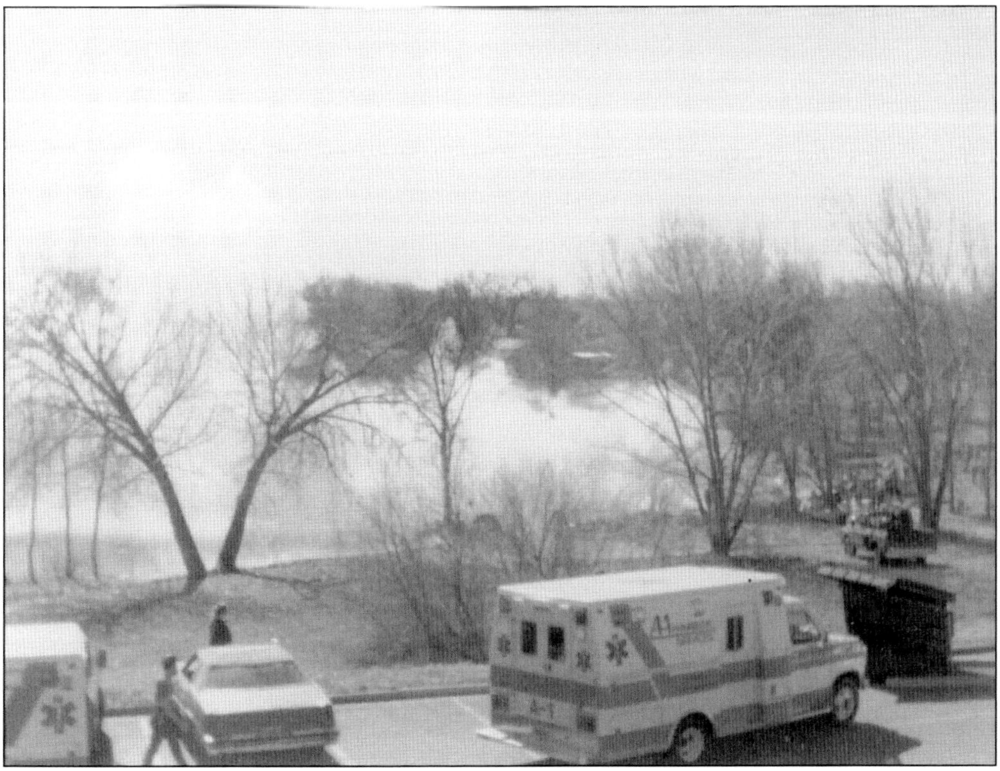

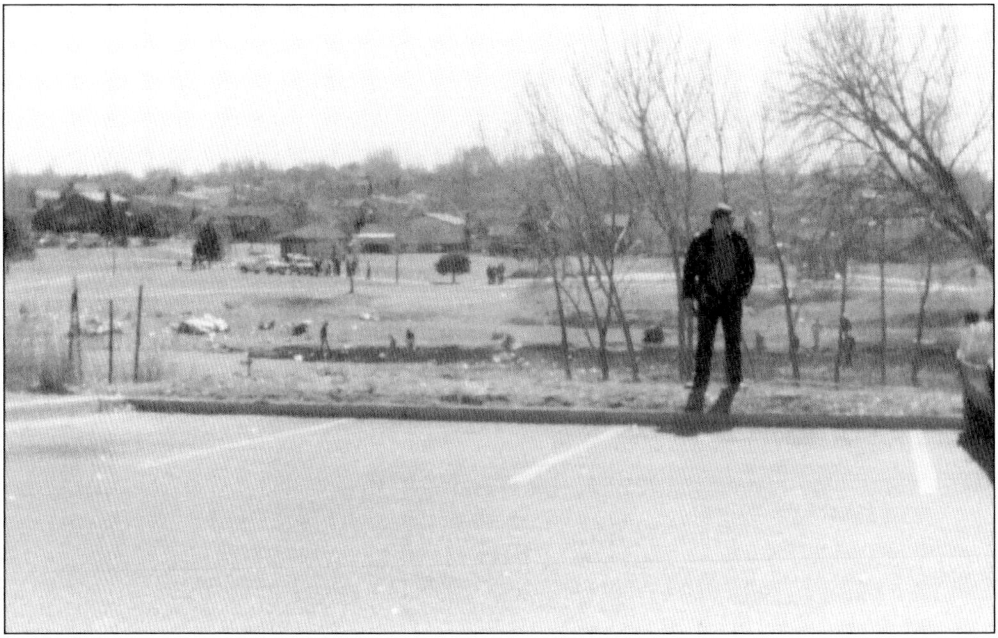

After the smoke cleared, all that remained from the wreckage of United Airlines Flight 585 were small bits of rubble. Heavy-equipment operators gathered up the crumpled material and hauled it off for the investigation team. They also disposed of large amounts of dirt contaminated with fuel and chemicals. A shaded resting spot was built at the crash site as a memorial to those who died. (KD.)

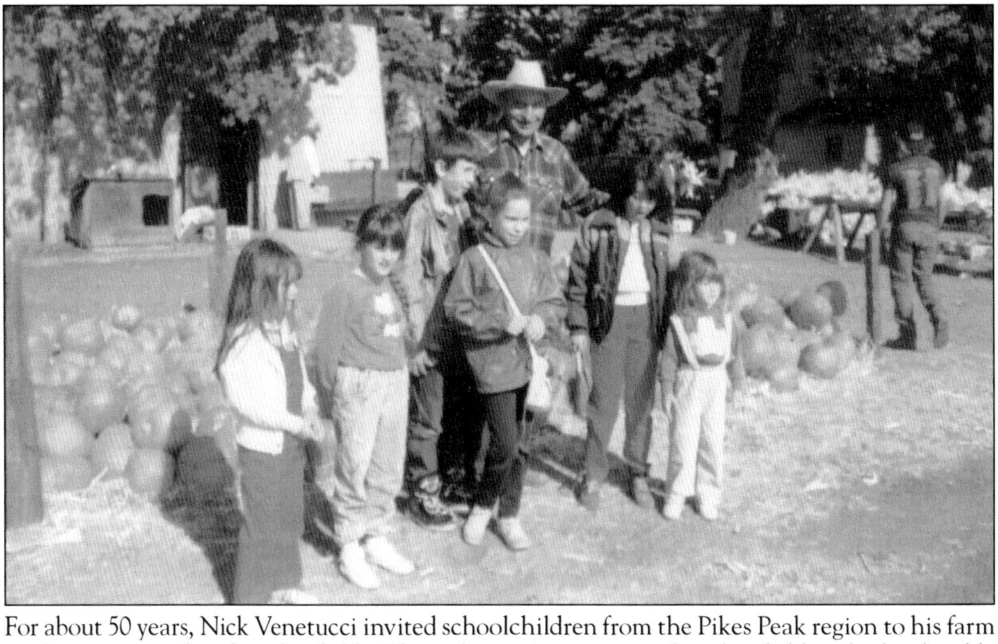

For about 50 years, Nick Venetucci invited schoolchildren from the Pikes Peak region to his farm to choose a pumpkin from his fields. The only requirement was that the children had to be able to carry their own pumpkins. Venetucci loved spending time with the children who visited his farm. Pictured in 1992 are, from left to right, Melanie Hahn, Jennifer Hahn, two unidentified children, Nick Venetucci, Maria Hahn, and Melissa Hahn. (ATH.)

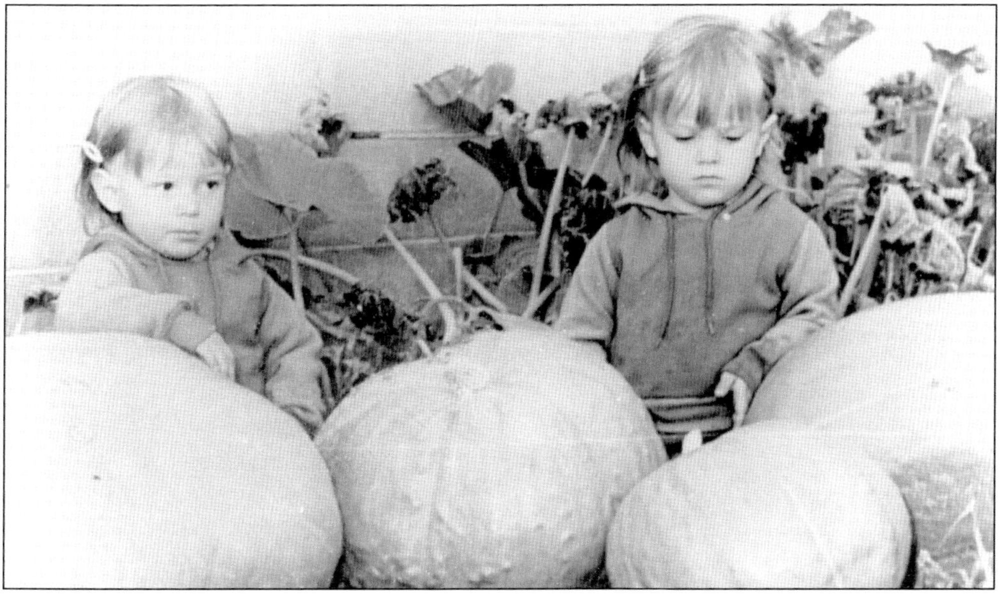

Nick Venetucci's pumpkin tradition began on Tejon Street in Colorado Springs where he brought vegetables to market. He spontaneously offered pumpkins from his truck to some children who had expressed delight in the bright-orange orbs. Later, a schoolteacher brought her class to the 60-acre pumpkin patch. Eventually, scores of school buses tied up the highway traffic each year as they entered and exited the farm. (FVM.)

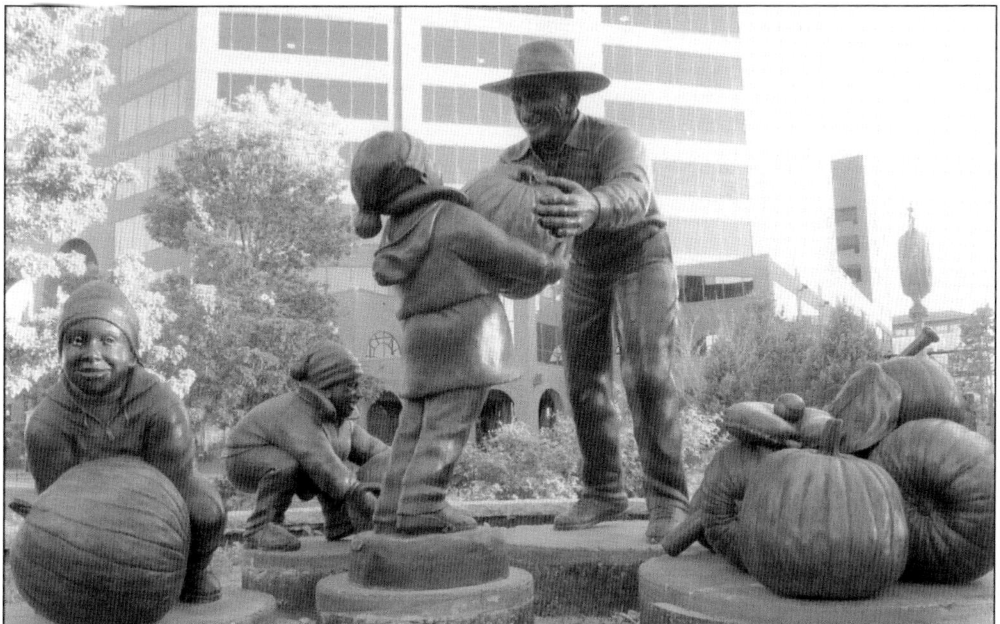

This statue of Nick Venetucci, installed in 2004 on the north side of the Pioneers Museum in Colorado Springs, depicts the joy on the faces of the farmer and the children. Venetucci's catcher's mitt and Yankees jersey lie beside him—a reference to his giving up a promising baseball career at his father's request to help on the family farm. Venetucci later explained that rows of pumpkins became his field of dreams. (ATH.)

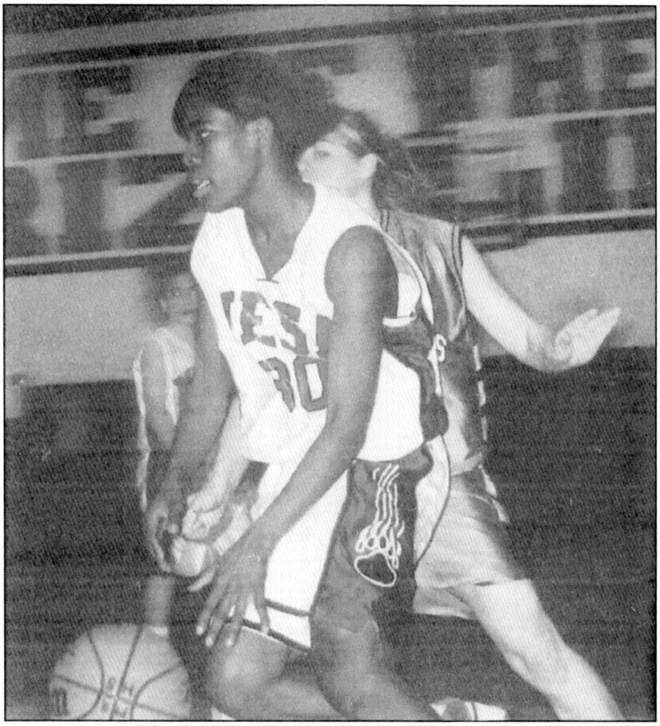

High school basketball star Fatima Mattox graduated from Mesa Ridge High in 2003. After finishing college, she became the ninth woman to ever play for the Harlem Globetrotters. (WSD.)

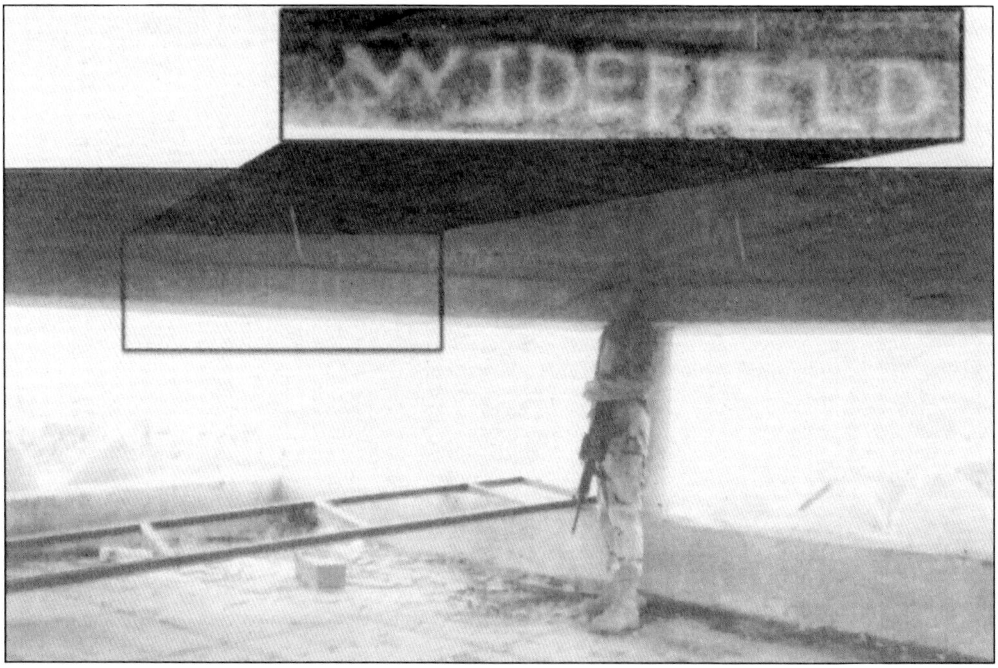

In 2007, Capt. Donald Martinez stands in a bombed-out structure in Iraq where he discovered the name Widefield etched among the graffiti. As there is no other municipality with the name Widefield, it is assumed that the scribe was a fellow citizen. Martinez attended Widefield schools and kept in touch with the students of Pinello Elementary through snapshots of his tour of duty in Iraq. (FVN.)

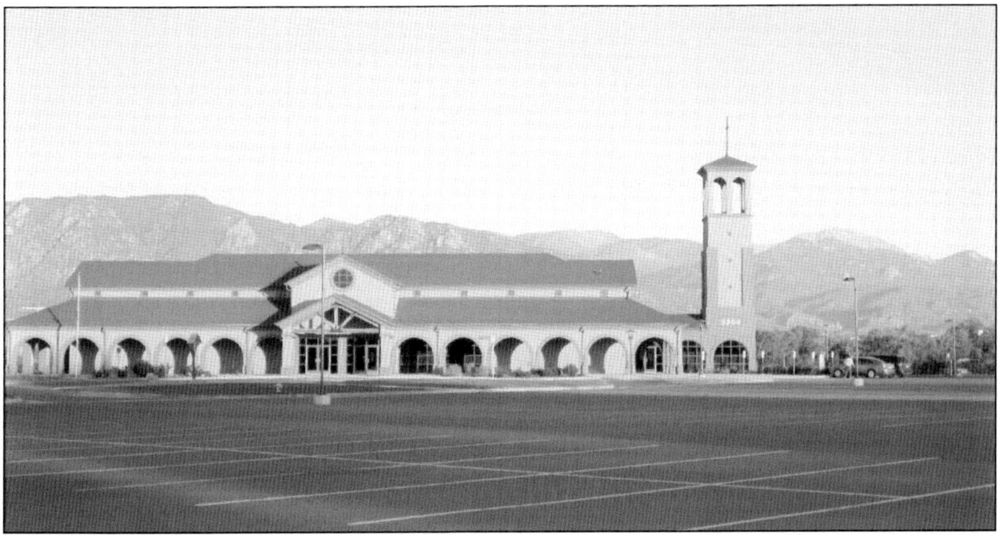

St. Dominic Parish meets in this beautiful church located on land donated by Nick and Bambi Venetucci. St. Dominic is the result of a 2008 merger between Holy Family Parish in Security-Widefield and St. Joseph Parish in Fountain. The bishop of Colorado Springs chose the new parish's name after reviewing three possibilities submitted by parishioners. Many feel the selection rightly honors the man Dominic "Nick" Venetucci. (ATH.)

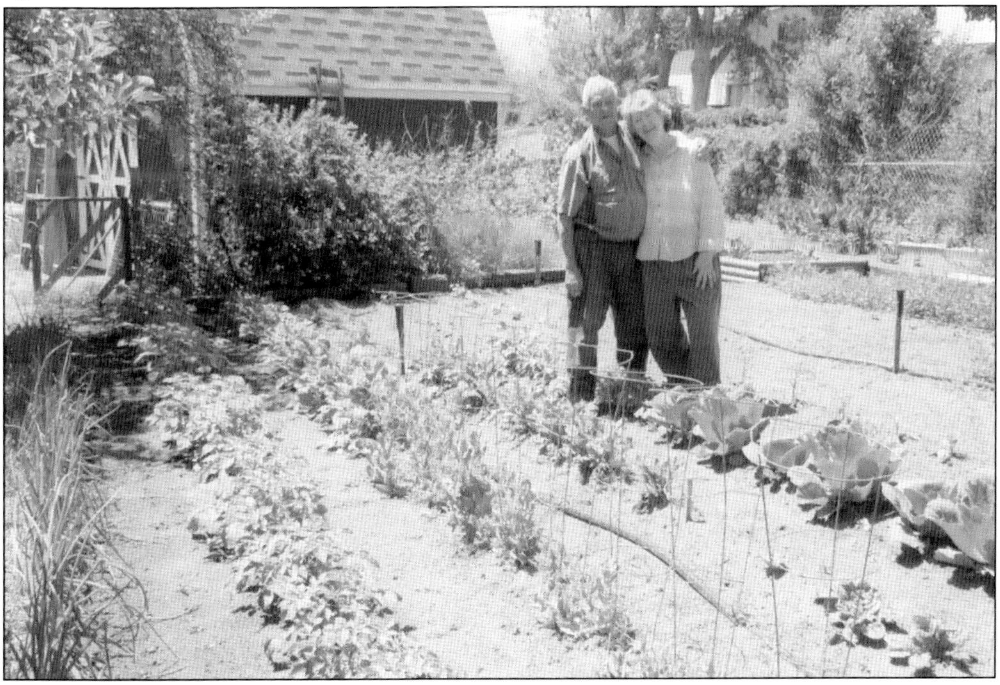

In the summer of 2011, the author's parents, Les and Nancy Thaden, stand in the vegetable garden in the large backyard at their Security home on Byron Place. Like many of the residents of Security-Widefield, they discovered the community's best-kept secrets in the early 1970s when they arrived at Fort Carson and chose to raise their family and retire in south Security. Now, they enjoy frequent visits from children, grandchildren, and great-grandchildren. (Photograph by Elizabeth Thaden, courtesy of NBT.)